OSCAR LEWIS was born in 1893, just as the era of the Wild West drew to a close, in San Francisco. He began his writing career at the age of twenty, and in recent years has specialized in books on Far Western themes—25 of them published to date. In 1924, he became secretary of the Book Club of California, and from 1933-1946 was editor of *News-Letter*. His books include: *Bay Window Bohemia; Sagebrush Casinos, The Story of Legal Gambling in Nevada, Sea Routes to the Gold Fields, The Town That Died Laughing.*

The
Autobiography
of the

Personal Narratives of the Discovery and
Settlement of the American West
Compiled and Annotated by

O S C A R   L E W I S

Henry Holt and Company   New York

Foreword

* One of the most interesting—and significant—chapters in our
national history is that which relates how, in a few decades,
the huge area that lies between the Rocky Mountains and the
shores of the Pacific was transformed from a virtually un-
trodden wilderness into the group of populous, forward-
looking states that today comprise the western third of the
nation.

On the pages that follow, an attempt has been made to re-
create the romance and drama of that achievement. The
story is an engrossing one, and in trying to capture for present-day readers its full excitement it has been deemed best
that it be told in the words of those pioneers, both men and
women, who had a part in bringing it about. For, in the
nature of things, few accounts of happenings long past, however skillfully they may be presented, can give readers quite
the same sense of reality, of closeness to the events described,
as do the chronicles of those who saw these events with their
own eyes and—as was usually the case—played a part in
bringing them to pass.

So here have been gathered a series of eye-witness accounts of how the primitive lands that once comprised our
far-western frontier were discovered, explored, settled, and

over the years converted into the enterprising and venturesome region we know today. Men of many occupations and widely different backgrounds had a hand in bringing this about, and their stories of what they saw and heard and did differ as widely one from the other as did their narrators themselves. But however much their writings vary in context or in manner of writing, they have one point in common. For whether they be hastily scrawled comments set down in diaries at the end of a long day's march, or the conclusions of trained observers, composed at leisure, they bear the unmistakable mark of authenticity.

Such first-hand accounts of the exploration and settlement of the Far West exist in great abundance, not only in the form of contemporary letters and journals and diaries, but in books of reminiscence written in later years, in official reports of early exploring expeditions, in the still-existing records of certain commercial organizations that then operated throughout the region, and elsewhere.

In choosing from this plentitude of material the items reprinted here, the aim has been to select those dealing with characteristic phases of the winning of the West. This is indeed a broad field, including as it does excerpts from the narratives of the first explorers to break new trails through the wilderness, of the far-ranging bands of hunters and trappers who follow them, and who were followed in turn by pioneer parties of emigrants heading westward both by land and sea to begin life anew on the far rim of the continent. The latter, few in numbers in the early years, abruptly grew to a mighty horde as a result of the finding, in 1848, of gold in the tailrace of Captain Sutter's new sawmill in the Sierra foothills. These and numerous other aspects of the area's transformation from primitive solitude to highly organized communities are all described—always in the words of men or women who wrote of what they themselves had seen and experienced.

The compiler's task has been made easier, and far more pleasurable, by the cooperation of numerous individuals and organizations in making available the material in their possession. Among those to whom special thanks are due are the staffs of the following institutions: The Bancroft Library, Berkeley, California, the California Room of the State Library, Sacramento, and the Sutro Library, the California Historical Society, and the Society of California Pioneers, all of San Francisco.

Oscar Lewis

San Francisco, California
February, 1958

Contents

THE AUTOBIOGRAPHY OF THE WEST

I
Widening Horizons

The lures that drew the first adventurers to what is now the western third of the nation, and that resulted in making the region known to the civilized world far earlier than would otherwise have been the case, were two.

One of the lures was the belief that a mythical passage, termed the Straits of Anian, joined the Atlantic and Pacific somewhere to the north. By means of this passage, it was maintained, early voyagers to the Indies could avoid the long and tedious passage round Cape Horn. The second lure was the belief in the existence of two fabulous kingdoms, those of Cibola and Quivira, reputed to be surpassingly rich in jewels and precious metals. They were said to lie somewhere in what is now the southwestern tier of states.

It was the second of these fantasies that, in the early half of the sixteenth century, drew two parties northward from Mexico City in search of the supposed treasure troves. One, under the command of Hernando de Alarcón, went by sea. His tiny ships reached the head of the Gulf of California, and he himself penetrated some distance up the Colorado River. At the same time, a land expedition was organized

and, headed by Francisco Vásquez Coronado, spent the next
three years in a fruitless quest for the wealthy cities, during
which time he, or his men, traversed much of present-day
Arizona, New Mexico, and Texas, discovered the Grand
Canyon, and pushed on northward as far as present-day
Oklahoma and Kansas.

Thus, although this part of the nation has long been
looked on as our "last frontier," a land that remained a
closed book to white men for many decades after the region
contiguous to the Atlantic Coast had been thoroughly explored, history records that large areas of that supposedly unknown land had become familiar to Europeans within the
first half century after Columbus' memorable voyage of 1492.

Among the several first-hand accounts of Coronado's historic expedition that have come down to us, the most de-
tailed and colorful is that of Pedro de Castaneda, a soldier
member of the party, and it is from his narrative that the
following excerpts are taken. The first is a description of
the Pecos pueblo—called Cicuye by Castaneda—which lies a
few miles to the southeast of present-day Santa Fe.

Cicuye [wrote Castaneda] is a village of nearly 500 warriors, who are feared throughout that country. It is square,
situated on a rock, with a large court, or yard, in the middle . . . The houses are all alike, four stories high. One can
go over the top of the whole village without there being a
street to hinder. There are corridors going all around it at
the first two stories, by which one can go around the whole
village. These are like outside balconies, and they are
able to protect themselves under these. The houses do not
have doors below, but they use ladders, which can be lifted
up like a draw-bridge, and so go up to the corridors which
are on the inside of the village. As the doors of the houses
open on the corridor of that story, the corridor serves as a
street. The houses that open on the plain are right back of

those that open on the court, and in time of war they go through those behind them. The village is inclosed by a low wall of stone. There is a spring of water inside, which they are able to divert. The people of this village boast that no one has been able to conquer them and that they conquer whatever villages they wish . . .

There is another large village farther on, entirely destroyed and pulled down, in the yards of which were many stone balls, as big as twelve-quart bowls, which seemed to have been thrown by engines or catapults. . . . All that I was able to find out about them was that, sixteen years before, some people called Teyas [a warlike tribe from the plains of Texas] had come to this country in great numbers and had destroyed these villages. They had besieged Cicuye but had not been able to capture it, because it was strong. . . . It seems as if they must have been a powerful people, and that they must have had engines to knock down the villages. The only thing they could tell about the direction these people came from was by pointing toward the north . . .

As Coronado's party continued farther eastward, they encountered vast herds of buffalo, some of which covered the plains as far as the eye could see. Here is Castaneda's description of these—to him and his companions—queer-looking beasts.

Now that I wish to describe the appearance of the bulls, it is to be noticed first that there was not one of the horses that did not take flight when he saw them first, for they have a narrow, short face, the brow two palms across from eye to eye, the eyes sticking out at the side, so that, when they are running, they can see who is following them. They have very long beards, like goats, and when they are running they throw their heads back with the beard dragging on the ground. There is a sort of girdle round the middle of the body. The hair is very woolly, like a sheep's, very fine . . . , in front the hair is very long and rough like a lion's. They have a great hump, larger than a camel's. The horns are short and thick, so that they are not much seen above the hair . . . They have a short tail, with a bunch of hair at the end. When they run, they carry it erect like a scorpion. It is worth noticing that the little calves are red and just like ours, but they change their color and appearance with time . . .

Another strange thing was that all the bulls that were killed had their left ears slit, although these were whole when young. The reason for this was a puzzle that could not be guessed. The wool ought to make good cloth on account of its fineness, although the color is not good . . .

Another thing worth noticing is that the bulls traveled without cows in such large numbers that nobody could have counted them, and so far away from the cows that it was more than forty leagues from where we began to see the bulls to the place where we began to see the cows. The country they traveled over was so level and smooth that if one looked at them the sky could be seen between their legs, so that if some of them were at a distance they looked like smooth-trunked pines whose tops joined, and if there was only one bull it looked as if there were four pines. When one was near them, it was impossible to see the ground on the other side of them. The reason for all this was that the country seemed as round as if a man should imagine himself in a three-pint measure, and could see the sky at the edge of it, about a crossbow shot from him, and even if a man only lay down on his back he lost sight of the ground.

ii

One of the most memorable journeys in the entire field of western exploration was that made during the years 1533-37 by the Spaniard Cabeza de Vaca, who with three companions traveled on foot from Florida to—or close to—the shores of the Pacific, thus becoming, so far as is known, the first white men to cross the continent. Cabeza de Vaca was a member of an expedition led by Pánfilo de Narváez which landed in Florida in 1528. When their attempt to found a colony there was abandoned due to the hostility of the natives, and they put forth in their ships, de Vaca and three others were the only survivors of the wreck of their vessels on an island off the coast of Texas.

Having been taken prisoner by the Indians of the mainland and held captive for more than five years, the four eventually made their escape and fled toward the west—not in any hope of re-establishing contact with other Europeans but because flight in any other direction was cut off. Later, after he returned to Spain, Cabeza de Vaca wrote an account of their adventures during their four years of wandering, some of the highlights of which are here given. One of the factors that gained them the friendship of the Pueblo Indians of the Southwest was the reputation their leader gained by his treatment of the sick and injured. Here is one instance of de Vaca's amazing doctoring which took place at one of the native settlements in the summer of 1535:

They fetched a man to me [wrote Cabeza de Vaca] and stated that a long time since he had been wounded by an arrow in the right shoulder, and that the point of the shaft was lodged above his heart, which, he said, gave him much pain, and in consequence, he was always sick. Probing the wound I felt the arrow head, and found it had passed

through the cartilage. With a knife I carried, I opened the
breast to the place, and saw the point was aslant and
troublesome to take out. I continued to cut, and, putting in
the point of the knife, at last with great difficulty I drew the
head forth. It was very large. With the bone of a deer, and
by virtue of my calling, I made two stitches . . . and with
hair from a skin I stenched the flow of blood. They asked
me for the arrow head after I had taken it out, which I gave,
when the whole town came to look at it. They sent it into the
back country that the people there might view it. In consequence of this operation they had many of their customary
dances and festivities . . . This cure gave us control
throughout the country in all that the inhabitants had power,
or deemed of any value, or cherished . . .

> Wherever they went, the customs of the Indians they en-
> countered aroused the interest of the wanderers, and in his
> reminiscences Cabeza de Vaca recorded some of the more
> curious of these. Thus while stopping with a tribe at a point
> that was probably somewhere in present-day New Mexico,
> he commented:

Their method of cooking is so new, that for its strangeness I
desire to speak of it; thus it may be seen and remarked how
curious and diversified are the contrivances and ingenuity
of the human family. Not having discovered the use of pip-
kins [small earthen pots] to boil what they would eat, they
fill half of a large calabash with water, and throw on the fire
many stones of such as are most convenient and readily take
the heat. When hot, they are taken up with tongs of sticks
and dropped into the calabash until the water in it boils from
the fervor of the stones. Then whatever is to be cooked is put
in, and until it is done they continue taking out cooled
stones and throwing in hot ones.

From time to time during the course of their wanderings, the wayfarers were thrilled by reports that men similar to themselves had been seen in the country ahead. At one point, having, in Cabeza de Vaca's words, observed "the buckle of a sword-belt on the neck of an Indian and stitched to it the nail of a horse-shoe," they plied the Indian with eager questions as to how he had come by them. Cabeza de Vaca continues thus:

We questioned him further, as to who had brought them thence: they all responded that certain men who wore beards like us, had come from heaven and arrived at that river; bringing horses, lances, and swords . . . In a manner of the utmost indifference we could feign, we asked them what had become of those men: they answered that they had gone to sea, putting their lances beneath the water; afterwards that they were seen on the surface going towards the sunset. For this we gave many thanks to God our Lord. We had before despaired of ever hearing more of Christians. Even yet we were left in great doubt and anxiety, thinking those people were merely persons who had come by sea on discoveries. However, as we had now such exact information, we made greater speed, and as we advanced on our way, the news of the Christians continually grew . . .

The end of their long odyssey and a return to their own kind took place toward the close of 1536. Their meeting with members of an expedition sent out from Mexico City and commanded by Diego de Alcarez is thus described by Cabeza de Vaca:

When we saw sure signs of Christians, and heard how near we were to them, we gave thanks to God our Lord for having chosen to bring us out of a captivity so melancholy and wretched. The delight we felt let each one conjecture, when he shall remember the length of time we were in that country, the suffering and perils we underwent. . . . The next morning . . . , following the Christians by their trail, I traveled ten leagues, passing three villages at which they had slept.

The day after, I overtook four of them on horseback, who were astonished at the sight of me, so strangely habited as I was, and in company with Indians. They stood staring at me a length of time, so confounded that they neither hailed me nor drew near to make an inquiry. I bade them take me to their chief: accordingly we went together half a league to the place where was Diego de Alcarez, their captain.

iii

The first Englishmen to set foot on the west coast of the continent were members of Francis Drake's party of buccaneers, whose ship, the 100-ton *Golden Hind,* having passed through the Straits of Magellan and plundered the Spanish ports of Valparaiso and Callao, proceeded up the coasts of South, Central, and North America, their leader's purpose to find an east-west passage that would enable him to return to England without having again to round the tip of South America. Having failed in that quest, Drake determined to proceed westward across the Pacific—a decision that resulted in his becoming the first English mariner to circumnavigate the globe.

In order to prepare for that long cruise, Drake decided that he must first clean and refit his vessel and take on needed supplies of food and water. Accordingly, toward the middle of June, 1579, the *Golden Hind* was beached on the shores of a bay on the northern California coast, where a stay of more than a month was made. Precisely where this landing was made has long been a matter of debate; some authorities maintain that the ship entered the harbor of San Francisco, while others claim it was the inlet some thirty miles to the north now known as Drake's Bay.

Several fragmentary accounts of their stay in California have come down to us, from one of which—that of the captain's nephew, John Drake, a member of the party—the following is taken:

Then [we] . . . sailed, always on a wind, in a north-west and north-north-westerly direction, for a thousand leagues . . . when the wind changed and he went to the Californias where he discovered land in forty-eight degrees. There he landed and built huts and remained for a month and a half, caulking his vessel. The victuals found were mussels and sea lions. During the time many Indians came there and when they saw the Englishmen they wept and scratched their faces and drew blood, as though this were an act of homage or adoration. But Captain Francis told them not to do that, for the Englishmen were not God. These people were peaceful and did no harm to the English, but gave them no food. They are the color of the Indians in Peru and are comely. They carry bows and arrows and go naked. The climate is temperate, more cold than hot. To all appearances it is a very good country . . . He departed leaving the Indians to all appearances sad . . .

A second account, based on notes made by Francis, chaplain of the expedition, and published in 1628, thus describes a trip Drake and others made into the back country:

After . . . our necessary businesses were all dispatched, our General, with his gentlemen and many of his company, made a journey up into the land, to see the manner of their dwelling, and to be the better acquainted with the nature and commodities of the country. Their houses are all such as we have formerly described, and being many of them in one place, made several villages. . . . The inland we found to be far different from the shore, a goodly country, and fruitful soil, stored with many blessings fit for the use of man: infinite was the company of very large and fat deer, which we saw by the thousands . . .

This country our General named *Albion,* and that for two causes; the one in respect to the white banks and cliffs, which lie toward the sea; the other, that it might have some affinity, even in name also with our own country, which was sometimes so called.

Before we went from thence, our General caused to be set up a monument of our being there, as also of her majesty's and successors' right and title to that kingdom; namely, a plate of brass, fast nailed to a great and firm post; whereon is graven her grace's name, and the day and year of our arrival there, and of the free giving up of the province and kingdom, both by the king and people, into her majesty's hands: together with her highnesses' picture and arms, in a piece of six-pence current English money, showing itself by a hole made of purpose through the plate; underneath was likewise engraven the name of our General, etc. . . .

The 23 of July they [the Indians] took a sorrowful farewell of us, but being loath to leave us, they presently ran to the top of the hills to keep us in their sight as long as they could, making fires before and behind, and on each side of them, burning therein (as is to be supposed) sacrifices at our departure.

iv

Before the end of the sixteenth century the exploration of
what is now our country's west coast had become a necessary
part of Spain's ambitious plan to control the commerce of
the Pacific. Trans-Pacific navigation, which had begun with
Magellan's voyage in 1520-21, had grown steadily; and by the
end of the century Spanish galleons were following regular
trade routes between Manila, China, and Panama. On their
eastward voyages it was the custom—because of prevailing
winds—for the ships to lay their courses so as to sight the
mainland about midway on the California shoreline, then to
follow the coast down to the Isthmus of Panama. These
passages often consumed more than six months, and both
men and vessels arrived at Panama—when they did arrive
—weakened by the strain of so long a period at sea.

The desirability of breaking the journeys at some point
near where the eastbound ships first sighted the mainland
was at length recognized by the Spanish authorities. It was
because of this need for a safe harbor on the northern coast
that the exploration of that area was undertaken so early.
The first attempt to locate such a stopping place failed
when, in 1595, Cermeno's ship, the *San Agustín,* ran ashore
and was wrecked on the northern California coast. Seven
years later, in 1602, a new expedition, commanded by Sebas-
tián Vizcaíno, was organized and dispatched northward.
During the months that followed Vizcaíno explored and
mapped the California coast from San Diego to Cape
Mendocino and beyond, conferring on many of its features
the picturesque names by which they are known to this day.

The most complete story of this venture is that written
by Father Antonio de la Ascensión, who accompanied Vizcaíno on his cruise. Father Antonio's story was first published
in 1615; here is his enthusiastic description of Monterey Bay,
into which the party put in mid-December of 1602:

This [he wrote] is an excellent harbor and secure against all winds. Near the shore are an infinite number of very large pines, strait and smooth, fit for masts and yards; likewise oaks of a prodigious size proper for building ships. Here likewise are rose-trees, white thorns, firs, willows, and poplars; large clear lakes, fine pastures, and arable lands. Wild beasts, particularly bears of an uncommon size, are found here, and a species of horned cattle resembling buffaloes, and about the same size; others as large as wolves, and shaped like a stag. . . . The country also abounds in deer, rabbits, hares, and wild cats, bustards, geese, ducks, pigeons, partridges, thrushes, sparrows, goldfinches; cranes and vultures are also found here, together with another kind of bird of the bigness of a turkey; and the largest seen during the whole voyage, being seventeen spans from the tip of one wing to that of the other . . . The sea abounds with oysters, lobsters, crabs, &c. Also huge sea wolves and whales. This harbor is surrounded with the rancherias of Indians, a well-looking affable people, and very ready to part with everything they have. They are also under some form of government. Their arms are bows and arrows. They expressed a great deal of concern when they perceived the Spaniards were going to leave them, which happened on the 3d of Jan. 1603 . . .

> Having proceeded up the coast to a point that some authorities believe may have been a bit beyond the present California-Oregon border, winter storms, plus the illness of many of the crew, caused the commander again to turn southward and head for Acapulco, the port from which the expedition had sailed. Their return trip down the coast was described by Father Antonio in these words:

[We] kept along so near the land as plainly to discern, whether anything worth noticing had escaped their first observations. In this latitude the country along the coast made a very verdant appearance, and that on the inland parts, which had all the signs of fertility, was also very populous, there being a great number of fires in all parts. The wind being now at northwest, very favorable, & the weather easy, we had a clear and continual view of every inch of ground along the shore. While the *Capitana* [their ship] was thus delightfully sailing along a very pleasant coast, a little distance from St. Barbara's channel, two canoes were seen coming towards the ship, each with three men without any other covering than a kind of goats' skins: and after rowing three times round the ship, without any further ceremony came on board, with the same freedom and cheerfulness as if coming into their own homes. Bisket and some other trifles were given them & they returned to the shore highly satisfied.

> During their stay at Monterey, Vizcaíno, on December 28, 1602, addressed a letter to a high official in Mexico City describing what he had thus far observed. This document, now preserved in the India Archives at Seville, reads in part as follows:

As to what this harbor of Monterey is, in addition to being so well situated in point of latitude for that which His Majesty intends to do for the protection and security of ships coming from the Philippines: In it may be repaired the damages which they may have sustained, for there is a great extent of pine forest from which to obtain masts, even though the vessel be of a thousand tons burthen . . . The harbor is very secure against all winds. The land is thickly peopled by Indians and is very fertile, in its climate and the quality of the soil resembling Castile, and any seed sown there will give fruit, and there are extensive lands for pasturage, and many kinds of animals and birds . . .

I advise His Majesty concerning the great extent of this land and its numerous population, and what promise it holds forth, and what the Indians have given me to understand concerning the people of the interior, and of how gentle and affable the people are, so that they will receive readily, as I think, the holy gospel and will come into subjection to the royal crown; and, since His Majesty is lord and master of all, let him provide as may seem best to him. As to what it behooves me to do on my part, I will serve him to the death . . .

II
Trail Breakers

i

Following the visits in the sixteenth and early seventeenth centuries of certain small groups of far-ranging adventurers —some of whose impressions are recorded in Chapter I— there came a period during which, for almost a century and a half, virtually no Europeans set foot on the territory that now comprises the western third of the nation. From one end to the other of that huge area the native Indian tribes remained in undisputed possession of the lands of their ancestors.

Then, in the final decades of the eighteenth century, the eyes of officials of the Spanish province of Mexico turned toward the north and a series of steps were taken, all designed to establish permanent outposts within the territory and thereby secure it as a permanent possession of the Spanish crown. Among the expeditions organized and dispatched northward during that period were two groups, one traveling by sea and the other by land. They both set off in 1769, their purpose to found military posts at strategic points along the coast of Alta California and to Christianize the natives of the region. The result was that within the next half century towns sprang up at a number of coastal points from San Diego to Monterey, and a series of missions—nineteen in all —were established in the area.

During that same period a like program of colonization was being carried out in the Southwest, with outposts being set up at various spots in present-day Arizona and New Mexico. After the revolution of 1822, by which Mexico gained its independence from Spain, the communities to the north continued to be administered from Mexico City. However, events were now fast moving toward a climax, for other nations had long been casting covetous eyes in the direction of these colonies, and it was growing clearer year by year that Mexico's hold on them could not be much longer maintained.

On the opposite coast of our continent, meanwhile, residents of the thirteen former British colonies had thrown off the yoke of the mother country and set up their own republic. The United States by the early 1800's had pushed its frontiers westward to and beyond the banks of the Mississippi, and interest in the region that lay beyond that stream was growing steadily stronger. It was indeed a desire for more definite information about that virtually unknown area west of the Mississippi that led to the memorable Lewis and Clark expedition of 1803-06.

That historic journey was undertaken at the behest of President Jefferson, who in 1803 obtained from Congress an appropriation of $2500 to cover the expense of sending an expedition westward from the Missouri River to the Pacific, its primary purpose to find "the most direct and practicable water communication across the continent. . . ."

To head the group, Jefferson appointed his 29-year-old secretary, Meriwether Lewis, and Lewis in turn selected his friend William Clark as joint leader of the 45-man party. After a winter of training near the mouth of the Missouri, the party set off in the spring of 1804, and proceeded up that stream to a point near the site of the present city of Bismarck, North Dakota, where a second winter was spent. With the coming of spring they again pressed on, following the Missouri to its source, then breaking a trail through the rugged Rocky Mountain country, searching for the headwaters of the Columbia. After more than two months of arduous travel they reached a tributary of that stream; there they built canoes and in them floated down to the Columbia's mouth, which was reached toward the middle of November, 1805.

Both Lewis and Clark kept day-by-day records of their travels, and from them one learns much of the tribulations and triumphs of their journey. Thus in the summer of 1805, while the party was struggling through what is now southern Montana, Lewis wrote:

August 10th: After passing a large creek at about 5 miles we fell in with the plain Indian road which led towards the point that the river entered the mountain. We therefore pursued the road. I sent Drewyer to the right to kill a deer which we saw feeding and halted on the river under an immensely high perpendicular clift of rocks where it entered the mountain. Here we kindled a fire and waited for Drewyer.

He arrived in about an hour and a half . . . with three deer skins and the flesh of one of the best of them; we cooked and ate a hasty meal and departed, returning a short distance to the Indian road which led us the best way over the mountains, which are not very high but rugged and approached the river closely on both sides . . .

The river below the mountains is rapid, rocky, very crooked, much divided by islands and withal shallow. After it enters the mountain its bends are not so circuitous and its general course more direct, but it is equally shallow, less divided, more rocky and rapid.

The mountains do not appear very high in any direction

tho' the tops of some of them are partially covered with snow.

This convinces me that we have ascended to a great height since we have entered the rocky mountains, yet the ascent has been so gradual along the valleys that it was scarcely perceptible . . . I do not believe that the world can furnish an example of a river running to the extent which the Missouri and Jefferson's rivers do through such a mountainous country and at the same time so navigable as they are.

If the Columbia furnishes us with such another example, a communication across the continent by water will be practicable and safe. But this I can scarcely hope from a knowledge of its having in its comparatively short course to the ocean the same number of feet to descend which the Missouri and Mississippi have from this point to the Gulf of Mexico.

Some two months later, having set off down the Snake River in their newly built canoes, Clark wrote in his diary:

October, 16th: A cool morning. Determined to run the rapids. Put our Indian guide in front of our Small Canoe next and the other four following each other.

The canoes all passed over Safe except the rear canoe which ran fast on a rock at the lower part of the Rapids. With the early assistance of the other Canoes & the Indians, who was extreamly ellert, every thing was taken out and the Canoe got off without any enjorie further than the articles which it was loaded all wet.

At 14 miles passed a bad rapid at which place we unloaded and made a portage of ¾ of a mile, haveing passed 4 smaller rapids, three Islands and the parts of a house above. I saw Indians and Horses on the South Side below. Five Indians came up the river in great haste. We smoked with them and gave them a piece of tobacco . . . and sent them back . . .

After getting safely over the rapid and haveing taken Diner, set out and proceeded on seven miles to the junction of this river and the Columbia which joins from the N.W. In every direction from the junction of those rivers the country is one continued plain, low, and rises from the water gradually, except a range of high Countrey on the opposite side . . .

Some three weeks later, on November 7, Clark's entry makes it clear that they were approaching the Columbia's mouth, their long and arduous trek nearing its end.

A cloudy foggey morning. Some rain. We set out early, proceeded under high rugged hills with steep assent, the shore bold and rocky, the fog so thick we could not see across the river. Two canoes of Indians met and returned with us to their village. They gave us to eate some fish, and sold us fish, *wap pato* roots, and I purchased 2 bever skins for the purpose of makeing me a robe, as the robe I have is rotten and good for nothing.

Opposit to this village the high mountaneous countrey leaves the river on the Larboard side below which the river widens into a kind of Bay & is crouded with low Islands subject to be covered by the tides.

We proceeded on about 12 miles below the Village . . . and encamped under a high hill opposit to a rock situated half a mile from the shore. . . . We with dificuelty found a place clear of the tide and sufficiently large to lie on and the only place we could get was on round stones on which to lay our mats . . .

Great joy in camp. We are [near] this great Pacific Ocean . . . and the roreing or noise made by the waves brakeing on the rockey shores (as I suppose) may be heard distinctly.

Not until November 18, however, did the group actually catch sight of the ocean toward which they had been struggling for more than eighteen months. The men, stated Clark, "appear much satisfied with their trip, beholding with estonishment the high waves dashing against the rocks & this emence Ocian."

There, at the mouth of the Columbia, the party built a series of rude shelters, which they called Fort Clatsop. Here they spent the winter of 1805-06, meanwhile hoping that a Yankee trading ship might arrive off the coast in which they could secure passage home. No such vessel appearing, they set off early the following spring on the long overland trek to St. Louis, which was reached in late September of 1806, the party thus becoming the first Americans to span the continent.

ii

In the exploration of the Far West no men played a larger part than did the traders and trappers. To these adventurous spirits the lure of new and greener fields to cultivate drew them ever farther into the unknown: to streams abounding in beaver and other animals the furs of which were in active demand in civilized centers both on the East Coast and abroad; to Indian tribes whose members would gather the valuable peltries and exchange them for bright-colored calicos, beads, blankets, firearms, powder, and other products of the white man's factories.

Two of the best-known members of that far-ranging band were William Henry Ashley and Jedediah Strong Smith, and fortunately both have left behind records of what they observed and what befell them on their wanderings. Ashley, a Virginian born in 1778, had by the 1820's become an im-

portant factor in the fur trade, yearly dispatching parties up
the Missouri River to the Yellowstone and beyond, and
building up an extensive and lucrative trade. During much
of 1824-25 Ashley was in the field with one of his parties,
following a great circle course that penetrated as far west
as present-day Utah. He then swung north to within a few
miles of the Canadian border, and followed the course of
the Missouri River more than a thousand miles to its con-
fluence with the Mississippi.

Upon his return to St. Louis toward the end of 1825,
Ashley wrote General Henry Atkinson, of the Adjutant-
General's office of the Army's Western Department at Louis-
ville, Kentucky, a 36-page letter describing his journey and
giving his impressions of the country traversed. From this,
these passages are quoted:

The following remarks [Ashley began] relating to my journey have been cursorily put together, but as they afford some
better information as to the practicability and means of traversing that region, at the season of the year presenting the
greatest privations, they may not be uninteresting to you.

I left Fort Atkinson on the 3rd November, 1824. On the
afternoon of the 5th, I overtook my party of mountaineers
(twenty-five in number), who had in charge fifty pack
horses, a wagon and teams, etc. On the 6th . . . it commenced snowing, and continued with but little intermission until the morning of the 8th. During this time my
men and horses were suffering for want of food, which, combined with the severity of the weather, presented rather a
gloomy prospect. I had left Fort Atkinson under the belief
that I could procure provisions at the Pawney villages to subsist my men until we could reach a point affording a suf-
ficiency of game; but in this I was disappointed, as I learned
by sending to the villages, that they were entirely deserted,
the Indians having . . . departed some two or three weeks

previous for their wintering ground. As the vicinity of those villages afforded little or no game, my only alternative was to subsist my men on horse meat, and my horses on cottonwood bark, the ground being at this time covered with snow about two feet deep. In this situation we continued for about the space of two weeks, during which time we made frequent attempts to advance and reach a point of relief, but, owing to the intense cold and violence of the winds, we had only succeeded in advancing some ten or twelve miles . . . Cold and hunger had by this time killed several of my horses, and many others were much reduced from the same cause.

> Throughout that winter on the open prairies both men and animals suffered severely from cold and hunger. An interest-ing—and at the same time amusing—picture of the hardships of the period is provided in the reminiscences of the noted frontiersman Jim Beckwourth, who was a member of the party. Because Beckwourth was an excellent marksman, Ashley frequently dispatched him on hunting forays along the snow-covered banks of the Platte River in the hope of bagging game that would augment the group's meager fare. On one such trip, Beckwourth relates that when only a few hundred yards from camp he had the good fortune to sight two teal ducks.

I levelled my rifle [he recalled] and handsomely shot one. This was a temptation to my constancy; and appetite and conscientiousness had a long strife as to the disposal of the booty.

> In the end appetite triumphed over moral scruples, and he forthwith kindled a fire and cooked and ate the duck, salv-ing his conscience with the reflection that "if, by fortifying myself, I gained ability to procure something more sub-stantial than a teal duck, my dereliction would be sufficiently

atoned, and my overruling appetite, at the same time, gratified." Fortified by his furtive meal, the hunter continued
and, as luck would have it, had an extraordinarily successful
hunt, bringing down three elk, a wolf, and a deer. When
these were dragged into camp the half-starved party happily
set about preparations for a banquet, and words of praise
for the mighty hunter were heard on all sides.

Amid all this gratulation [continued Beckwourth] I could
not separate my thoughts from the duck which had supplied
my clandestine meal in the bushes. I suffered them to ap-
pease their hungers with the proceeds of my toil before I
ventured to tell my comrades of the offense I had been guilty
of. All justified my conduct, declaring my conclusions ob-
vious . . . Since that time, I have never refused to share
my last shilling, my last biscuit, or my only blanket with a
friend, and I think the recollection of that "temptation in the
wilderness" will ever serve as a lesson to more constancy in
the future.

Throughout the winter of 1824-25 Ashley's party pushed its
way westward across the bleak, snow-covered countryside,
and the spring found the caravan trooping through Bridger's
Pass, Ashley and his men being the first to cross the Continental Divide by that route. Arriving in early April on the
banks of the Green River in what is now southwest Wyoming, Ashley set about exploring the area.

I determined [he wrote] to relieve my men and horses of
their heavy burdens, to accomplish which, I concluded to
make four divisions of my party, send three of them by land
in different directions, and with the fourth party, descend the
river myself with the principal part of my merchandise. Accordingly, some of the men commenced making a frame
about the size and shape of a common mackinaw boat, while

others were sent to procure buffalo skins for a covering. On
the 21st of April, all things being ready for our departure,
I dispatched six men northwardly to the sources of the river;
seven others set out for a mountain bearing S.S.W., and
N.N.E., distant about thirty miles; and six others were sent
in a southern direction. After selecting one of the most intelligent and efficient of each party as partizans, I directed
them to proceed to their respective points of destination and
thence in such direction as circumstances should dictate for
my interest. At the same time they were instructed to en-
deavor to fall in with two parties of men that were fitted out
by me the year previous, and who were then, as I supposed,
beyond the range of mountains appearing westwardly. The
partizans were also informed that I would descend the river
to some eligible point about one hundred miles below, there
deposit a part of my merchandise, and make such marks as
would designate it as a place of general rendezvous for the
men in my service in that country, and where they were all
directed to assemble on or before the 10th July following.

Upon arriving back at St. Louis in October of 1825 Ashley
carried with him a hundred or more packs of beaver skins,
having a value estimated at from forty to eighty thousand
dollars—which he considered ample compensation for the
privations and dangers he had faced during his eleven
months in the wilderness. The following year he led a
second expedition westward, this time advancing to the
vicinity of Great Salt Lake—which one of his men, Jim
Bridger, is credited with having discovered—and once more
returning with a plentitude of beaver pelts. Having by that
time acquired an ample fortune in the fur trade, the 48-
year-old Ashley gradually withdrew from active business and
thereafter devoted his abundant energies to politics. Twice
defeated for governor of Missouri, he served three terms in
Congress (from 1831 to 1837), where he was regarded by

his fellows as a prime authority on matters pertaining to the Far West. He died in 1838 at the age of sixty.

Although, as stated earlier, Ashley's second expedition— that of 1826—ended his personal acquaintance with the frontier, during the next several years the activity he had set in motion was to continue on an ever widening scale. It is recorded that prior to leaving St. Louis on his final west- ward trip in the spring of 1826, Ashley had agreed to sell his trading company to three of his employees, namely, Jedediah Smith, David Jackson, and William L. Sublette. Of these the best remembered is Jedediah Smith, whose subsequent travels covered so large an area of virgin territory as to place him in the front rank of far western trail breakers.

Born in 1798 of sturdy New England stock, the adven- ture-loving Smith early headed west, where while still a youth he held a succession of progressively more important posts. Hence, when in 1822 he joined the first of Ashley's expeditions, he was already an experienced frontiersman, and—as we have seen—during the next several years he be- came one of his employer's most trusted lieutenants. When, in the summer of 1826, the Ashley party reached Great Salt Lake and its leader set off on the long trek back to St. Louis, the three new owners of this far-flung fur-trading empire laid plans to increase still further the scope of its operations. This was no less than to seek out new beaver hunting grounds that they assumed must lie farther to the west in the vast region that lay between the Rockies and the shores of the Pacific.

Accordingly, while his two partners, Jackson and Sublette, continued trading operations in their already established frontier stations, Smith and a picked group of fifteen men set off on a journey that during the course of the next year was to carry them over huge areas of country never before traversed by white men. Upon his return to the starting place on the shores of Salt Lake in July of 1827, Smith wrote

a letter to General William Clark, Superintendent of Indian
Affairs, describing his journey. Some of the high points of
that narrative are quoted here.

My situation in this country [he began] has enabled me to
collect information respecting a section of the country which
has hitherto been measureably veiled in obscurity to the
citizens of the United States. I allude to the country S.W. of
the Great Salt Lake west of the Rocky Mountains . . .

> After giving an account of his party's three-month-long pas-
> sage down the Virgin and Colorado rivers, and their crossing
> of the latter stream into California near the present site of
> Needles, he continued thus:

I travelled a west course fifteen days over a country of complete barrens [the Mojave Desert] generally travelling from
morning to night without water. I crossed a salt plain about
20 miles long and 8 wide; on the surface was a crust of
beautiful white salt, quite thin. Under this surface there is
a layer of salt from a half to one and a half inches in depth;
between this and the upper layer there is about four inches
of yellowish sand.

On my arrival in the province of Upper California, I was
looked upon with suspicion, and was compelled to appear in
the presence of the governor of the Californias residing at
San Diego, where, by the assistance of some American
gentlemen . . . , I was enabled to obtain permission to return with my men by the route I came, and purchased such
supplies as I stood in want of . . . I returned to my party
. . . and went eastward of the Spanish settlements on the
route I had come in. I then steered my course N.W., keeping from 150 miles to 200 miles from the sea coast. A very
high range of mountains [the Sierra Nevada] lay on the
east. After travelling three hundred miles in that direction

through a country somewhat fertile, in which there were a great many Indians, mostly naked and destitute of arms, with the exception of a few bows and arrows and, what is very singular amongst Indians, they cut their hair to the length of three inches; they proved to be friendly; their manner of living is on fish, roots, acorns and grass.

On my arrival at the river which I named the Wimulche (after a tribe of Indians which resides on it, of that name) I found a few beaver, and elk, deer, and antelope in abundance. I here made a small hunt and attempted to take my party across the mountain . . . which I called Mount Joseph, to come on and join my partners at the Great Salt Lake.

Crossing the towering bulk of the Sierra at that season of the year proved a formidable undertaking, one that called forth all the skill and endurance of Smith and his men. His letter to General Clark continues thus:

I found the snow so deep on Mount Joseph that I could not cross my horses, five of which starved to death; I was compelled therefore to return to the valley which I had left, and there, leaving my party, I started with two men, seven horses and two mules, which I loaded with hay for the horses and provisions for ourselves, and started on the 20th of May, and succeeded in crossing it in eight days, having lost only two horses and one mule. I found the snow on the top of this mountain from 4 to 8 feet deep, but it was so consolidated by the heat of the sun that my horses only sank from half a foot to one foot.

Thus briefly and casually did Smith describe this momentous first crossing of the Sierra Nevada range. Of the hardly less gruelling final leg of his journey—from the eastern base of the mountains across the arid wastes of present-day Nevada

and western Utah to his starting point—he wrote in a manner equally matter-of-fact.

After travelling twenty days from the east side of Mount
Joseph [he stated], I struck the S.W. corner of the Great
Salt Lake, travelling over a country completely barren and
destitute of game. We frequently travelled without water
sometimes for two days over sandy deserts, where there was
no sign of vegetation and when we found water in some of
the rocky hills, we most generally found some Indians who
appeared the most miserable of the human race having nothing to subsist on (nor any clothing) except grass seed,
grass-hoppers, etc. When we arrived at the Salt Lake, we
had but one horse and one mule remaining, which were so
feeble and poor that they could scarce carry the little camp
equipage which I had along; the balance of my horses I was
compelled to eat as they gave out.

> We of today, fortunately, do not have to depend exclusively
> on Smith's letter for a first-hand account of that journey of
> the first overland party of Americans to reach California.
> For one of the fifteen men who accompanied him was Harri-
> son G. Rogers, the company clerk, and Rogers kept a daily
> record of happenings, part of which has survived. This, as
> the following excerpts reveal, was far more detailed and
> colorful than that of the party's leader. Thus, on November
> 28, 1826, the group having arrived, travel-weary and hungry,
> at the Mission San Gabriel, they were hospitably greeted by
> the padres, who supplied food and shelter for the men and
> took Smith as their guest in the mission itself. Rogers' entry
> of that date reads thus:

Mr. S[mith] wrote me this morning, stating that he was received as a gentleman and treated as such, and that he
wished me to go back and look for a pistol that was lost, and

send the company on to the missionary establishment. I com-
plied with his request, went back, and found the pistol, and
arrived late in the evening, was received very politely, and
showed into a room and my arms taken from me. At about
ten o'clock at night supper was served, and Mr. S. and myself sent for. I was introduced to the 2 priests over a glass
of good old whiskey and found them to be very jovial
friendly gentlemen, and supper consisted of a number of
different dishes, served different from any table I ever was at.
Plenty of good wine during supper, and before the cloth was
removed sigars was introduced. Mr. S. has wrote to the governor, and I expect we shall remain here some days.

> The next day's entry gives further details of the hospitality
> of the mission friars to these strangers from beyond the
> mountains.

29th. . . . We was sent for about sunrise to drink a cup of
tea, and eat some bread and cheese. They all appear friendly
and treat us well; although they are Catholicks by profession,
they allow us the liberty of conscience, and treat us as they
do their own countrymen, or breathren.

About 11 o'clock, dinner was ready, and the priest come
after us to go and dine; we were invited into the office and
invited to take a glass of gin and water and eat some bread
and cheese; directly after we were seated at dinner, and
everything went on in style, both the priests being pretty
merry, the clerk and one other gentleman, who speaks some
English. They all appear to be gentlemen of the first class,
both in manner and habits . . .

> Little escaped the eye of this observant young man, and
> what he saw was faithfully recorded on the pages of his
> journal. Here is his picture of the complex establishment
> the padres presided over at San Marino:

The mansion, or mission, consist of 4 rows of houses forming a complete square, where there is all kinds of macanicks at work; the church faces the east and the guard house the west; the N. and S. line composes the work shops. They have large vineyards, apple and peach orchards, and some orrange and some fig trees. They manufacture blankets, and sundry other articles; they distill whiskey and grind their own grain, having a water mill, of a tolerable quality; they have upwards of 1,000 persons employed, men, women, and children, Indians of different nations. The situation is very handsome, pretty streams of water running through from all quarters, some thousands of acres of rich and fertile land as level as a die in view, and a part under cultivation . . . The mission has upwards of 30,000 head of cattle, and horses, sheep, hogs, etc. in proportion . . . They slaughter at this place from 2 to 3,000 head of cattle at a time; the mission lives on the profits.

The party's stay at San Gabriel lasted much longer than had been planned, the delay being occasioned by a reluctance of the Mexican governor to grant Smith and his party permission to leave California by a different route than that by which they had come. Not until mid-January of 1827 did the group set off on the long tramp eastward, progressing by easy stages up the province's central valley to the point where the Stanislaus River flows into the San Joaquin, then following up the canyon of the latter stream toward the snowy crest of the Sierra.

When it was found impossible to move the entire party, men, animals, and equipment, over the summit, Smith and two companions, as we have seen, set off on the long trek to Salt Lake while the others made camp in the foothills to await their leader's return. Having after an extremely arduous march gained the shores of Salt Lake and kept the rendezvous with his partners, Jackson and Sublette, Smith

began preparations for a return to California. Accordingly
in mid-July he again headed westward, this time with a party
of nineteen men and, following much the same trail he had
broken the year before, in mid-September joined the original
group at their camp on the Stanislaus.

After a delay of some weeks devoted to replenishing their
supplies and equipment, the united party got under way on
their return trip eastward. Having learned from his experience the previous spring that it would be impossible to
transport so large a group across the Sierra, Smith reached
a bold decision, namely, to head northward into the unknown territory between central California and the Hudson's
Bay Company's trading posts on the banks of the Columbia
River. The result was another notable trail-breaking journey, passing up the Sacramento Valley in March and April,
1828, crossing over to the coast the following month, and
proceeding up the shoreline of present-day Oregon for several weeks before again turning inland.

The story of the latter part of that long march has also
been preserved in Rogers' journal. This document makes
clear that that part of the trip was likewise an uncommonly
arduous one, with only infrequent Indian trails to aid their
progress through a rugged, heavily wooded country, and a
succession of streams that had to be crossed and recrossed
on their progress up the coast. Much of June and July were
thus consumed. It was then, after the party has turned inland toward the Willamette Valley—from which a few days'
easy travel would have brought them to the trading outposts on the Columbia—that disaster struck.

What happened was thus described by Jedediah Smith
to an official of the Hudson's Bay Company after Smith and
two companions reached safety at Fort Vancouver:

Finding myself among Indians whom, from their possession
of many articles of European merchandize, and frequently

naming you and several other gentlemen, I began to consider no longer as enemies, I relaxed my usual vigilance. Having prolonged my stay for two days, to recruit the worn-out animals I had purchased at San Gabriel, on the third morning I directed Mr. Rogers, my assistant, to have everything in readiness, desiring the men to clean their rifles, preparatory to a start on the morrow. I then, accompanied by two men, embarked in a canoe, and proceeded in search of a suitable crossing place [of the Umpqua River], the banks opposite our encampment being too steep for the horses to surmount. On my return, after an absence of three hours, when within half a mile of the tents, I observed a number of Indians running towards us along the bank, yelling most fearfully. Immediately suspecting what had happened, we crossed over, and secreted ourselves in the bushes, the Indians discharging their guns at us without effect. Anxious to ascertain the fate of my party, I then ascended an eminence, from whence I could plainly perceive that the camp was destroyed, and not a vestige of man, horse, or mule, to be seen.

Though conscious that the wretches would not dare to pursue us, in a country so thickly wooded, I yet considered it to be most prudent to be concealed during the day, and to travel only under cover of the night. On the second day we perceived some of the Company's servants, who conducted us safely to Vancouver.

The official to whom Smith related the above [supposedly Peter Skeene Ogden] thus continued the narrative:

The day preceding Mr. Smith's arrival under these circumstances, one of his party named John Black, who had escaped the massacre at the camp, had also made his way to Fort Vancouver, and preparations had at once been commenced by the superintendent of the Company's affairs, to ascertain the fate of Mr. Smith and his two men. This party was on the eve of setting out, when the arrival of the fugitives relieved us of that anxiety. From Black we elicited the particulars of the massacre in the following words: "Soon after Mr. Smith's departure, while some of the men were cleaning their rifles, some cooking, and others trafficking with the natives, on a sudden the latter, in number exceeding two hundred, with dreadful shouts, rushed on us, before any one was prepared for defence. I," said the poor fellow, "escaped the general fate, being wounded and left for dead, but recovering, succeeded in effecting my retreat hither."

The Hudson's Bay Company official then added this postscript:

Thus fell eighteen men, far from their homes, their relations and their friends. As for the survivors, they met with every attention from us which their destitute condition demanded. Decisive measures were adopted to recover Mr. Smith's property. All the furs, with most of the horses and mules, were recovered and restored to their right owners, who subsequently made them over to the Company at a valuation rather exceeding the current price, which the agents for the Company cheerfully offered to the adventurer, in sympathy for his forlorn condition. . . .

The rest can be briefly told. Smith eventually made his way back to St. Louis and the following year (1831) again headed westward, this time over the Santa Fe Trail. Late in May, while in search of water for the men and animals of his party, he pushed on in advance of the main group and was set on by a band of Comanche Indians and slain. During his brief life—he was only thirty-three at the time of his death—Smith played an outstanding role in the story of the opening of the West, he having been, so far as is known, not

only the first white man to cross the Sierra range but likewise the first to travel up the west coast from the Mexican
province of California to the mouth of the Columbia River.
Surely these two exploits, to say nothing of others with which
his name is associated, are sufficient to place him high on
any list of the country's trail blazers.

iii

Another name inseparably associated with the exploration
of the early West is that of John C. Frémont, who between
1842 and 1848 led no less than five expeditions into the
wilderness, during which he and his companions (one of
whom was the famous scout, Kit Carson) met with a long
series of adventures. One of the most formidable of these
took place early in 1844, in the course of Frémont's second
exploring trip. On this, he and his party made the arduous
trek westward into the Oregon country, then turned south,
following the eastern base of the Cascades; finally, again
heading west, they attempted a winter crossing of the towering Sierra Nevada range.

    In his account of that passage, which first appeared in his
*The Exploring Expedition to the Rocky Mountains, Oregon
and North California,* published in 1849, Frémont gave a
day-by-day description of its hardships and perils. His entry
for February 4, 1844, reads thus:

I went ahead early with two or three men, each with a lead
horse to break the road. We were obliged to abandon the
hollow entirely and work along the mountainside, which was
very steep, and the snow covered with an icy crust. We cut a
footing as we advanced, and trampled a road through for
the animals, but occasionally one plunged outside the trail

and slid along the field to the bottom, a hundred yards below.

Toward a pass which the guide indicated here, we attempted in the afternoon to force a road, but after a laborious plunging through two or three hundred yards our best horses gave out, entirely refusing to make any further effort, and for a time we were brought to a stand. The guide informed us that we were entering the deep snow, and here began the difficulties of the mountain; and to him, and almost to all, our enterprise seemed hopeless.

Tonight we had no shelter, but we made a large fire around the trunk of one of the huge pines and, covering the snow with small boughs, on which we spread our blankets, soon made ourselves comfortable. The night was very bright and clear, though the thermometer was only ten degrees. Strong wind, which sprang up at sundown, made it intensely cold, and this was one of the bitterest nights during the journey.

The Indians joined our party here, and one of them, an old man, immediately began to harangue us, saying that ourselves and animals would perish in the snow, and that if we would go back, he would show us another and better way across the mountain. He spoke in a very loud voice, and there was a singular repetition of phrases and arrangement of words, which rendered his speech striking and not unmusical.

We now began to understand some words and with the aid of signs easily comprehended the old man's simple ideas.

"Rock upon rock—rock upon rock—snow upon snow," said he; "even if you get over the snow, you will not be able to get down from the mountains." He made us the sign of precipices and showed us how the feet of the horses would slip and throw them off from the narrow trails that led along their sides. Our Chinook, who comprehended even more readily than ourselves and believed our situation hopeless, covered his head with his blanket and began to weep and lament. "I wanted to see the whites," said he; "I came away from my own people to see the whites, and I wouldn't care to die among them, but here"—and he looked around into the cold night and gloomy forest and, drawing his blanket over his head, began again to lament.

Seated around the tree, the fire illuminating the rocks and the tall bolls of the pines round about and the old Indian haranguing, we presented a group of very serious faces . . .

Frémont's narrative continues thus:

February 5th. —The night had been too cold to sleep, and we were up very early. Our guide was standing by the fire with all his finery on, and seeing him shiver in the cold, I threw on his shoulders one of my blankets. We missed him a few minutes afterwards and never saw him again. He had deserted. His bad faith and treachery were in perfect keeping with the estimate of Indian character which a long intercourse with his people had forced upon my mind.

While a portion of the camp were occupied in bringing up the baggage to this point, the remainder were busy making sledges and snowshoes. I had determined to explore the mountain ahead, and the sledges were to be used in transporting the baggage.

6th. —Accompanied by Mr. Fitzpatrick, I set out today with a reconnoitering party on snowshoes. We marched all in single file, trampling the snow as heavily as we could. Crossing the open basin, in a march of about ten miles, we reached the top of one of the peaks to the left of the pass indicated by our guide. Far below us, dimmed by the distance, was a large snowless valley, bounded on the western side, at a distance of about a hundred miles, by a low range of mountains, which [Kit] Carson recognized with delight as the mountains bordering the coast . . . Between us, then, and this low coast range, was the valley of the Sacramento, and no one who had not accompanied us through the incidents of our life for the last few months could realize the delight with which at last we looked down upon it.

All our energies are now directed to getting our animals across the snow, and it was supposed that after all the baggage had been drawn with the sleighs over the trail we had made, it would be sufficiently hard to bear our animals . . . On our way across we had set on fire several broken stumps and dried trees to melt the snow for the camps. Its general depth was five feet, but we passed over places where it was twenty feet deep, as shown by the trees. . . .

9th. —During the night the weather changed, the wind rising to a gale, and commencing to snow before daylight; before morning the trail was covered. We remained quiet in camp all day, in the course of which the weather improved. Four sleighs arrived toward evening with bedding for the men. We suffer much from the want of salt, and all the men are becoming weak from insufficient food.

10th. —The elevation of the camp . . . is 8050 feet. We are now 1000 feet above the level of the South Pass in the Rocky Mountains, and still we are not done ascending. The top of a flat ridge near was bare of snow and very well sprinkled with bunch grass, sufficient to pasture the animals two or three days, and this was to be our main support.

11th. —In the evening I received a message from Mr. Fitzpatrick, acquainting me with the utter failure of his attempt to get our mules and horses over the snow—the half-hidden trail had proved entirely too slight to support them, and they had broken through and were plunging about or lying half buried in the snow. He was occupied in endeavoring to get them back to his camp and in the meantime sent to me for further instructions. I wrote to him to send the animals immediately back to their old pastures and, after having made mauls and shovels, turn in all the strength of his party

to open and beat a road through the snow, strengthening it
with branches and boughs of pines.

13th. —We continued to work on the road, and in the
course of the day had the satisfaction to see the people working down the face of the opposite hill, about three miles distant. . . . A party of Indians had passed on snowshoes,
who said they were going to the western side of the mountain
after fish. This was an indication that the salmon were coming up the streams, and we could hardly restrain our im-
patience as we thought of them, and worked with increased
vigor.

The meat train did not arrive this evening, and I gave
Godey leave to kill our little dog (Tlamath), which he prepared Indian fashion, scorching off the hair and washing the
skin with soap and snow, and then cutting it up into pieces,
which were laid on the snow. Soon afterwards the sleigh arrived with a supply of horse meat, and we had tonight an
extraordinary dinner—pea soup, mule, and dog.

16th. —We had succeeded in getting our animals safely
to the first grassy hill, and this morning I started with Jacob
on a reconnoitering expedition beyond the mountain. We
traveled along the crest of narrow ridges extending down the
mountain in the direction of the valley from which the snow
was fast melting away. On the open spots was tolerably good
grass, and I judged we should succeed in getting the camp
down by way of these. Toward sundown we discovered some
icy spots in a deep hollow and, descending the mountain, we
encamped on the headwater of a little creek, where at last the
water found its way to the Pacific.

The night was clear and very long. We heard the cries of
some wild animals which had been attracted by our fire, and
a flock of geese passed over during the night. Even these
strange sounds had something pleasant to our senses in this
region of silence and desolation.

We started again early in the morning. The creek acquired a regular breadth of about twenty feet, and we soon began to hear the rushing of water below the icy surface over which we traveled to avoid the snow; a few miles below we broke through where the water was several feet deep, and halted to make a fire and dry our clothes. We continued a few miles further, walking being very laborious without snowshoes.

I was now perfectly satisfied that we had struck the stream on which Mr. Sutter lived, and turning about, made a hard push and reached the camp at dark. . . .

On the 19th the people were occupied in making a road and bringing up the baggage; and on the afternoon of the next day, February 20, 1844, we encamped with the animals and all the *materiel* of the camp on the summit of the PASS in the dividing range . . .

21st. We now considered ourselves victorious over the mountain, having only the descent before us, and the valley under our eyes, we felt strong hope that we should force our way down. But this was a case in which the descent was *not* facile. Still deep fields of snow lay between, and there was a large intervening space of rough looking mountains, through which we had yet to wind our way. Carson roused me this morning with an early fire, and we were all up long before day, in order to pass the snow fields before the sun should render the crust soft . . .

We had hard and doubtful labor yet before us, as the snow appeared to be heavier where the timber began further down, with few open spots. Ascending a height, we traced out the best line we could discover for the next day's march, and had at least the consolation to see that the mountain descended rapidly. . . .

23rd. This was our most difficult day; we were forced off the ridges by the quantity of snow among the timber, and obliged to take to the mountain sides, where occasionally, rocks and a southern exposure afforded us a chance to

scramble along. But these were steep, and slippery with
snow and ice; and the tough evergreens of the mountain im-
peded our way, tore our skins, and exhausted our patience.
Some of us had the misfortune to wear mocassins with *par-
fleche* soles, so slippery that we could not keep our feet, and
generally crawled across the snow beds. . . .

> Thus day by day the laborious descent continued, men and
> animals cautiously making their way down toward the low-
> lands. Not until early March did the party leave the snows
> behind and gratefully set off across the valley's floor.

iv

Not only were the breakers of new trails throughout the
West obliged to contend with deep snows, waterless deserts,
mighty mountain ranges, swift-flowing streams, and numerous other natural features of the land, but they also faced
the hazard of surprise attacks by the Indian tribes through
whose hereditary hunting grounds they passed. One such
raid was, as we have seen, launched against Jedediah
Smith's party as they were approaching Fort Vancouver on
the Columbia River in the spring of 1828. That, however,
was not the Smith group's first disastrous brush with the
savages. The other had taken place months earlier, while
that far-ranging expedition was making its way through the
Southwest, headed for California. What transpired was thus
described in the leader's own words:

After suffering severely in crossing the barren desert [wrote
Smith], I was truly pleased to discover a fine stream of fresh
water, which proved to be the north branch of the Rio

Colorado. On sounding it, I found it too deep to ford, and as grass, which my lean horses much required, appeared to be far more abundant on the opposite side, I ordered ten men of the party to get them across, which they accordingly did, by driving them into the water, and accompanying them swimming. For several days I had been unsuccessfully searching above and below our position for a fording place, without discovering a vestige of any human inhabitants; but no sooner had my men landed on the opposite shore, than upwards of a hundred Indians rushed on them, from behind a thicket of willows, and murdered the whole. My horses were speedily secured and driven from sight, and it is scarcely necessary to say that any attempt at pursuit under such circumstances had been in vain. Such was the situation in which I found myself, with property to the value of ten thousand dollars; and rather than the villains who had so deeply injured me should reap any benefit from it, I had the whole thrown into the river. We then made a raft, and crossed over, when we found the bodies of my unfortunate men so mutilated as to be scarcely recognizable. We consigned them also to the keeping of the deep, for as you well know, not even the dead are respected by the wild tribes in these parts.

> One prime reason for Indian attacks against parties of whites who penetrated into their territory was to possess themselves of the invaders' livestock, horses and mules being highly prized by the natives, both for transportation and food. The story of one such raid, and its aftermath—this one also in the arid country of the Southwest—is told by John C. Frémont in the report of his historic expedition to the Oregon country, Nevada, and California in 1843-44. It was while returning via a southern route that the episode occurred. Under the date of April 24, 1844, Frémont wrote in his journal:

In the afternoon we were surprised by the sudden appearance in the camp of two Mexicans—a man and a boy. The name of the man was Andreas Fruentes; that of the boy (a handsome lad, eleven years old) Pablo Hermandez. They belonged to a party consisting of six persons . . . with a cavalcade of about thirty horses; they had come out from Puebla de Los Angeles, near the coast, to travel more at leisure, and obtain better grass. Having advanced as far into the desert as was considered consistent with their safety, they halted at the Archilette, one of the customary camping grounds, about eighty miles from our encampment, where there is a good spring of water, with sufficient grass, and concluded to wait there the arrival of the great caravan. Several Indians were soon discovered lurking about the camp, who, in a day or two after, came in, and after behaving in a very friendly manner, took their leave, without awakening any suspicions. Their deportment begat a security which proved fatal. In a few days afterward, suddenly a party of about one hundred Indians appeared in sight, advancing toward the camp. It was too late, or they seemed not to have presence of mind to take proper measures of safety; and the Indians charged down into the camp, shouting as they advanced, and discharging flights of arrows. Pablo and Fruentes were on horse-guard at the time, and mounted according to the custom of the country.

One of the principal objects of the Indians was to get possession of the horses, and part of them immediately surrounded the band; but in obedience to the shouts of Giacome, Fruentes drove the animals over and through the assailants, in spite of their arrows; and, abandoning the rest to their fate, carried them off at speed across the plain. Knowing that they would be pursued by the Indians, without making any halt, except to shift their saddles to other horses, they drove them on for about sixty miles, and this morning left them at a watering-place upon the trail called Agua de

Tomaso. Without giving themselves any time for rest, they hurried on, hoping to meet the Spanish caravan, when they discovered my camp. I received them kindly, taking them into my own mess, and promised them such aid as circumstances might put it in my power to give.

The following day, April 25, Frémont told the aftermath.

After traveling about twenty-five miles [he wrote] we arrived at the Agua de Tomaso—the spring where the horses had been left; but as we expected, they were gone. A brief examination of the ground convinced us that they had been driven off by the Indians. Carson and Godey volunteered with the Mexican to pursue them; and, well mounted, the three set off on the trail. In the evening Fruentes returned, his horse having failed; but Carson and Godey had continued the pursuit. In the afternoon of the next day, a war-whoop was heard, such as Indians make upon returning from a victorious enterprise; and soon Carson and Godey appeared, driving before them a band of horses recognized by Fruentes to be part of those they had lost. Two bloody scalps dangling from the end of Godey's gun, announced that they had overtaken the Indians as well as the horses. They informed us that, after Fruentes left them from the failure of his horse, they continued the pursuit alone, and toward nightfall entered the mountains, into which the trail led. After sunset the moon gave light, and they followed the trail by moonshine until late at night, when they entered a narrow defile, and it was difficult to follow. Afraid of losing it in the darkness of the defile, they tied up their horses, struck no fire, and lay down to sleep in silence and darkness . . .

At daylight they resumed the pursuit, and about sunrise discovered the horses; and immediately dismounting and tying up their own, they crept cautiously to a rising ground which intervened, from the crest of which they perceived the

encampment of four lodges close by. They proceeded quietly
and had got within thirty or forty yards of their object, when
a movement among the horses discovered them to the Indians. Giving the war-shout, they instantly charged into the
camp, regardless of the number which the four lodges would
imply. The Indians received them with a flight of arrows
shot from their long bows, one of which passed through Godey's shirt collar, barely missing his neck; our men fired their
rifles with a steady aim, and rushed in. Two Indians were
stretched upon the ground, fatally pierced with bullets; the
rest fled, except a lad that was captured. The scalps of the
fallen were instantly stripped off . . .

They were now masters of the camp, which was a pretty
little recess in the mountain, with a fine spring, and apparently safe from all invasion. Great preparations had been
made to feast a large party, for it was a very proper place for
a rendezvous, and for the celebration of such orgies as robbers of the desert would delight in. Several of the best horses
had been killed, skinned, and cut up; for the Indians, living
in the mountains, and only coming into the plains to rob and
murder, make no other use of horses than to eat them. Large
earthen vessels were on the fire, boiling and stewing the
horse-beef; and several baskets, containing fifty or sixty pairs
of moccasins, indicated the presence, or expectation, of a
considerable party . . .

Their object accomplished, our men gathered up all the
surviving horses, fifteen in number, returned upon their trail,
and rejoined us at our camp in the afternoon of the same
day. They had rode about one hundred miles in the pursuit
and return, and all in thirty hours. The time, place, object,
and numbers considered, this expedition of Carson and Godey may be considered among the boldest and most disinter-
ested which the annals of western adventure, so full of dar-
ing deeds, can present. Two men, in a savage desert, pursue
day and night an unknown body of Indians—attack them at

night, without counting numbers—and defeat them in an instant, and for what? To punish the robbers of the desert, to avenge the wrongs of Mexicans whom they did not know. I repeat, it was Carson and Godey who did that—the former an American, born in the Boon's Lick county of Missouri; the latter a Frenchman, born in St. Louis; and both trained to Western enterprise from early life.

I I I
Under Four Flags

i

When the first parties of explorers to touch at one or another
point in the Far West returned to their home bases, it was
not long before both the extent and resources of the regions
they had discovered were made known throughout the
civilized world, whereupon several of the great European
powers began laying plans to add these newly explored sections to their already large holdings in the New World.

The first to take definite steps in that direction was, as we
have seen, Spain, which had set up permanent outposts
both in California and the Southwest well before the close
of the eighteenth century. Spain, however, presently had
rivals. To the north, Great Britain, through the far-flung
Hudson's Bay Company, had by 1825 established a trading
post at Fort Vancouver and for the next two decades laid
claim to a huge area that included present-day Washington
and Oregon. A third claimant was Russia, which, already
firmly established in Alaska, in 1812 founded an outpost
colony on the California coast a few miles above San Francisco Bay. Farther to the east, France claimed ownership to
the vast region that lay between the Mississippi and the

Rocky Mountains—an empire that did not pass to the control
of the United States until the consummation of the Louisiana Purchase in 1803.

Most firmly established within the area during the earliest
period were the Spaniards, who by the beginning of the
eighteenth century had numerous flourishing settlements
both in southern and central California and at various points
throughout the Southwest. That these outposts were not
free from molestation by raiding parties belonging to other
nations is, however, made clear by an episode that took place
at the California port of Monterey in the fall of 1818. This
was no less than an attack on that peaceful settlement by two
shiploads of brigands under the command of the French
buccaneer Hypolyte Bouchard. The pirates sacked the town,
set fire to its principal buildings, and made off with such
loot as they could gather up during the week of their stay.

Later, in a book bearing the innocuous title *Early Northern Pacific Voyages,* published in London in 1833, a member
of the raiding party, Peter Corney, gave this account of the
exploit:

We [wrote he] carried a complement of 100 men, thirty of
whom were Sandwich Islanders, the remainder were composed of Americans, Spaniards, Creoles, Negroes, Portu-
guese, Manila men, Malays and a few Englishmen. The *Argentina* had 260 men, fifty of whom were Islanders, and the
remainder a mixed crew, nearly similar to that of the *Santa
Rosa.*

On our passage towards California we were employed ex-
ercising the great guns and putting the ships in good condition for fighting.

After getting a supply of eggs, oil, etc., from the Russians
at Fort Ross [where they had first touched the mainland] we
made sail for the bay of Monterey. The Commodore ordered
me into the bay, and to anchor in a good position to cover the

landing, while he would keep his ship under weigh, and send his boats in to assist me. Being well acquainted with the bay, I ran in and came to at midnight, under the fort; the Spanish hailed me frequently to send a boat on shore, which I declined. Before morning they had the battery manned, and seemed quite busy.

I got a spring on the cable, and at daylight opened fire on the fort, which was briskly returned by two batteries. Finding it useless to fire at the batteries, the one being so much above us that our fire had no visible effect, the Commodore came in with his boats, and we landed on Point Pinos, about three miles to the westward of the fort; and before the Spaniards had time to bring their field-pieces to attack us, we were on our march against it.

We halted at the foot of the hill where it stood, for a few minutes, beat a charge and rushed up, the Sandwich Islanders in front with pikes. The Spaniards mounted their horses and fled; a Sandwich Islander was the first to haul down their colors. We then turned our guns on the town, where they made a stand, and after firing a few rounds, the Commodore sent me with a party to assault the place, while he kept possession of the fort.

As we approached the town, the Spaniards fled again, after discharging their field-pieces, and we entered without opposition. It was well stocked with provisions and goods of every description, which we commenced sending on board the *Argentina*.

The Sandwich Islanders, who were quite naked when they landed, were soon dressed in the Spanish fashion, and all the sailors were employed in searching the houses for money, and breaking and ruining everything. We took several Creole prisoners, destroyed all the guns in the fort, etc.

We had three men killed and three taken; next day a party of horsemen came in sight, to whom the Commodore sent a flag of truce, requiring the governor to give up our people and save the town. Three days were granted to consider this proposition, and on the third day, not receiving an answer, he ordered the town to be fired, after which we took plenty of livestock on board, wood, water, etc., and on the 1st day of December got under weigh from Monterey and stood along the coast to the southland.

ii

Another account of Bouchard's raid, this one from the viewpoint of the dispossessed Spanish residents, is contained in a reminiscence written years later by Maria Antonia Pico, member of one of the first families of the province, who was then a young girl.

It was about the middle of November, 1818 [she recalled], and I was sixteen years of age. A vessel brought the report to Monterey that a whole fleet of pirates were coming. Every one, in great fright, commenced to move and hide the most valuable things. Carts were used to carry them to the ranches. My father was not at home, but my mother and I packed many articles in rawhide bags, to send them twelve miles inland to the *cañada preita,* or black ravine. My brother, sister, and myself went with the carts; mother was to come next day, with a servant. Night came on before we fairly started, and it began to rain, for it was late in the year, and the first frosts were in the deeper cañons. As we went on the rain grew worse; the oxen wanted to turn about because of the rain in their faces, but we three children pushed on to carry out our mother's orders. About midnight we reached a large, broken oak tree where our mother had told us to camp. We let the oxen loose to graze, and crawled under the cart, wet to the skin.

My little sister was afraid of bears in the chaparral. I tried to comfort her, but she would not listen; she was sure we would be eaten up, and at last her persistence frightened my little brother till he cried out. In an hour or so they went to sleep beside me, but I lay awake and wished my father and the men-servants had been at home. They were all in the hills, gathering up the cattle. Though I had been over the road many times, it had never before seemed at all dangerous. While I was thinking of these things, a wild, strange noise was heard approaching, and one of our oxen, running through the thicket, fell over the tongue of the cart, rose, ran a little way off, and again fell, with a scream. I knew that something must have attacked the animals; I believed it was a big bear. We heard the other ox rushing into a gulch, and we all three set up and said our prayers to the saints, to be delivered from *El Feroz,* which was the name the hunters had given to a very large and dangerous grizzly that was known to roam about this cañon of the broken oak. I did not remember until we had camped there, or indeed until the oxen made such an uproar, but now I was very sure it was nothing but *El Feroz.*

The morning was dawning when this happened, and in a few minutes I could see a hundred feet down the cañon. An indistinct form began to be revealed there, and I hushed the children to watch and listen. There, as we soon saw, was a large California lion, or puma, pulling the meat from one of our oxen. Then I hoped that mother, and José, the peon, might soon come along the trail. José, who carried a gun, and was a brave man, would kill the wild animal, but we could see no one to help us. I whispered to the others to lie still, because we had no place to hide in, nor was it any use to try to climb a tree, for the California lion will climb like a cat. So we saw the lion finish his meal on our ox. It grew very light, near sunrise, before he took any notice of us, where we sat under the ox-cart. As soon as he saw us he walked up very close, with a curious, wondering expression on his face, and went all about the cart, looking us over, and making a purring sound. We sat close with our arms about one another, but we did not say a word. He then came up so close that I felt his breath on me, and finally he put his nose against my ankle. I had no stockings on, only home-made shoes, and his nose felt very strange, and made me expect to be eaten up at once. But I thought it best to lie still, and not cry out. After what seemed a long time, the lion went back and lay down beside the dead ox, about a hundred feet distant, keeping his eyes on us most of the time. He sometimes walked around the ox; then he went off a little way to a spring; then he came back and walked around the cart. At last he lay down by the ox, shut his eyes, and seemed asleep. The sun was now high, and we were very hungry and thirsty, and when we moved a little to rest our limbs the lion opened his eyes and looked very bad.

We lay there under the cart all the morning, and until about the middle of the afternoon, and the lion lay under the shade of a tree, watching us, ate some more beef, and went to the spring as often as he chose. About three o'clock mother and José, the peon, came down from the coast way, and when they were on the ridge they could look into the cañon and see the whole situation at a glance—the lion, the dead ox, the cart, and the three of us huddled together under it. José ran forward and fired two shots, wounding the lion, but he got away in the rocks.

Since one of our oxen was dead, and the other had escaped, we hid our goods as best we could in the bushes. Then mother told me, as we made a camp, that she had forgotten a family book, with writing of her father's in it. It was on a shelf in the house, and she wanted to ride back and obtain it. I told her that I was not afraid to go; so, after we had our meal, I mounted her horse, and galloped off to Monterey. After a little while I heard a cannon shot, then another, and

then a great many. I thought that now the pirates had come,
and would perhaps land, and burn the town and our house;
so I rode faster. At last I reached the *lomita* near the Plaza de
Doña Brigida, and there were boats and men on the beach.
Some of the houses were on fire, and that seemed dreadful. I
turned a little and rode across the ridge, and down a cañon
to our own house, which was about a mile from the beach,
and I ran in and found the old book where mother said, and
wrapped it in a piece of calfskin to tie behind the saddle. But
when I went out of the door I saw my horse running off,
frightened by the noise of the firing.

It was very hard to know what to do. There was no other
horse at the house—all had been turned loose. I ran over a
little hill to the next ranch house, but all the people had gone.
Then the firing stopped, and pretty soon I heard a band of
music, and the next minute a man dashed by on horseback
and shouted to me that Ignacio Vallejo was a prisoner and
that all the people had fled. I determined to catch a horse
somehow, but just as I was planning how it might be done
two men came out of the bushes and spoke to me. They were
armed strangers, and very wild, so I fell on my knees and
prayed to them to do me no harm. One of them asked me my
name, and why I was there; so I told him and showed the
book, but I did not reveal the course to our other ranch. He
laughed and said I was a good girl, and he sent his man to
catch my horse. Then he dismounted while I still knelt there
by the doorway of the deserted adobe, hardly believing my
own eyes, and he came up to me and kissed me on the fore-
head and called me Senorita, which frightened me very
much. Then the man came up with my horse, and I looked
at the leader of the two, and asked what he was going to do
with me?

He looked at me and swore a great oath. "My girl," he
said, "you are more brave than some of your people were on
the beach when we landed. You shall go back." He put me on

my horse, and kissed my hand, and said, "Ride fast; there are others of Bouchard's men who would not treat you so well." I thanked him briefly, and he added as he let got the bridle that his name was Pedro Condré, and that he already had two wives on board his ship, or he would have taken me there. This last made me ride in great terror and with fright- ful speed down the gulches and up the hills. When I reached mother's camp I was crying, and so terribly excited that I could not say anything but "Hasten, hasten!" We left all our things hidden in the bushes, and went on to Salinas. We met many families of fugitives. For nearly two weeks we lived in huts near the river, but early in December the frightened people began to move back to Monterey.

The padres had the floors and walls of all the houses sprinkled with holy water before anyone would live there again. At Christmas time the good padre called me out be- fore the congregation and gave me a gold cross because of what he called my courage with the lion and with the pirate. It does not seem to me that I was very brave, for I only took things as they happened, but I was very much pleased with the cross and the words of praise.

iii

An engaging picture of life as lived in California seacoast towns during the period when the province was ruled by Spain and Mexico was recalled years later by an anonymous Spanish woman who had grown up in that environment.

The ladies of Monterey in 1827 [wrote she] were rarely seen in the street, except very early in the morning on their way to church. We used to go there attended by our servants, who carried small mats for us to kneel upon, as there were

no seats. A tasteful little rug was considered an indispensable
part of our belongings, and every young woman embroidered
her own. The church floors were cold, hard, and damp, and
even the poorer classes managed to use mats of some kind,
usually of tule woven by the Indians.

The dress worn in the mornings at church was not very becoming; the *rebozo* and the petticoat being black, always of
cheap stuff, and made up in much the same way. All classes
wore the same; the padres told us we must never forget that
all ranks of men and women were equal in the presence of
the Creator, and so at the morning service it was the custom
to wear no finery whatever. One mass was celebrated before
sunrise, for those whose duties compelled them to be at work
early; later masses took place at every hour of the morning.
Every woman in Monterey went daily to church, but the men
were content to go once a week.

For home wear and for company we had many expensive
dresses, some of silk, or of velvet, others of laces, often of our
own making, which were much liked. In some families were
imported laces that were very old and valuable. The rivalry
between beauties of high rank was as great as it could be in
any country, and much of it turned upon attire, so that those
who had small means often underwent many privations in
order to equal the splendor of the rich.

Owing to the unsettled state of affairs in Mexico and in all
the provinces, and the great difficulty of obtaining teachers,
most of the girls of the time had scanty educations. Some of
my playmates could speak English very well, and quite a
number knew something of French. One of the gallants of the
time said that "dancing, music, religion, and amiability" were
the orthodox occupations of the ladies of Alta California. Visitors from other countries have said many charming things
about the manners, good health, and comeliness of these
ladies, but it is hardly right for any of us to praise ourselves.
The ladies of the province were born and educated here;

here they lived and died, in complete ignorance of the world outside. We were in many ways like grown-up children.

Our servants were faithful, agreeable, and easy to manage. They often slept on mats on the earthen floor, or, in the summertime, in the courtyards. When they waited on us at meals we often let them hold conversations with us, and laugh without restraint. As we used to say, a good servant knew when to be silent and when to put in his *cuchara* (or spoon).

iv

No less than other aspects of California life during "the Days of the Dons," the social customs of the residents make interesting—and curious—reading today. Here is how another Spanish lady, Brigida Briones, pictured the polite behavior of those attending a social function at Monterey more than a century and a quarter ago.

The first carnival ball that I ever attended [she recalled] took place near Monterey about 1829, when I was Señorita Brigida Cañes. I do not remember my age at the time, but I think I was about eighteen. I was invited by a friend in Monterey to visit her, as she had arranged to give a carnival ball . . . I left my home with the usual attendants at about eleven o'clock the day before, for our ranch was many miles distant. We met numbers of persons going to the party, all on horseback, and full of gaiety. . . . The pranks of the gentlemen were so numerous and amusing that it makes me laugh now to think of them. Every one could ride perfectly, and could pick up a leaf or a flower from the ground as he galloped past. Good riding was expected as a matter of course. On this occasion they all had red, black, and green paint (for the most part colored earths, powdered), and *cascarones* (egg-shells filled with finely cut gold and silver paper), and vials of different colored liquids, all harmless. It was the great sport to ride against each other, each endeavoring to stain his opponent's face while himself escaping. As we neared Monterey the carnival spirit grew wilder, and the ladies' dresses and faces suffered, but we all took it in good part.

On our arrival at the ranch near Monterey where the festivities took place we found everyone already dancing. The assembled guests, rushing to us, lifted us from our horses and led us in, smearing our faces with more paint and breaking *cascarones* on our heads with much laughter, while we defended ourselves in the same manner. It was my first experience of so wild a scene, and the red, green and black paint on my face made me uglier than a Yuma Indian. But as long as the others were in as bad a case, I could not complain.

A few minutes later a Mexican colonel came in and was immediately surrounded by ten or twelve ladies, and in a moment his face, cravat and vest looked like a rainbow. There was a severe struggle between his politeness and his dignity; but he remembered the old adage, yielded to the inevitable, and played his part in the grotesque farce. I also had a little courage, and I went up and cracked a *cascarone* on a young officer's head, but he was so busy rubbing the paint from his face that my faint-hearted attack passed unnoticed.

Next came the old alcalde of Monterey, a very stiff and dignified man. The first one to attempt to meddle with him was the governor's secretary, who was so awkward that he hurt the alcalde's face, and they retired to the courtyard of the ranch-house. This frightened the hostess, who feared a quarrel, and she went out at once. Of course their warm words stopped immediately and they came in together, but the old alcalde kept his face and dignity unchanged the rest of the night and no one lifted a *cascarone* against him.

The next arrival was a beautiful lady, almost a stranger to

us all, but known in Monterey as *"La Española,"* because she
had recently come from Spain. She came to me, and in a very
sweet voice asked me to uncork a cologne bottle she carried
in her hands, which in my simplicity I did. Then everyone
laughed as she sprinkled me from head to foot with the contents. She came in an elegant ball dress, but in a moment the
roses and lilies of her beautiful face and neck were hidden
under red, black, and green paint laid on heavily. She broke
many *cascarones,* and she also had two bottles, one of cologne
for the ladies, and one of scented ammonia. At last she made
her prayer, *"por el amor de Dios,"* and everyone ceased, with
gracious bows and smiles, leaving her to put on her dancing
slippers.

All this was in the afternoon. Then we washed our hands
and faces and sat down to a banquet in the old adobe. After
that some more dancing. The annual carnival ball was a
great feature of the social life of the times, and often lasted
all night. The wild revel of the early part of the ball was succeeded by the most courtly behavior.

V

Yet another revealing picture of the times has been preserved by General Mariano Guadalupe Vallejo, who himself
had played an important part in the affairs of the remote
province.

It seems to me [he recalled years later] that there never was
a more peaceful or happy people on the face of the earth
than the Spanish, Mexican, and Indian population of Alta
California before the American conquest. We were the pioneers of the Pacific Coast, building towns and Missions while

General Washington was carrying on the war of the Revolution, and we often talk together of the days when a few hundred large Spanish ranches and Mission tracts occupied the whole country from the Pacific to the San Joaquin . . . Indeed, our social life still [that is, in the early 1890's] tends to keep alive the spirit of love for the simple, homely outdoor life of our Spanish ancestors on this coast, and we try, as best we may, to honor the founders of our ancient families, and the saints and heroes of our history since the days when Father Junipero planted the cross at Monterey . . .

No one need suppose that the Spanish pioneers of California suffered many hardships or privations, although it was a new country. They came slowly, and were well prepared to become settlers. All that was necessary for the maintenance and enjoyment of life according to the simple and healthful standards of those days was brought with them. They had seeds, trees, vines, cattle, household goods, and servants, and in a few years their orchards yielded abundantly and their gardens were full of vegetables . . .

The houses of the Spanish people were built of adobe, and were roofed with red tile. They were very comfortable, cool in summer and warm in winter. The clay used to make the bricks was dark brown, not white or yellow, as the adobes in the Rio Grande region and in parts of Mexico. Cut straw was mixed with the clay, and trodden together by the Indians. When the bricks were laid, they were set in clay as in mortar, and sometimes small pebbles from the brooks were mixed with the mortar to make bands across the house. All the timber of the floors, the rafters and crossbeams, the doorways, and the window lintels were "built in" as the house was carried up. After the house was roofed it was usually plastered inside and out to protect it against the weather and make it more comfortable. A great deal of trouble was often taken to obtain stone for the doorsteps, or for gate-posts in front of the dwelling.

After describing the artisans to be found plying their trades
in the workrooms attached to the missions—a group that
included masons, millwrights, tanners, shoemakers, saddlers,
potters, and weavers—Vallejo continued thus:

The settlers themselves were obliged to learn trades and
teach them to their servants, so that an educated young gentleman was well skilled in many arts and handicrafts. He
could ride, of course, as well as the best cowboy of the Southwest, and with more grace; and he could throw the lasso so
expertly that I never heard of any American who was able to
equal it. He could also make soap, pottery, and bricks, burn
lime, tan hides, cut out and put together a pair of shoes,
make candles, roll cigars, and do a great number of things
that belong to different trades.

The Indian vaqueros, who lived much of the time on the
more distant cattle ranges, were a wild set of men. I remember one of them, named Martin, who was stationed in Amador
Valley and became a leader of the hill vaqueros, who were
very different from the vaqueros of the large valley near the
Missions. He and his friends killed and ate three or four
hundred young heifers belonging to the Mission, but when
Easter approached he felt that he must confess his sins, so he
went to Father Narciso and told all about it. The father for-
gave him, but ordered him to come in from the hills to the
Mission and attend school until he could read. The rules were
very strict; whoever failed twice in a lesson was always
whipped. Martin was utterly unable to learn his letters, and
he was whipped every day for a month; but he never com-
plained. He was then dismissed, and went back to the hills. I
used to question Martin about the affair, and he would tell
me with perfect gravity of manner, which was very delight-
ful, how many calves he had consumed and how wisely the
good father had punished him. He knew now, he used to say,
how very hard it was to live in the town, and he would never

steal again lest he might have to go to school until he had learned his letters. . . .

In the old days, everyone seemed to live out-doors. There was much gaiety and social life, even though people were widely scattered. We traveled as much as possible on horse-back. Only old people or invalids cared to use the slow cart, or *carreta*. Young men would ride from one ranch to another for parties, and whoever found his horse tired would let him go and catch another. . . . Horses were given to the runaway sailors, and to trappers and hunters who came over the mountains, for common horses were very plentiful, but fast and beautiful horses were never more prized in any country than in California, and each young man had his favorites . . .

Family life among the old Spanish pioneers was an affair of dignity and ceremony, but it did not lack in affection. Children were brought up with great respect for their elders. It was the privilege of any elderly person to correct young people by words, or even by whipping them, and it was never told that any one thus chastised made a complaint. Each one of the old families taught their children the history of the family, and reverence towards religion. A few books, some in manuscript, were treasured in the household, but children were not allowed to read novels until they were grown. They saw little of other children, except their near relatives, but they had many enjoyments unknown to children now, and they grew up with remarkable strength and healthfulness.

In these days of trade, bustle, and confusion, when many thousands of people live in the Californian valleys, which formerly were occupied by only a few Spanish families, the quiet and happy domestic life of the past seems like a dream. We, who loved it, often speak of those days, and especially of the duties of the large Spanish households, where so many dependents were to be cared for, and everything was done in a simple and primitive way.

There was a group of warm springs a few miles distant from the old adobe house in which we lived. It made us children happy to be waked before sunrise to prepare for the "wash-day expedition" to the *Agua Caliente*. The night before, the Indians had soaped the clumsy carreta's great wheels. Lunch was packed in baskets, and the gentle oxen were yoked to the pole. We climbed in, under the green cloth of an old Mexican flag which was used as an awning, and the white-haired Indian *ganan*, who had driven the carreta since his boyhood, plodded beside with his long *garrocha*, or ox-goad. The great piles of soiled linen were fastened on the backs of horses, led by other servants, while girls and women who were to do the washing trooped along by the side of the carreta. All in all, it made an imposing cavalcade, though our progress was slow, and it was generally sunrise before we had fairly reached the spring . . .

The group of hot sulphur-springs, so useful on wash-days, was a famed resort for sick people, who drank the water, and also buried themselves up to the neck in the soft mud of the slope below the spring, where the waste waters ran. Their friends brought them in litters and scooped out a hole for them, then put boughs overhead to shelter them from the hot sun, and placed food and fresh water within reach, leaving them sometimes thus from sunrise to sunset. The Paso Robles and Gilroy Springs were among the most famous on the coast in those days, and after the annual *rodeos* people often went there to camp and to use the waters. But many writers have told about the medicinal virtues of the various California springs, and I need not enlarge upon the subject. To me, at least, one of the dearest of my childish memories is the family expedition from the great, thick-walled adobe, under the olive and fig trees of the Mission, to the *Agua Cal-*

iente in early dawn, and the late return at twilight, when
the younger children were all asleep in the slow carreta, and
the Indians were singing hymns as they drove the linen-
laden horses down the dusty ravines.

vi

Although Spain was the first to establish itself on the West
Coast, it was presently followed by two other nations, namely,
England and Russia. The agency by which the British moved
into the territory was the long-established Hudson's Bay
Company, which in 1825 founded Fort Vancouver on the
Columbia River. By means of this fort it sought to control the
then booming fur trade throughout the Northwest. Long
the Company's chief agent there was Dr. John McLoughlin,
a shrewd and able administrator who for the next twenty
years made the Fort the most important trading and trapping center on the entire West Coast.

   Of the hospitality extended by Dr. McLoughlin to early
wayfarers who visited the area, we have already seen an example in the treatment accorded Jedediah Smith and his
two companions who sought refuge there following the
disastrous attack on his party by the Indians on the nearby
Umpqua River in the spring of 1828. A reception no less
amicable was extended to Captain John C. Frémont when,
on November 6, 1843, he and his travel-worn group reached
the Fort.

I [wrote Frémont] immediately waited upon Dr. McLoughlin, the executive officer of the Hudon's Bay Company, in the
territory west of the Rocky Mountains, who received me
with the courtesy and hospitality for which he has been em-
inently distinguished, and which makes a forcible and de-

lightful impression on a traveler from the long wilderness
from which we had issued. I was immediately supplied by
him with the necessary stores and provisions to refit and support my party in our contemplated winter journey to the
States; and also with a Mackinaw boat and canoes, manned
with Canadian and Iroquois Indians, for their transportation to the Dalles of the Columbia. In addition to this efficient kindness in furnishing me with these necessary supplies, I received from him a warm and gratifying sympathy
in the suffering which his great experience led him to anticipate for us in our homeward journey, and a letter of recom-
mendation and credit for any officers of the Hudson's Bay
Company into whose posts we might be driven by unexpected misfortune . . .

vii

England, however, was not the first European nation eager
to establish itself on the northwest coast. For, in the fall of
1812, a Russian explorer, Ivan Kuskof, landed a party on
northern California's rugged shore and proceeded to found
an outpost settlement that became known as Fort Ross. Intended originally as a source of food and other supplies
for their fur-trading posts far to the north in Alaska, the
Russians maintained their settlement there for close to three
decades—to the intermittent concern of the Spanish officials
at Monterey, who in the name of their king had long since
laid claim to the territory occupied by the intruders. That
source of alarm, however, was presently removed, for in
1841, the Tsar having ordered the withdrawal of his subjects, the property—lands, buildings, and livestock—was sold
to the Swiss adventurer John A. Sutter, founder of Sacramento, and Fort Ross was abandoned.

An interesting picture of the settlement as it appeared during its heyday was given by Auguste Duhaut-Cilly, commander of the French trading ship, *Lé Heros,* who visited the spot in the summer of 1828. Having landed at Bodega Bay a few miles to the south and proceeded on horseback over the rugged intervening countryside, he and his companion, the ship's doctor, reached their destination on June 4.

At eleven in the morning [wrote he] we arrived at the colony the Russians called Ross. It is a large square enclosure, surrounded by a palisade of thick planks twenty feet high, firmly built, and finished with a *cheval-defrise* of proportionate weight and size. At the northeast and southwest corners are two turrets hexagonal in shape, pierced with portholes, loopholes and barbicans. On the four sides corresponding to the four cardinal points are four doors, each one defended by a mortar with fixed breeching, showing at a port-hole, as in a ship; inside also were two field pieces of bronze, with their gun-carriages. A fine house for the commandant or director, pretty lodgings for the subordinate chiefs, large storehouses and workshops take up the square. A chapel newly built serves as a bastion at the southeast corner.

This citadel is constructed upon the edge of the wall of rock, on a high flat piece of ground about two hundred feet above the level of the sea; to right and left are gorges protecting it from Indian attacks from the north and south, while the rocky wall and the sea defend it on the side to the west. The two gorges open out into two little creeks serving as a shelter and landing place to the boats belonging to the colony.

All the buildings of Ross are of wood, but well built and well taken care of. In the apartments of the director are found all the conveniences which Europeans value, and which are still unknown in California. Outside the square are disposed or scattered the pretty little houses of sixty Russian colonists, the flattened cabins of eighty Kodiaks, and the cone shaped huts of as many indigenous Indians.

To the east of the establishment the land rises gradually, and gains great heights covered with thick forests which shelter it from the winds. . . . All of these slopes are divided into fields of corn, French beans, oats, potatoes, etc., surrounded with palisades, not to put the harvests beyond the reach of thieves, but to protect them from the cattle and the wild beasts. . . .

Much order and discipline appear to exist at Ross; and though the director is the only chief who is an officer, everywhere is noticed the effects of a minute care. The colonists, at once workmen and soldiers, after being busied all day with the labors of their various occupations, mount guard during the night. Holidays they pass in reviews and in gun and rifle practice.

Although this colony . . . appears to lack nothing, it cannot be of great account to the company [that is, the Russian-American Fur Company] which founded it. The principal revenue upon which they had reckoned was based upon the sea otter and seal fishing. The first is about exhausted, and no longer supplies anything. As for the other, the director maintains the whole year a hundred Kodiaks upon the Farallones . . . This fishing, which was at first very productive, becomes less plentiful from day to day, and within some years will be entirely null; but the director . . . has been for several years busied chiefly with husbandry. Not only does he produce corn and vegetables which heretofore he obtained from California, but he also supplies the larger colony of Sitka. With only six hundred cows, he procured more butter and cheese than entire Upper California with her numberless herds . . .

We went with M. Shelikof [the commandant of the col-

ony] to see his felling of wood. Independently of the needs
of the establishment, he cuts a great quantity of boards,
small beams, thick planks, etc., which he sells in California,
the Sandwich Islands and elsewhere; he has even entire
houses built which may then be transported taken apart. The
trees he cuts are almost all firs of various species, and in particular the one called *palo colorado* [redwood]. This . . .
is the largest tree I have ever seen. M. Shelikof made me observe the cut trunk of a fir of this species recently felled: it
was twenty feet in diameter, taking this measurement two
feet from the ground . . . I measured two hundred and
thirty feet from the stump to the beginning of the top, remaining where it had been parted from the trunk. Think of
the enormous quantity of boards that a tree of this size
should produce! The piles of them made from it covered a
considerable extent of ground. All the *palos colorados* are
not so immense; but it is very common to see those which
three men would have difficulty in clasping, and which
would make, in one single piece, the lower masts of our largest warships.

> Having thus been one of the first to describe to the world
> the great size of California's coastal redwoods, M. Duhaut-
> Cilly concluded the account of his visit to Fort Ross in these
> words:

We were treated with the most distinguished hospitality by
M. Shelikof, and we passed a very pleasant night at his
house. Unfortunately neither Dr. Botta nor I understood
Russian, and the director spoke neither French nor English
nor Spanish. This inconvenience made us lose a large part of
the charm his company would have afforded us. It was, however, in Spanish that we succeeded the best to make ourselves
understood. I did but little business with him: an American
ship had preceded me hither, and had gathered almost all

the furs this settlement had. I sold him only to the value of
some hundreds of sealskins. The next day I arose early, and
went to a hill to the east to make a drawing of the citadel.
After breakfast we mounted our horses to return to the port,
whence we set sail the next morning.

vii

Not only French trading ships but those of the Yankees
too from time to time visited the West Coast in the early
nineteenth century, supplying the Spanish ranchers with
manufactured goods in exchange for hides and tallow. Many
years later one such visit was thus recorded by a resident of
the town of Martinez, who had witnessed it as a girl:

In the autumn of 1840 [wrote she] my father lived near
what is now called Point Pinole, in Contra Costa County,
California. I was then about twelve years old, and I remember the time because it was then that we saw the first American vessel that traded along the shores of San Pablo Bay.
One afternoon a horseman from the Peraltas, where Oakland
now stands, came to our ranch, and told my father that a
great ship, a ship "with two sticks in the center," was about
to sail from Yerba Buena into San Pablo and Suisun, to buy
hides and tallow.

The next morning my father gave orders, and my brothers, with the peons, went on horseback into the mountains
and smaller valleys to round up all the best cattle. They
drove them to the beach, killed them there, and salted the
hides. They tried out the tallow in some iron kettles that my
father had bought from one of the Vallejos, but as we did
not have any barrels, we followed the common plan in those
days. We cast the tallow in round pits about the size of a

cheese, dug in the black adobe and plastered smooth with clay. Before the melted tallow was poured into the pit an oaken staff was thrust down in the center, so that by the two ends of it the heavy cake could be carried more easily. By working very hard we had a large number of hides and many pounds of tallow ready on the beach when the ship appeared far out in the bay and cast anchor near another point two or three miles away. The captain soon came to our landing with a small boat and two sailors, one of whom was a Frenchman who knew Spanish very well, and who acted as interpreter. The captain looked over the hides, and then asked my father to get into the boat and go to the vessel. Mother was much afraid to let him go, as we all thought the Americans were not to be trusted unless we knew them well. We feared they would carry my father off and keep him a prisoner. Father said, however, that it was all right: he went and put on his best clothes, gay with silver braid, and we all cried, and kissed him good-by, while mother clung about his neck and said we might never see him again. Then the captain told her: "If you are afraid, I will have the sailors take him to the vessel, while I stay here until he comes back. He ought to see all the goods I have, or he will not know what to buy." After a little my mother let him go with the captain, and we stood on the beach to see them off. Mother then came back, and had us all kneel down and pray for father's safe return. Then we felt safe.

He came back the next day, bringing four boat-loads of cloth, axes, shoes, fish-lines, and many new things. There were two grindstones and some cheap jewelry. My brother had traded some deerskins for a gun and four tooth-brushes, the first ones I had ever seen. I remember that we children rubbed them on our teeth until the blood came, and then concluded that after all we liked best the bits of pounded willow root that we had used for brushes before. After the captain had carried all the hides and tallow to his ship he came back, very much pleased with his bargain, and gave my father, as a present, a little keg of what he called Boston rum. We put it away for sick people.

After the ship sailed my mother and sisters began to cut out new dresses, which the Indian women sewed. On one of mine mother put some big brass buttons about an inch across, with eagles on them. How proud I was! I used to rub them hard every day to make them shine, using the tooth-brush and some of the pounded egg-shell that my sisters and all the Spanish ladies kept in a box to put on their faces on great occasions. Then our neighbors, who were ten or fif-teen miles away, came to see all the things we had bought. One of the Moragas heard that we had the grind-stones, and sent and bought them with two fine horses.

Soon after this I went to school, in an adobe, near where the town of San Pablo now stands. A Spanish gentleman was the teacher, and he told us many new things, for which we remember him with great respect. But when he said the earth was round we all laughed out loud, and were much ashamed. That was the first day, and when he wrote down my name he told me that I was certainly "La Cantinera, daughter of the regiment." Afterwards I found out it was because of my brass buttons. One girl offered me a beauti-ful black colt she owned for six of the buttons, but I con-tinued for a long time to think more of those buttons than of anything else I possessed.

IV

Hunters, Traders, and Trappers

i

During the early decades of the last century fashion decreed that well-dressed men both in Europe and the eastern part of the United States must wear hats made of beaver fur, and it is one of the ironies of history that this custom was responsible for ushering in a truly great period in the exploration of the West.

For when the demand for beaver fur sent the price of skins to above $5 a pound at trading posts all over the frontier, it set in motion a search that sent bands of men pressing ever farther into the unknown to hunt out new streams in which to set their traps. It was this—the first widespread commerce of the plains and mountains—that hastened the exploration of vast areas all over the West and added to our national heritage scores of frontiersmen whose deeds are too little known today.

One member of that picturesque band was "Old Bill" Williams, a native of North Carolina, who came west as a youth, married an Osage Indian, became a member of that tribe, and as trapper and trader spent many years breaking new trails through the wilderness. A friend who had known

him well during his later years thus described his picturesque appearance as he led parties of trappers on their far-
ranging expeditions:

Williams always rode ahead [he wrote], his body bent over
his saddlehorn, across which rested a long heavy rifle, his
keen gray eyes peering from under the slouched brim of a
flexible felt-hat, black and shining with grease. His buckskin
hunting shirt, bedaubed until it had the appearance of pol-
ished leather, hung in folds over his bony carcass; his nether
extremities being clothed in pantaloons of the same material (with scattered fringes down the outside of the leg,
which ornaments, however, had been pretty well thinned to
supply "whangs" for mending moccasins or pack saddles),
which, shrunk with wet, clung tightly to his long, spare,
sinewy legs. His feet were thrust into a pair of Mexican stirrups made of wood, and as big as coal-scuttles; and iron
spurs of incredible proportions, with tinkling drops attached to the rowels, were fastened to his heel—a bead-
worked strap, four inches broad, securing them over the in-
step. In the shoulder belt which sustained his powder-horn
and bullet-pouch, were fastened the various instruments essential to one pursuing his mode of life. An awl, with deer-
horn handle, and a point defended by a case of cherry-wood
carved by his own hand, hung at the back of his belt, side
by side with a worm for cleaning the rifle; and under this was
a squat and quaint-looking bullet-mold, the handles guarded
by strips of buckskin to save his fingers from burning when
running balls, having for its companion a little bottle made
from the point of an antelope's horn, scraped transparent,
which contained the "medecine" used in baiting traps.
    The old coon's face was sharp and thin, a long nose and
chin hob-nobbing each other; and his head was always bent
forward giving him the appearance of being hump-backed.
He appeared to look neither to the right nor the left, but,

in fact, his little twinkling eye was everywhere. He looked
at no one he was addressing, always seeming to be thinking
of something else than the subject of his discourse, speaking
in a whining, thin, cracked voice, and in a tone that left the
hearer in doubt whether he was laughing or crying . . .

> In the early 1830's, one of these far-ranging groups of trap-
> pers, this one led by Joseph Reddeford Walker, pushed on
> westward until they reached the far rim of the continent.
> That the larger significance of their journey was not lost on
> some of their number will be seen from this excerpt from
> the journal kept by Zenas Leonard, clerk of the expedition:

Most of this vast waste of territory [wrote Leonard] belongs
to the Republic of the United States. What a theme to con-
template its settlement and civilization! Will the jurisdic-
tion of the federal government ever succeed in civilizing the
thousands of savages now roaming over these plains, and her
hearty freeborn population here plant their homes, build
their towns and cities, and say here shall the arts and sci-
ences of civilization take root and flourish? Yes, here, even
in this remote part of the great west before many years, will
these hills and valleys be greeted with the enlivening sound
of the workman's hammer, and the merry whistle of the
ploughboy. But this is left undone by the government, and
will only be seen when too late to apply the remedy. The
Spaniards are making inroads in the South—the Russians
are encroaching with impunity along the sea shore to the
North, and further North-east the British are pushing their
stations into the very heart of our territory, which, even at
this day, more resemble military forts to resist invasion, than
trading stations. Our government should be vigilant. She
should assert her claim by taking possession of the whole
territory as soon as possible—for we have good reason to
suppose that the territory *west* of the mountains will some

day be equally as important to the nation as that on the *east*.

Among the many hazards faced by the beaver-trappers on their months-long forays into the backcountry were encounters with two dangerous foes; namely, hostile Indians and wild animals. A meeting with one of the last-named, a California grizzly bear, by a member of Walker's party (whose name was Philips) is thus described in Zenas Leonard's journal:

It appeared that Philips had been out hunting deer, and having killed one, took out the insides and hung it upon a tree, and started to camp to get a horse to bring it home. After travelling a mile or so, whilst ascending a hill, he came suddenly upon an old bear and two cubs. The bear immediately on seeing Philips, as is their custom, reared on her hind feet, and being very close, commenced growling most furiously. This our hero could not brook, and fearing the consequences if he should shoot and wound her, lost his presence of mind, and started to run. The bear immediately pursued and caught him. He now found it quite useless to attempt to get loose, and only saved his life by sinking to the ground and affecting to be dead. The bear then left him, but not without wounding him to such a degree that it was a long time before he could collect strength enough to raise to his feet. It was late at night when he reached the camp, and was so far gone, from hunger and loss of blood, that his life was despaired of at first. One of his arms was broke and his body most shockingly cut and mangled.

ii

It was not alone the hunt for beaver that sent parties of trappers breaking new trails throughout the Far West; the

furs of other animals—notably that of the marten, or sable—
were likewise much prized and brought high prices at the
frontier trading posts. The lonely lives lived by the early-day
sable-hunters were graphically portrayed by Isaac Wistar,
who, with a single companion, spent several winters in the
solitudes of the Rocky Mountains.

Before settling down to our winter's work [wrote he] it may
be well to describe what a sable trapper's work is like. It is
totally different from beaver trapping, which requires an
outfit of steel traps and must be pursued along streams and
rivers which are also frequented during the winter by Indians, whose hostility is often extremely dangerous. The
marten, or sable, is a small animal of the weasel tribe that
lives well up in the middle district of the mountains, where
the Indians, unless traveling, rarely come in winter. The
trapper, having deposited his livestock in a safe place and
laid up either pemmican or smoked dried meat for provisions, sets down on some remote, difficult, and well-con-
cealed stream, well up, though not too high among the mountains, and makes a small brush shelter, open in front, and if
possible with plenty of dry, well-felled timber close by. Here
he can have as much fire as he chooses at night, when the
smoke cannot be seen, but if he is prudent and regards his
scalp, he will not risk much of it during the day. Nor will he
ever discharge his gun either by night or day except in circumstances of stringent necessity.

Here he is soon snowed in and shut off from all the world,
provided he has been sufficiently careful of his trail and the
marks and signs he has left behind him. His horses, turned out
in some distant valley, may be and often are discovered and
stolen, in which event he must, when spring comes, replace
them in the same way or abandon all the proceeds of his
winter's labor. Having made his quarters comfortable, safely
disposed of his provisions, and prepared snowshoes and trap-

sticks, one of the pair starts off, taking a long leading ridge for forty miles or more, setting traps in favorable places as he goes, crossing over and returning by some similar ridge as far as practicable. Each of such trips may occupy a week or more—sometimes, if fresh snow falls, considerably more— and on his return his partner does the same. Thus they alternate all winter, setting and resetting traps, skinning and packing the skins. While in camp there is plenty of work, fleshing, drying, stretching, and packing the skins and trapping small game for fresh provisions when it can be had.

But if a *carcajou* or, as the Americans call them, wolverine gets on the line of traps, or if quarters have to be moved in midwinter in consequence of scarcity of martens, or worst of all, should the sign of some prowling Indian be detected, it may become necessary to move the camp . . . far away to another district, in which case the skins already collected must be cashed and protected from the weather and from hungry prowlers and every other asset packed on snowshoes through the wildest . . . of mountains covered deep with snow. Supposing, however, that such accidents and removals can be avoided, the mere routine of trap setting and attendance gives but little trouble except after fresh falls of snow, especially when caught by storms far away from camp . . .

Marten traps in themselves are simple enough; it is the locality, lines, directions, and modes of concealment from uninvited guests that the trapper's skill consists. They are made by arranging a small enclosure of driven stakes with a single opening. Across that is laid as threshold a log, stone, or even a flat chunk of ice, upon which at one end rests the movable deadfall, the other end of the latter supported by some of the various kinds of trap sticks, the common "figure four" being usually preferred. A small bait of fresh or dried meat, the former preferable when it can be had, is carried by the trigger stick inside the inclosure, where the marten can only reach it by introducing his long neck through the entrance. As soon as he seizes it, conscious of the suspicious character of the arrangement, he quickly backs out, bringing down the fall, which breaks his neck or his back on the lower log without marking the skin, which in that climate, even when covered by snow, will keep fresh a long time . . .

After the trapper has laid in his provisions, disposed of his horses, and settled down in his solitary winter quarters, incidents are few; and as none of a pleasant character are likely to occur, the fewer they are, the better for him.

> In Wistar's case, the first of his winters was far from uneventful. For, finding few marten in the area they had originally chosen, he and his companion—a French trapper named Francois—carrying their belongings, including a small amount of provisions, set off in search of a new location.

But with ground covered by heavy snow [Wistar's narrative continues], streams hard bound with ice, and frequent windstorms which at the low prevailing temperatures none can face and live, our progress was slow and no place looked very attractive. Hence no great time had elapsed before we found our provisions exhausted, in a difficult country with game not to be had. Making a temporary shelter . . . we proceeded to devote our whole attention to hunting, till after some days we became aware of the fact that the district was absolutely without game . . .

After trying in vain all the resources practised by trappers in such straits, all of which were well known to Francois, we ate the grease in our rifle stocks, all the fringes and unnecessary parts of our buck-skin clothes, gun and ammunition bags, and every scrap of eatable material, boiling it down in an Assinaboine basket with hot stones, and were finally reduced to buds and twigs. After many days of this extreme privation, no longer possessing strength to travel or hunt, I became discouraged; and as we lay down one night I determined to abandon the struggle and remain there, enduring with such fortitude as I might the final pangs . . .

At this last stage of the struggle, an event occurred of the most extraordinary character. . . . Notwithstanding our exhaustion and my desperate conclusion of the night before, Francois rose at daylight, made up the fire as well as his strength permitted, blazed a tree nearby on which he marked with charcoal a large cross, and carefully reloading and standing his gun against that emblem, proceeded to repeat . . . all the scraps of French and Latin prayers he could remember . . . When he got through he remarked with much cheerfulness that he was now sure of killing something and urged me to make one more effort with him, which I rather angrily refused, and bade him lie down and take what had to come, like a man. . . . Then, desisting from his useless effort to get me up, Francois, leaving his heavy snowshoes behind, directed himself with weak and uneven steps down the little stream in the deep gorge of which our camp was made; and never expecting to see him again, my mind relapsed into an idle, vacuous condition. . . . But scarcely a few minutes had elapsed and he had hardly traversed a couple of hundred yards when I heard his gun, which I knew never cracked in vain.

I had thought myself unable to rise, but at that joyful sound promptly discovered my mistake. I found Francois in the spot from which he had fired, leaning against a tree in such deep excitement that he could speak with difficulty. On that rugged sidehill apparently destitute of all life, in that most improbable of all places, within sound and smell of our camp, he had seen not a squirrel or rabbit, but a deer. Attempting to climb for a better shot, the deer jumped, and with terrible misgivings he had fired at it running. He had heard it running after his shot but was sure he had made a killing hit. Scrambling with difficulty up the hill, we found a large clot of blood and a morsel of "lights," which we divided and ate on the spot. After taking up the trail we soon found the animal.

> Having regained their strength, the pair returned to their original camp, where they remained until spring, subsisting on animals and birds they trapped, then returned to the lowlands, grateful for having survived their ordeal.

iii

Because of the vastness of the country in which they operated, meetings between parties of fur trappers were infrequent, but on those rare occasions when they took place, they were a source of gratification to all concerned, providing as they did an opportunity for an exchange of information concerning the country each had traversed, the Indians encountered, the furs gathered, and—most welcome of all—news of the outer world from which they had been for so long shut off.

One of the most dramatic of such encounters occurred in the spring of 1826, when a party of trappers led by Miguel Robidoux, and of which James Ohio Pattie was a member, made camp one night in a village of the Papagos Indians at the juncture of the Salt and Gila rivers in what is now Arizona. Suspecting treachery on the part of their Indian hosts, Pattie advised against stopping there, and, when his warnings were ignored, he and a single companion withdrew and camped some distance away. True to his prediction, the savages that night fell on the sleeping trappers, slaying all but their leader, Robidoux. The latter, badly wounded, managed to escape and the following morning made his way to the spot where Pattie and his companion had camped.

The three remained hidden all that day, planning to try an escape when darkness fell, and quite unaware that another party of trappers—a numerous company led by Ewing Young—was in the vicinity. What happened next is told in Pattie's own words.

When it became dark [wrote he] we descried three fires close together, which we judged to be those of savages in pursuit of us . . . We concluded that my companion and myself should leave our wounded companion to take care of the horses, and go and reconnoitre the camp, in which were these fires, and discover the number of the Indians, and if it was great, to see how we could be most likely to pass them unobserved. When we arrived close to the fires, we discovered a considerable number of horses tied, and only two men guarding them. We crawled still closer, to be able to discern their exact number and situation.

In this way we arrived within fifty yards of their camp, and could see no one, but the two, any where in the distance. We concluded that all the rest of the company were asleep in some place out of our view. We presumed it would not be long before some of them would awake, it being now ten at night. Our intention was to take aim at them, as they should pass between us and their fire, and drop them both together. We could distinctly hear them speaking about their horses. At length one of them called to the other, in English, to go and wake their relief guards. Words would poorly express my feelings, at hearing these beloved sounds. I sprang from my crouching position, and ran towards them. They were just ready to shoot me, when I cried "a friend, a friend!" One of them exclaimed, "Where in God's name did you spring from . . . you seem to have come out of the earth!" The surprise and joy upon mutual recognition was great on both

sides. I gave him a brief sketch of the recent catastrophe of
our company, as we followed them to camp.

At once plans were made to avenge the massacre of the
previous night. Accordingly, a surprise attack was launched
against the Papagos, during which many of the warriors were
slain, the white men's property recovered, the victims buried, and the village burned to the ground.

iv

Of the pioneers who ventured into the Far West during
the early days, the majority traveled light, carrying with
them only such necessities as the clothes they wore, blankets
to warm them at night, guns and ammunition, knives, a
water canteen, and a blackened pot in which they prepared
their meals. Their supply of foodstuffs was likely to be limited to sugar, salt, a few condiments, and a bag of flour. The
country through which they passed was expected to provide
the rest. Hunting, hence, occupied an important part in
every frontiersman's life, for it was mainly on the birds and
animals he shot that he depended to keep him and his
companions from starvation.

Some interesting comments on the high degree of skill required in stalking game on the western plains have been
preserved in a reminiscence by Henry Hastings Sibley
(1811-91), who during his later years was a leading citizen
of Minnesota, where he served as that state's first governor.

In the month of October, 1842 [wrote he], I took with me
eight horses and carts, in charge of five Canadians and one
American, and with my old hunting companions, Alex

Faribault and Jack Frazer, wended my way towards the buffalo region. We expected to find these animals at or about the *Minday Mecoche Wakkon*, or Lake of the Spirit Land, a distance of about a hundred and fifty miles . . . On the seventh day out, Jack Frazer reported that he had seen some game, but whether buffalo or elk he could not tell, as they were too far off. Our glass being put in requisition, we soon found them to be a small herd of the latter, lying down at the base of a hill about six miles off . . .

Alex, Jack Frazer, and myself, as the only experienced hunters, were to approach and fire, while the others of the party mounted their horses and were stationed under the cover of the hill, except one man, who remained in charge of the carts and baggage. With this man I left my hunting horse, ready saddled, with instructions to mount as soon as he heard our guns, and come with all speed to my stand. These precautions taken, and having stripped ourselves of all superfluous clothing, we commenced the delicate operation of approach. A few yards brought us in full view of the herd, which, unsuspicious of danger, were lolling lazily in the sunshine. Throwing ourselves flat on the ground, we wormed ourselves with Indian stealthiness, under cover of the short grass.

We had proceeded thus about half a mile, when we came to a marsh, which it was found we must necessarily pass. The water here was two feet deep, and the exertion of crawling through the knotted grass, and securing, at the same time, our guns from moisture, while we kept ourselves concealed, was excessively severe. By dint of unremitting efforts we passed through this serious obstacle, and emerged upon dry ground within sixty yards of the game.

We here examined our arms, renewed our primings, and sprang upon our feet, not wishing to fire until the elk rose. As these magnificent creatures bounded off in great confu-

sion, our double barrels were discharged, and three elk fell
dead . . . Unfortunately, Alex, F., and myself had aimed
our second barrels at the same large animal, which came to
the ground riddled with balls and buckshot, otherwise we
might have secured a fourth . . . My horse was presently at
my side, and as soon as I was mounted, the noble animal
entering into the spirit of the chase, set off at racing speed.
The elk were now a mile ahead, and I passed successively
each of the Canadians on their jaded horses, vainly struggling to keep with the chase. Wright, the American, who was
well mounted, was thrown headlong from the saddle, and
when I overtook the herd after a run of six miles, I perceived his horse running side by side with the elk.

I had left my double barrel behind, trusting to a revolv-
ing pistol to do execution. But my hands were so benumbed
by long immersion in the cold water that I could not pull the
trigger. Shifting the revolver to my left hand, I managed
to discharge it at a large female elk, at a distance of not
more than ten feet. The ball took effect *a posteriori*, and the
animal was so much wounded that she plunged headlong
into a wide boggy stream, through which, with incredible
efforts, she succeeded in passing, leaving me no other alternative than to abandon the chase, the nature of the ground
rendering it impossible to cross.

I succeeded in securing the runaway horse, with which I
returned to my companions, who had already made preparations to encamp on the border of the lake. Here we spent one
day preserving the meat of the slain elk, which was accomplished by cutting it into thin slices, when it was spread
out upon a scaffold, and a fire kindled under, which soon
dried it thoroughly.

The party's next objective was buffalos, and on the evening
of the following day a group of three of the animals was
sighted.

After holding a *consiel de guerre* [Sibley's narrative contin-
ues], we concluded not to follow them until the next morning, as the day was already far spent. Selecting a favorable
spot, we encamped, and the arms of the party were put in
order for the expected sport. A large buck came out of the
woods at the opposite side of the stream, without perceiving
us. We could not allow him to be fired at. The next morning
Jack Frazer was dispatched with the most active of the Canadians to reconnoitre. In a short time they returned, and reported that three buffalo were lying down in one of the low
places . . . Two men were placed in charge of the carts,
with directions to proceed slowly along at an angle slightly
deviating from the line of the buffalo, while the rest of us,
seven in number, mounted our horses and prepared for the
chase.

Approaching the bulls within three hundred yards, we
charged down the hill upon them at full speed. The first
flight of the buffalo is comparatively slow, but when pressed
by the huntsman, the rapidity with which these apparently
unwieldy animals get over the ground is amazing. Alex, F.,
and myself having the fleetest horses, each of us singled out
a victim, leaving the third to be dealt with by the remainder.
We were shortly alongside, and our double barrels told with
deadly effect, the huge beasts rolling on the ground in death,
within a hundred yards of each other. The other horsemen
followed the remaining buffalo, discharging numberless
shots at him, but . . . the bull got clean off, and his pursu-
ers were brought to a sudden halt by the sight of a large
herd, which they were unwilling to disturb until we
joined them . . .

When about half a mile distant, the huge mass set itself
in motion, and the herd, composed of several hundreds, took
to flight. We were soon among them, and the discharge of
fire-arms from all the horsemen was incessant and well-sus-
tained . . .

There was a very fine fat cow in the center of the band, which I made several attempts to separate from the others, but without effect. She kept herself close to an old bull, who, by his enormous size, appeared to be the patriarch of the tribe. Being resolved to get rid of this encumbrance, I shot the old fellow behind the shoulder. The wound was mortal, and the bull left the herd, and went off at a slow gallop in a different direction. As soon as I fired I slackened the speed of my horse to enable me to reload, determining to pursue the retiring mass, trusting to find the wounded animal on my return. Unfortunately I changed my mind, and rode after the bull to give him the *coup de grace*. I rode carelessly along with but one barrel of my gun loaded, when, upon getting near the buffalo, he turned as quick as lightning to charge. At this critical instant I had risen in my stirrups, and released my hold on the bridle rein. At the moment the buffalo turned, my horse, frightened out of his propriety, gave a tremendous bound sidewise, and, alas! . . . threw me clear out of the saddle, and within ten feet of the enraged monster!

Here was a predicament! Imagine your humble servant face to face with the brute, whose eyes glared through the long hair which garnished his frontlet like coals of fire—the blood streaming from his nostrils. In this desperate situation I made up my mind that my only chance of escape was to look my enemy in the eye: as any attempt to run would only invite attack. Holding my gun ready cocked to fire if he attempted a rush, I stood firmly, although I must confess I was awfully frightened, and thought my last hour had come! How long he stood there pawing and roaring, I have now not the least idea, but certainly thought he was a long time making his decision what he should do. At last he turned slowly away, and I gave him a parting salute, which let out the little blood left in his body. He went a short distance and fell dead.

V

The Yankees Head West

The first parties of fur traders to break new trails into the
Far West found their progress toward the shores of the
Pacific blocked by the towering barrier of the Sierra range,
the lofty, snow-covered crests of which presented an obstacle so formidable as to deter all but the most resolute.
Among the first to make the crossing were a group of trappers and traders under the leadership of Joseph Reddeford
Walker, and the story of the perils and privations they encountered during their weeks-long ordeal is graphically described by Zenas Leonard, clerk of the expedition.

Leading a party of sixty trappers, Walker had set forth in
the summer of 1833 to reconnoitre the unknown country to
the southwest of Great Salt Lake. They crossed the arid
plains of present-day Nevada, and in the late fall scouting
parties were sent on ahead to search out a feasible route
through the Sierra range. On the return of one, which reported the finding of an Indian trail that appeared to lead
upward toward the summit, preparations got under way.

At an early hour the next morning [wrote Leonard] we
started on our journey along the foot of the mountain in

search of the path discovered the previous day, and found it. On examination we found that horses travelled it, and must of course come from the west. This gave us great encouragement, as we were very fearful we would not be able to get our horses over at all. Here we camped for the night. In the morning we started on our toilsome journey. Ascending the mountain we found it to be very difficult from the rocks and its steepness. This day we made but poor speed and encamped on the side of the mountain.

> As they made their way upward toward the crest, the party's difficulties multiplied. Leonard's journal entry some days later reads:

The next morning it was with no cheerful prospect that each man prepared himself for travelling, as we had nothing to eat worth mentioning. As we advanced, in the hollows sometimes we would encounter prodigious quantities of snow. When we would come to such places, a certain portion of the men would be appointed alternately to go forward and break the road, to enable our horses to get through; and if any of the horses would get swamped, the same men were to get them out. In this tedious and tiresome manner we spent the whole day without going more than 8 or 10 miles . . . This day's travel was very severe on our horses, as they had not a particle to eat. They began to grow stupid and stiff, and we began to despair of getting them over the mountain. We encamped this night on the south side of the peaks or ridges without anything to eat, and almost without fire . . .

> The journey continued thus day after day, the cold and hungry men subsisting on the "black, tough, lean" flesh of two of their broken-down animals, which they had slain. Leonard's narrative continues:

In the morning, after freely partaking of the horse meat . . . , we renewed our journey, now and then coming onto an Indian path, but as they did not lead in the direction we were going, we did not follow them—but the most of the distance we this day travelled, we had to encounter hills, rocks and deep snows . . . About the middle of the afternoon we arrived at a small lake or pond, where we concluded to encamp, as at this pond we found a small quantity of very indifferent grass, but which our horses cropped off with great eagerness. Here we spent the night, having as yet seen nothing to create a hope that we had arrived near the opposite side of the mountain—and what was equally as melancholy, having yet discovered no signs of game. . . .

> Their difficulties, then, were far from over, for they had penetrated into the midst of one of the most rugged areas of the entire range; that is, the maze of deep canyons and serrulated ridges that lie to the north of the Tuolumne River.

The prospect at this time [continued Leonard] began to grow somewhat gloomy . . . We were at a complete stand. No one was acquainted with the country, nor no person knew how wide the summit of the mountain was. We had travelled for five days since we arrived at what we supposed to be the summit—were now still surrounded with snow and rugged peaks—the vigor of every man almost exhausted . . .

> In a final, desperate attempt to extricate themselves, the party turned toward the south—and in so doing won for themselves the distinction of becoming the first white men to lay eyes on one of the most spectacular natural wonders in all America: the Yosemite Valley. Here is the passage in which Leonard described the phenomenon:

We travelled a few miles every day, still on the top of the mountain, and our course continually obstructed with snow, hills and rocks. Here we began to encounter in our path, many small streams which would shoot out from under these high snow-banks, and after running a short distance in deep chasms which they have through the ages cut in the rocks, precipitate themselves from one lofty precipice to another, until they were exhausted in rain below. Some of these precipices appeared to us to be more than a mile high. Some of the men thought that if we could succeed in descending one of these precipices to the bottom, we might thus work our way into the valley below—but on making several attempts we found it utterly impossible for a man to descend, to say nothing of our horses. We were then obliged to keep along the top of the dividing range between two of these chasms which seemed to lead pretty near in the direction we were going—which was West—in passing over the mountain, supposing it to run north and south.

> The search for a way down into the San Joaquin Valley continued, with scouts being sent on ahead in the hope of discovering a feasible route.

These [wrote Leonard] returned after an absence of a few hours and reported that they had discovered a pass or Indian trail which they thought would answer our purpose, and also some signs of deer and bear, which was equally as joyful news—as we longed to have a taste of some palatable food . . . The mountain was extremely steep and difficult to descend, and the only way we could come by any speed was by taking a zigzag direction; first climbing along one side and then turning to the other, until we arrived at a ledge or precipice of rocks, of great height, and extending eight to ten miles along the mountain . . .

Down this declivity the men of the party cautiously made
their way, lowering their horses by means of ropes over a
succession of nearly vertical cliffs, and that night camped in
a grove of stunted oaks, feeling "more cheerful and in better
heart than we had . . . for a long time."

Moreover, before they at last gained the floor of the valley,
the party won another distinction, that of being the first of
their kind to see another of the Sierra's outstanding natural
attractions, the *Sequoia gigantea,* the world's largest tree.
Leonard's description of that find reads thus:

We continued down the side of the mountain at our leisure,
finding the timber much larger and better, game more
abundant and the soil more fertile . . . On the evening of
the 30th [of October] we arrived at the foot or base of this
mountain—having spent almost a month in crossing over
. . . In the last two days travelling we have found some
trees of the Redwood species, incredibly large—some of
which would measure from 16 to 18 fathom round the
trunk at the height of a man's head above the ground.

From the route they followed, it is assumed that the party
passed through either the Merced or the Tuolumne groves,
both of which contain trees of the prodigious size mentioned by Leonard.

ii

As the 1840's opened, tales of the attractions—and opportunities—awaiting those pioneers who would make their way
to the Pacific slope began to circulate among residents of
the trans-Mississippi frontier. One of the first to turn the

eyes of the settlers in that region to the far rim of the continent was a trapper, Antoine Robidoux, who appeared at a meeting in Platte County, Missouri, late in 1840, and described the manner of life to be lived in California in such glowing terms that an organization called the Western Emigration Society was promptly formed, the members of which proposed to set off for the new Promised Land. Within a short time more than five hundred men, women, and children had joined up and agreed to assemble the next spring at Sapling Grove, prepared to embark on the long overland trek.

However, during the winter that followed, the Platte County merchants, alarmed at this threatened exodus of so many of their customers, spread reports dealing unfavorably with conditions on the West Coast. These proved so effective that of the five hundred who had agreed to gather at Sapling Grove, by the time the designated day had rolled around, only one person had appeared. This lone exception was a youth named John Bidwell, a schoolteacher who was destined to become one of California's most eminent citizens and to serve a term as governor of the state. But this desertion of all but one of the original group did not cause the abandonment of the project, for a considerable number of others appeared to take their places, and when the party set off on their historic march it numbered close to a hundred members.

Several first-hand accounts of the adventures met with by this first party of settlers to make their way overland to California have been preserved. One is that of John Bidwell; another is by a second member of the group, also an ex-schoolteacher, whose name was Nicholas Dawson. It is from the latter's narrative that the following excerpts are taken. Dawson, a native of western Pennsylvania, had left home at the age of nineteen, his purpose being, in his own words, "to spend about six years seeing the world." The first half of that period he tramped here and there over the western frontier, mainly in Missouri, Arkansas, and Louisiana, pausing from time to time to recoup his fortunes by teaching in early-day schools.

After wandering up and down and around and across [Dawson later recalled], I finally found relief for my blistered feet and slender purse in Sevier county, Arkansas. Here I remained nine months, teaching . . .

As my school neared its end, I began to take stock: nearly three years had passed out of the six I had planned to spend in travel, so I thought it time I should set out for foreign lands. My plan was to go to Independence, Mo., where I should most likely find a company going to Oregon. I could take in the Rocky Mountains and buffaloes on the way, and go on to the Pacific.

Young Dawson accordingly made his way northward, and his narrative continues thus:

Learning here that a company was soon to go to California and Oregon, I soon decided to make one of the company, and remained . . . until the crowd should be made up. Some doubt existed as to whether a sufficient number would congregate to make it safe to go, but as the time drew near (May 1st, 1841) men began to drop in until, when we started, there were about one hundred.

It was a very mixed crowd. There were heads of families going out first to find a spot to bring their families to, and heads of families taking the families along to share whatever fortune might bring. There were many adventurous youths like myself and John Bidwell . . . , who wanted nothing but to see and experience. There were gentlemen seeking health, and an English lord, Lord Romain, going out with a half-breed hunter, John Grey, to shoot buffalo. Among the last to come in were some priests, bound for the Flathead Mission. They had with them a fine pilot, Fitzpatrick. The modes of transportation were as mixed as the crowd. Some had wagons drawn by oxen; others wagons drawn by horses; a few had hacks; and the priests had carts; many were to make the journey on horseback; and a few brought nothing but themselves. I had traded my horse for an old mule and had bought an interest in Bartleson's wagon and team. When this and my share of the provisions was paid for, I had seventy-five cents left—and I had it still when I reached California in November. . . .

On May 12, 1841, we set out, Fitzpatrick in the lead. A little before night, he would gallop on ahead and select a camping place. When the camping place was reached, the wagons were placed in a hollow square, leaving a space between each two for tents and campfires. The horses were grazed outside until night, then they were picketed inside, and a guard kept outside all night.

Before we passed beyond the range of friendly Indians, I made a trade which, as it brought in what proved to be a very important member of our company, I will tell of. The old mule I had traded my horse for proved very unsatisfactory. When I wanted him to go to water he wanted to go to grass; and when I wanted him to go to grass, he wanted water . . . One day we met a gang of Indians. The leader was riding a spirited white pony, which I at once coveted. Riding up alongside the Indian, I drew my forefingers across each other and holloed "swap!" "Swap," grunted the Indian. He jumped from his horse, I from my mule. He took off his saddle, I took off mine. He fastened his saddle upon my old mule, and I girthed mine around the white pony. Then we each sprang into our saddles and rode off. Thus came into my possession, "Monte." This is the only trade I remember ever to have made in which I did not get the worst of the bargain . . .

Our route soon crossed the Kansas river, and then passed over to the Platte. While we were in the Platte valleys a little incident occurred that gave me a nickname for the rest of the journey: we were now in the country of hostile Indians, and Fitzpatrick had warned us not to stray beyond sight of the wagon train. But one day, curious to see the country that lay beyond a range of hills, I had ventured farther than usual, and coming upon a herd of antelope I, in my eagerness to get a shot at them, had followed them still farther. I was . . . trying to get near enough for a shot, when I was startled by an Indian whoop. I sprang upon my mule, but he perversely wheeled and ran toward the sound, I pulling desperately at the reins. Finally, I got his head in the direction I wanted to go, but no amount of urging could get that mule to hurry, and in an instant I was surrounded by Indians. One galloped by me, thrust a spear along my back, and motioned me to disembark. I did so. They seized my gun and knife, stripped me of my outer clothing, and taking my mule, left me. I hurried after our train, and overtaking it, told my story. The alarm spread along the line, and all was confusion. Fitzpatrick galloped back, calling out the horsemen as he came, and was off with them to find the Indians, and, if necessary, give them battle. I was very angry now, and intent on vengeance, so hastily borrowing a horse and gun, I hurried after the party. I came on at full speed and was aiming at the first Indian within range, when I was stopped by some forcible language from Fitzpatrick, and perceived that Fitzpatrick and the Indians were engaged in friendly pow-wow. It proved to be a band of Cheyennes, friendly but thievish. They camped near us that night, and Fitzpatrick attempted to get back my property. He and I and the Indians sat around in a circle, and for every article to be returned, gifts of blankets, clothes, etc., had to be thrown down, a peace pipe smoked by all, and much haranguing done. Fitzpatrick's patience gave out before all was got back, and declaring that I ought to be satisfied to have got off with my life, he refused to intercede further. I chafed under my enforced friendliness, and after that, to distinguish me from another Dawson in the company known as Bear Dawson, I was called Cheyenne Dawson.

> The caravan pushed steadily on, following the Sweetwater River for several weeks, then passing through South Pass, in late July it reached the Green, a tributary of the Colorado.

Our journey from here to Soda Springs [wrote Dawson] was more difficult—more mountains and fewer valleys. Ours, I presume, were the first wagons to pass over this route. At times we could pass along the mountain sides only by having fastened to the top of our loads ropes to which men clung to keep loads from tipping the wagons over, and we descended steeps by having behind the wagons men clinging to ropes.

At Soda Springs [in the southern part of present-day Idaho] we parted company with the crowd that was going to Oregon, which crowd included Fitzpatrick and the priests. Thirty-one of us, including one woman (Mrs. Benjamin Kelsey) and her child, decided to strike out for California. We knew nothing positive of the route, except that it went west.

> Then began what was by far the most difficult part of their memorable journey. Heading southwest, they made their way across many miles of barren, waterless land that is now central Nevada before eventually reaching the Carson River and the base of the Sierra. On the way they had been forced to abandon their vehicles, discard the major part of their possessions, and tie the remainder to the backs of their horses, oxen, and mules. Before them, moreover, still lay the formidable barrier of the mountains.

By this time [continues Dawson's account] short rations and toil had reduced both man and beast to a very weakened condition. The animals began to drop down. They would be relieved by distributing their loads among others. Occasionally a horse or mule could go no farther, and had to left behind. Some of the crowd started the practise of knocking these on the head, cutting off the flesh and eating it. This soon became general. About the middle of October, we came into oak timber, with acorns lying on the ground. The first tree we found with acorns under it we camped at, although it was early in the day. We feared we might not find another.

> In all, three weeks were spent seeking a pass over the mountains and a route down their western side. Fortunately winter storms were late that year, for it was then near the end of October, and had the weakened party been caught in snowstorms they would almost surely have perished. Eventually, after many hardships, the party made their way down into the foothills and out on to the floor of the San Joaquin Valley, where food for man and beast was plentiful.

So [concludes Dawson] we had reached California—the first truly distinctive American emigrant train to do so . . .

iii

> A second graphic account of that journey was written years later by John Bidwell, who, then a youth in his early twenties, had joined the party in the fall of 1840.

The plan [he recalled] had its inception when there appeared among the homesteaders of Platte County [Missouri] a French trader named Robidoux, who had been a recent visitor to the West Coast Mexican province . . .

His [Robidoux's] description of California was in the superlative degree favorable. So much so that I resolved if possible to see that wonderful land, and with others helped to get up a meeting at Weston and invited him to make a statement before it in regard to the country. At that time when a man moved out West, as soon as he was fairly settled he wanted to move again, and naturally every question imaginable was asked. Robidoux described it as one of perennial spring and boundless fertility, and laid stress on the countless thousands of wild horses and cattle. Every conceivable question that we could ask was answered favorably. Generally the first question which a Missourian asked about a country was whether there was any fever and ague. I remember his answer distinctly. He said there was but one man in California that ever had a chill there, and it was a matter of so much wonderment to the people of Monterey that they went eighteen miles into the country to see him shake. Nothing could have been more satisfactory on the score of health. He said that the Spanish authorities were most friendly; that you could travel all over California and it would cost you nothing for horses or food. Even the Indians were friendly . . .

> The result of this glowing account was that plans at once got under way to organize a group to make their way to that promised land.

A pledge was drawn up [continued Bidwell] in which every signer agreed to purchase a suitable outfit, and to rendezvous at Sapling Grove in what is now the State of Kansas, on the 9th of the following May, armed and equipped to cross the Rocky Mountains to California . . . In a short time I think within a month, we had about five hundred names; we also had correspondence with people all over Missouri, and even as far east as Illinois and Kentucky, and as far south as Arkansas . . .

This being the first movement to cross the Rocky Mountains to California, it is not surprising that it suffered reverses before we were fairly started. One of these was the publication of a letter in a New York newspaper giving a depressing view of the country for which we were all so confidently longing . . . The merchants of Platte County had all along protested against our going . . . , saying it was the most unheard-of, foolish, wild-goose chase that ever entered the brain of man for five hundred people to pull up stakes, leave that beautiful country, and go away out to a region that we knew nothing of. But they made little headway until this letter . . . appeared. They republished it in a paper in the town of Liberty in Clay County, and sent it broadcast all over the surrounding region. The result was that as the people began to think more seriously about the scheme the membership of the society began dropping off, and it so happened at last that of all the five hundred that signed the pledge I was the only one that got ready; and even I had hard work to do so, for I had barely means to buy a wagon, a gun, and provisions. Indeed, the man who was going with me, and who was to furnish the horses, backed out, and there I was with my wagon!

At the last moment before the time to start for the rendezvous at Sapling Grove—it seemed almost providential—along came a man named George Henshaw . . . I persuaded him to let me take his horse and trade him for a yoke of steers to pull the wagon and a sorry-looking, one-eyed mule for him to ride. We went via Weston to lay in some supplies. One wagon and four or five persons here joined us . . . When we reached Sapling Grove in May 1841, there was but one wagon ahead of us. For the next few days one or two wagons would come each day . . . Everyone furnished

his own supplies. Our teams were oxen, mules, and horses
. . . My gun was an old flint-lock rifle, but a good one. Old
hunters told me to have nothing to do with cap or percussion locks, that they were unreliable, and that if I got my
caps or percussion wet I could not shoot, while if I lost my
flint I could pick up another on the plains. I doubt if there
was one hundred dollars in money in the whole party, but
all were enthusiastic and anxious to go . . .

In general our route lay from near Westport, where Kansas City now is, northwesterly over the prairie, crossing
several streams till we struck the Platte River . . . Then
crossing the South Fork of the Platte, and following up the
north side for a day or so, we went over to the North
Fork and camped at Ash Hollow; thence up the north side
of that fork . . . , till we came to Fort Laramie, a trading
post of the American Fur Company . . . Thence after several days we came to another noted landmark called Independence Rock, which we followed up to the head. . . . Next
we crossed Green River to Black Fork, which we followed
till we came to Ham's Fork, at the head of which we crossed
the divide between Green and Bear rivers. Then we followed Bear River down to Soda Springs . . . which we
continued to follow down on the west side till we came to
Salt Lake. Then we went around the north end of the lake
and struck out to the west and southwest.

> During this part of their journey the group had grown accus-
> tomed to life on the far frontier, had had their share of ad-
> ventures and hardships en route, and became reasonably
> skilled in the ways of the wilderness. Beyond Salt Lake, how-
> ever, they had to cope with a variety of more formidable diffi-
> culties. Because by then summer was far advanced, and
> haste would be necessary in order to get over the Sierra
> range before the passes were blocked by winter snows, it
> was decided to abandon their wagons.

So [wrote he] we stopped one day and threw away everything we could not carry, made pack-saddles and packed the
oxen, mules, and horses, and started. On Green River we
had seen the style of pack-saddles used by the trapping party,
and had learned a little about how to make them. Packing is
an art, and something that only an experienced mountaineer
can do well. We were unaccustomed to it, and the difficulties
we had at first were simply indescribable. The trouble began the very first day. But we started—most of us on foot,
for nearly all the animals, including several of the oxen, had
to carry packs. It was but a few minutes before the packs began to turn; horses became scared, mules kicked, oxen
jumped and bellowed, and articles were scattered in all
directions.

> Nonetheless the diminished party—for, as stated earlier, half
> their number had abandoned their intention of going to Cal-
> ifornia and joined a group of trappers bound for Oregon—
> the remainder, numbering thirty-two, including one woman
> and child, pushed on into the unknown. Having crossed
> many miles of hot and waterless desert they eventually
> reached a branch of the Humboldt River, the bed of which
> was dry at that time of year.

On the Humboldt [continued Bidwell] we had a further division of our ranks . . . We were getting tired, and some
were in favor of leaving the oxen, of which we had only
about seven or eight, and rushing on into California. They
said there was plenty of beef in California. But some of us
said: "No; our oxen are now our only supply of food. We
are doing well, making eighteen or twenty miles a day."
One morning . . . the captain and two of his mess came to
us and said: "Boys, our animals are better than yours, and
we always get out of meat before any of the rest of you. Let
us have the most of the meat this time, and we will pay you
back the next ox we kill." We gladly let them have all

they wished. But as soon as they had taken it, and were mounted ready to start, the captain in a loud voice exclaimed: "Now we have been found fault with long enough, and we are going to California. If you can keep up with us, all right; if you cannot, you may go to ——"; and away they started, the captain and eight men . . .

In a short time they were out of sight. We followed their trail for two or three days, but after they had crossed over to the south side of the Humboldt and turned south we came into a sandy waste where the wind had entirely obliterated their tracks. We were then thrown entirely upon our own resources. It was our desire to make as great speed as possible westward, deviating only when obstacles interposed, and in such case bearing south instead of north, so as to be found in a lower latitude in the event that winter should overtake us in the mountains . . . So, perforce, we followed down the Sink of the Humboldt and were obliged to drink its water, which in the fall of the year becomes stagnant and of the color of lye, and not fit to drink or use unless boiled. Leaving the Sink of the Humboldt, we crossed a considerable stream . . . and followed it to where it came out of the mountains, which proved to be the Sierra Nevada.

We were now camped on the Walker River, at the very eastern base of the Sierra Nevada, and had only two oxen left. We sent men ahead to see if it would be possible to scale the mountains, while we killed the better of the two oxen and dried the meat in preparation for the ascent. The men returned towards evening and reported that they thought it would be possible, though very difficult. We had eaten our supper, and were ready for the climb in the morning. Looking back on the plains we saw something coming, which we decided to be Indians.

However, these proved to be the eight men who had deserted the party nine days earlier. They had swung farther to

the south, there met a party of Indians camped beside a stagnant lake, and been supplied by them with a quantity of fish
caught in its waters. Having eaten heartily of these, the
group had become violently ill, from the effects of which
they were still suffering when they gratefully rejoined the
original party. Thereupon the united group pushed on into
the lofty Sierra. Fortunately, the winter snows came late that
year and although many difficulties were encountered during
the weeks-long passage, the feat was eventually accomplished.

The evening of the day we started down into the valley
[wrote Bidwell] we were very tired, and when night came
our party was strung along for three or four miles, and
every man slept right where darkness overtook him. He
would take off his saddle for a pillow and turn his horse or
mule loose, if he had one. His animal would be too poor to
walk away, and in the morning he would find him, usually
within fifty feet. The jaded horses nearly perished with hunger and fatigue. When we overtook the foremost of the
party the next morning we found they had come to a pond
of water, and one of them had killed a fat coyote; when I
came up it was all eaten except the lights and windpipe, on
which I made my breakfast . . . From that camp we saw
timber to the north of us, evidently bordering a stream running west. It turned out to be the stream that we had followed down in the mountains—the Stanislaus River. As soon
as we came in sight of the bottom land of the stream we saw
an abundance of antelopes and sandhill cranes. We killed
two of each the first evening.

Several days later the bedraggled party reached the outpost
ranchhouse of Dr. John Marsh, their historic six-month trek
at an end.

iv

Tales of human beings who spend long periods cut off from all contacts with their fellows have always been a favorite with authors and readers alike, the best-known example being, of course, *Robinson Crusoe*. Nor have all such stories been a product of the fiction-writer's imagination. Indeed, in the annals of the West can be found the authenticated records of many real-life Crusoes. One of the most dramatic of these tales relates to the adventures of a 17-year-old youth named Moses Schallenberger, who spent the winter of 1844-45 marooned on the shores of a lake high on a shoulder of the Sierra Nevada range.

Schallenberger was a member of a group of emigrants who set off early in 1844 from Council Bluffs, Missouri, bound for California. During the major part of their long journey the party met no unusual difficulties. However, on reaching the body of water now known as Donner Lake the snow was so deep that it was decided to leave their wagons and other possessions there and continue on to Sutter's Fort, where they hoped to procure fresh horses to draw their wagons down to the lowlands.

Young Schallenberger volunteered to remain behind and watch over the property during the absence of his fellows. His own story, written years later, thus explains his reasons for reaching that decision:

There seemed little danger to me in undertaking this. Game seemed to be abundant. We had seen a number of deer, and one of our party had killed a bear, so I had no fears of starvation. The Indians in that vicinity were poorly clad, and I therefore felt no anxiety in regard to them, as they probably would stay further south as long as cold weather lasted. Knowing that we were not far from California, and being unacquainted, except in a general way, with the climate, I did not suppose that the snow would at any time be more than two feet deep, or that it would be on the ground continually.

After I had decided to stay, Mr. Joseph Foster and Mr. Allen Montgomery said that they would stay with me, and so it was settled, and the rest of the party started across the mountains. They left us two cows, so worn out and poor that they could go no further. We did not care for them to leave us any cattle for food, for, as I said, there seemed to be plenty of game, and we were all good hunters, well furnished with ammunition, so we had no apprehension that we would not have plenty to eat . . .

The morning after the separation of our party, which we felt was only for a short time, Foster and Montgomery and myself set about making a cabin, for we determined to make ourselves comfortable as possible . . .

On the evening of the day we finished our little house it began to snow, and that night it fell to a depth of three feet. This prevented a hunt which we had in contemplation for the next day. It did not worry us much, however, for the weather was not at all cold and we thought the snow would soon melt. But we were doomed to disappointment. A week passed, and instead of any snow going off more came. At last we were compelled to kill our cows, for the snow was so deep that they could not get around to eat . . . We hung them up on the north side of the house and covered them with pine brush. That night the meat froze, and as the weather was just cold enough to keep it frozen, it remained fresh without salt. It kept on snowing continually, and our little cabin was almost covered. It was now about the last of November or first of December, and we began to fear that we should all perish in the snow.

The snow was so light and frosty that it would not bear us up, therefore we were not able to go out at all except to cut wood for the fire, and if that had not been near at hand I do not know what we should have done. None of us had ever seen snow-shoes and of course had no idea how to make them, but finally Foster and Montgomery managed to make something they called a snow-shoe . . . We were now able to walk on the snow to bring in our wood, and that was about all there was to do. There was no game. We went out several times but never saw anything. What could we expect to find in ten feet of snow? . . .

We now began to feel very blue, for there seemed no possible hope for us. We had already eaten about half our meat, and with the snow on the ground getting deeper and deeper each day there was no chance for game. Death, the fearful, agonizing death by starvation, literally stared us in the face. At last, after due consideration, we determined to start for California on foot. Accordingly we dried some of our beef, and each of us carrying ten pounds of meat, a pair of blankets, a rifle and ammunition, we set out on our perilous journey. Not knowing how to fasten snow-shoes to our feet made it very fatiguing to walk with them. We fastened them to heel and toe, and thus had to lift the whole weight of the shoe at every step, as the shoe would necessarily sink down somewhat, the snow would crumble in on top of it, and in a short time each shoe weighed about ten pounds.

Foster and Montgomery were matured men, and could consequently stand a greater amount of hardship than I . . . Consequently when we reached the summit of the mountain about sunset that night, having traveled a distance of about fifteen miles, I was scarcely able to drag one foot after the other . . .

When night came on we cut down a tree and with it built a fire on top of the snow. We then spread some pine boughs for our beds, and after eating a little jerky and standing around our fire in a vain attempt to get warm, we laid down and tried to sleep. Although we were thoroughly exhausted, sleep would not come . . . Every now and then we would rise and replenish the fire, which, though it kept us from freezing, could not make us comfortable. When daylight came . . . our fire was so far down that we could not get to it, but as we had nothing to cook, it made but little difference. We ate our jerky while we deliberated as to what we should do next. I was so stiff that I could hardly move, and my companions had grave doubts as to whether I could stand the journey. If I should give out they could afford me no assistance, and I would necessarily be left to perish in the snow. I fully realized the situation, and told them that I would return to the cabin and live as long as possible on the quarter of beef that was still there, and when it was all gone I would start out again alone for California. They reluctantly assented to my plan, and promised that if they ever got to California and it was possible to get back, they would return . . .

My companions had not been long out of sight before my spirits began to revive, and I began to think, like Micawber, that something might "turn up." So I strapped on my blankets and dried beef, shouldered my gun, and began to retrace my steps to the cabin. It had frozen during the night and this enabled me to walk on our trail without the snow-shoes. This was a great relief, but the exertion . . . of the day before had so weakened me that I think I was never so tired in my life as when, just a little before dark, I came in sight of the cabin. The door-sill was only nine inches high, but I could not step over it without taking my hands to raise my leg. As soon as I was able to crawl around the next morning I put on my snow-shoes, and, taking my rifle, scoured the country thoroughly for foxes. The result was as I had expected . . . plenty of tracks but no fox.

Then began the youth's grim, months-long struggle for survival. Throughout that period his major task was to procure enough food to ward off starvation, and when successive attempts to bag foxes with his gun uniformly failed it oc-

curred to him that he might have better luck trying to trap
them. He accordingly hunted out two steel traps that had
been left behind in one of the wagons, set them out, and
hopefully awaited the result.

When daylight came [his reminiscence continues] I went
out to inspect the traps. I was anxious to see them and still
dreaded to look. After some hesitation I commenced the examination, and to my delight found in one of them a
starved coyote. I soon had his hide off and his flesh roasted
in a Dutch oven. I ate this meat, but it was horrible. I next
tried boiling him, but it did not improve the flavor. I cooked
him in every possible manner my imagination, spurred by
hunger, could suggest, but could not get him into a condition where he could be eaten without revolting my stomach.
But for three days that was all I had to eat. On the third
night I caught two foxes. I roasted one of them, and the
meat, though entirely devoid of fat, was delicious. I was so
hungry I could easily have eaten a fox at two meals, but I
made one last me two days . . .
   It is strange that I never craved anything to eat but fat
meat. For bread and vegetables I had no desire. Salt I had
in plenty, but never used. I had just coffee enough for one
cup, and that I saved for Christmas . . .
   The daily struggle for life and the uncertainty under
which I labored were very wearing. I was always worried
and anxious, not about myself alone, but in regard to the
fate of those who had gone forward. I would lie awake
nights and think of these things, and revolve in my mind
what I would do when the supply of foxes became exhausted . . .
   Fortunately, I had plenty of books, Dr. Townsend [the
leader of the expedition] having brought out quite a library. I used often to read aloud, for I longed for some

sound to break the oppressive stillness. For the same reason I would talk aloud to myself. At night I built large fires and read by the light of the pine-knots as late as possible, in order that I might sleep late the next morning, and thus cause the days to seem shorter. What I wanted most was enough to eat, and the next thing I tried hardest to do was to kill time. I thought the snow would never leave the ground, and the few months I had been living there seemed years.

Not until the end of February, 1845, did the youth's long ordeal come to a close.

One evening a little before sunset [stated he] as I was standing a short distance from my cabin I thought I could distinguish the form of a man moving towards me. At first I thought it was an Indian, but very soon I could recognize the familiar face of Dennis Martin. My feelings can be better imagined than described. He relieved my anxiety about those of our party who had gone forward with the wagons. They had all arrived safely in California and were then in Yuba . . . Mr. Martin had brought a small amount of provisions on his back . . . My sister, Mrs. Townsend, hearing that Mr. Martin was about to return to pilot the emigrants out of the wilderness, begged him to extend his journey a little further and lend a helping hand to her brother . . . He consented to do so, and here he was. Being a Canadian, he was accustomed to snow-shoes, and soon showed me how to fix mine so I could travel with less than half the labor . . .

Next morning the pair set off to rejoin the main party, which was encamped on the Yuba River. Their journey seems to have been accomplished without incident, and on March 1 the entire group pushed on to Hock Farm. There Captain

Sutter's vaqueros slaughtered a fat cow, which provided the newcomers with what Schallenberger described as "a good square meal." The trials and privations of the "Sierra Crusoe" were happily over.

V

Although the annals of the West are replete with tales of the hardships and privations suffered by those who first ventured into the wilderness, perhaps the most widely known of these is the tragic story of the Donner party. This group, numbering thirty-one men, women, and children, set off from Springfield, Illinois, in the spring of 1846, bound for California. After proceeding as far as Fort Bridger, in what is now southwestern Wyoming, the party—which then, having been joined by other groups, numbered close to a hundred—was persuaded to abandon the well-marked overland trail and take a cut-off that led south of Great Salt Lake. There they lost their way and encountered so many delays that by the time they reached the base of the Sierra the season had far advanced. Nonetheless they pushed on into the mountains, hoping to get safely over the crest before their way was blocked by winter storms. In this they were disappointed, for an abundance of early snowfall descended upon them, first slowing their progress, then stopping it entirely. Thereupon panic seized them; some fashioned crude snowshoes and pushed ahead on foot, while others set up a makeshift camp at the edge of the mountain lake that has ever since borne the party's name.

One survivor of the ordeal that followed was a child named Virginia Reed. Nearly a half-century later she recalled her experiences in a narrative from which the following excerpts are taken.

Winter had set in a month earlier than usual [wrote she].
All trails and roads were covered; and our only guide was
the summit which it seemed we would never reach. Despair
drove many frantic. Each family tried to cross the mountains but found it impossible. When it was seen that the
wagons could not be dragged through the snow, their goods
and provisions were packed on oxen and another start was
made, men and women walking in the snow up to their
waists, carrying their children in their arms and trying to
drive the cattle. The Indians [who were acting as guides]
said they could find no road, so a halt was called, and Stanton went ahead . . . and came back and reported that we
could get across if we kept right on, but that it would be impossible if snow fell. He was in favor of a forced march until
the other side of the summit should be reached, but some of
our party were so tired and exhausted with the day's labor
that they declared they could not take another step; so the
few who knew the danger that the night might bring
yielded to the many, and we camped within three miles of
the summit.

That night came the dreaded snow. Around the camp-fires
under the trees great feathery flakes came whirling down.
The air was so full of them that one could see objects only a
few feet away. The Indians knew we were doomed, and one
of them wrapped his blanket about him and stood all night
under a tree. We children slept soundly on our cold bed of
snow with a soft white mantle falling over us so thickly that
every few moments my mother would have to shake the
shawl—our only covering— to keep us from being buried
alive. In the morning the snow lay deep on mountain and
valley. With heavy hearts we turned back to a cabin that had
been built by the Murphy-Schallenberger party two years
before. We built more cabins and prepared as best we could
for the winter. That camp, which proved the camp of death
to many in our company, was made on the shore of a lake,

since known as "Donner Lake." The Donners were camped in Alder Creek Valley below the lake, and were, if possible, in a worse condition than ourselves. The snow came on so suddenly that they had no time to build cabins, but hastily put up brush sheds, covering them with pine boughs.

Three double cabins were built at Donner Lake, which were known as the "Breen Cabin," the "Murphy Cabin," and the "Reed-Graves Cabin." The cattle were all killed, and the meat was placed in snow for preservation. My mother had no cattle to kill, but she made arrangements for some, promising to give two for one in California. Stanton and the Indians made their home in my mother's cabin . . .

The misery endured during those four months at Donner Lake in our little dark cabin under the snow would fill pages and make the coldest heart ache. Christmas was near, but to the starving its memory gave no comfort. It came and passed without observance, but my mother had determined weeks before that her children should have a treat on this one day. She had laid away a few dried apples, some beans, a bit of tripe, and a small piece of bacon. When this hoarded store was brought out, the delight of the little ones knew no bounds. The cooking was watched carefully, and when we sat down to our Christmas dinner mother said, "Children, eat slowly, for this one day you can have all you wish." So bitter was the misery relieved by that one bright day, that I have never since sat down to a Christmas dinner without my thoughts going back to Donner Lake . . .

The storms would last ten days at a time, and we would have to cut chips from inside the logs which formed our cabins, in order to start a fire. We could scarcely walk, and the men had hardly strength to procure wood. We would drag ourselves through the snow from one cabin to another, and some mornings snow would have to be shoveled out of the fireplace before a fire could be made. Poor little children were crying with hunger, and mothers were crying because they had so little to give their children. We seldom thought of bread, we had been without it so long . . .

Time dragged slowly along till we were no longer on short allowance but were simply starving. My mother determined to make an effort to cross the mountains. She could not see her children die without trying to get them food. It was hard to leave them but she felt it must be done. She told them she would bring them bread, so they were willing to stay, and with no guide but a compass we started—my mother, Eliza, Milt Elliot and myself. Milt wore snow shoes and we followed in his tracks. We were five days in the mountains; Eliza gave out the first day and had to return, but we kept on and climbed one high mountain after another only to see others higher still ahead. Often I would have to crawl up the mountains, being too tired to walk . . . One morning we awoke to find ourselves in a well of snow. During the night, while in the deep sleep of exhaustion, the heat of the fire had melted the snow and our little camp had gradually sunk many feet below the surface until we were literally buried in a well of snow. The danger was that any attempt to get out might bring an avalanche upon us, but finally steps were carefully made and we reached the surface. My foot was badly frozen, so we were compelled to return, and just in time, for that night a storm came on, the most fearful of the winter, and we should have perished had we not been in the cabins.

We now had nothing to eat but raw hides and they were on the roof of the cabin to keep out the snow; when prepared for cooking and boiled they were simply a pot of glue. When the hides were taken off our cabin and we were left without shelter Mr. Breen gave us a home with his family, and Mrs. Breen prolonged my life by slipping me little bits of meat now and then when she discovered that I could not eat the hide. Death had already claimed many in our party and it seemed as though relief would never reach us.

Meantime news of the plight of the marooned group had reached Sutter's Fort and at once plans to rescue them got under way, though it was recognized that at best this would be a dubious gamble. The first attempt, led by Virginia Reed's father—who had gone on ahead—ended in failure.

On his arrival at Sutter's Fort [wrote Virginia] my father made known the situation of the emigrants, and Captain Sutter offered at once to do everything possible for their relief. He furnished horses and provisions and my father and Mr. McClutchen started for the mountains, coming as far as possible with horses and then with packs on their backs proceeding on foot; but they were finally compelled to return. Captain Sutter was not surprised at their defeat. . . . He advised my father to go to Yerba Buena, now San Francisco, and make his case known to the naval officer in command. My father was in fact conducting parties there—when the seven members of the Forlorn Hope arrived from across the mountains. Their famished faces told the story. Cattle were killed and men were up all night drying beef and making flour by hand mills, nearly 200 pounds being made in one night, and a party of seven, commanded by Captain Reasen P. Tucker, was sent to our relief by Captain Sutter and the alcalde, Mr. Sinclair. On the evening of February 19th, 1847, they reached our cabins, where all were starving. They shouted to attract attention. Mr. Breen clambered up the icy steps from our cabin, and soon we heard the blessed words, "Relief, thank God, relief!" There was joy at Donner Lake that night, for we did not know the fate of the Forlorn Hope and we were told that relief parties would come and go until all were across the mountains. But with the joy sorrow was strangely blended. There were tears in other eyes than those of children; strong men sat down and wept. For the dead were lying about on the snow, some even unburied, since the living had not the strength to bury their dead.

Their trials, however, were not yet at an end. For not until weeks later were the last of the survivors brought down over the snowy trails, and during that passage both rescued and rescuers suffered many hardships. But eventually all found safe refuge within the hospitable walls of Sutter's Fort, where, in Virginia Reed's words, "the generous hearted Captain did everything possible for the sufferers."

Out of the eighty-three persons who were snowed in at Donner Lake [wrote she] forty-two perished, and of the thirty-one emigrants who left Springfield, Illinois, that spring morning, only eighteen lived to reach California.

V I

Gold on the American River!

i

As recorded earlier, the first group of emigrants made their way from the Mississippi Valley to the West Coast in the fall of 1841. The hardships and privations met with by that pioneer party failed to deter others from following in their footsteps; indeed, each year thereafter saw a growing number of heavily laden wagons and carts rolling westward over the trail they had broken.

While many of these newcomers headed for the Oregon country, a majority made their way to California, and it was not long before this heavy influx of Yankees began to arouse the concern of officials of that Mexican province, and certain steps were taken that were designed to discourage further immigration. These measures, however, completely failed to stem the tide, for the American frontiersman was first of all an individualist, and the surest way to arouse his ire was to attempt to hamper his freedom of movement. The result was that as the 1840's advanced, their resentment against the restrictive rules imposed by the Mexican rulers grew from year to year.

One of the few letters extant that gives an eye-witness ac-

count of what followed is that of E. M. Kern, an officer of
the exploring expedition headed by John C. Frémont which
was then passing through the province. Written from "Fort
Sacramento" [Sutter's Fort] in late July of 1846 and addressed to a friend on the East Coast, Kern's letter begins by
stating that while Frémont and his men were proceeding
north, bound for the Oregon country, they were overtaken by
Lieutenant Gillespie, bearing a message from U.S. Consul
Thomas O. Larkin at Monterey, ordering the party to return
to California.

What we were to return for [he wrote] no one knows . . .
We had been ordered out on March last, and abused by a
Proclamation [by Colonel José Castro, Mexican Comman-
der-in-Chief of the Department of California] and left the
country without a fight. It [that is, their return] appeared
equivalent to a declaration of war. When fairly down in the
Valley, couriers were running here and yon and nobody
knew what for. At last word was sent to José Castro that we
had returned. Then came a rumor that he was marching
against us with a force of 300 men. Then the foreigners living around the upper part of the Country, about 20 or 25,
were called into camp—as a Proclamation had been issued
stating that all foreigners, Americans in particular, should
leave the country at once, leaving their property to be disposed of as Govt. should think fit or abide by the consequence. Indians were bribed to burn the crops as soon as
they should be ripe enough, thereby cutting off all supplies
for the Emigrants when they should arrive this fall . . .

Now to the commencement of hostilities. Having collected
what forces could be raised in the upper country, [we]
moved . . . towards the fort. The Spaniards were reported
to be on the west side of the Sacramento River. We supposed they would move upwards & sweep the country down,
attacking us in the rear, defeat us (of course easily) & have

possession of the whole upper country. But . . . it turned
out to be a corporal with 12 men driving a band of horses
for the use of Castro. Here was an opening to commence business, & Merrit [Ezekiel Merritt] a R [ocky] Mountain man
at the head of 12 men started and returned with the whole
Cavillarda. Not a blow was struck. He [Frémont] sent word
to Castro that he was there, that he took the horses, and that
if he(C) wanted them, to come and get them . . .

The next move was the attack and taking of Sonoma, a
bold and beautifully managed affair. Our information [was]
that this post was garrisoned with about 80 or 100 men &
about 200 Indians. We had every reason to suppose that
they were on the alert, as the business had commenced. Merrit started with 25 men to the place, his forces increasing to
45 all told when he arrived there. The charge was made but
there was no resistance, simply because there was no one to
resist. A garrison was stationed under the command of one
[William B.] Ide, a Mormon, while our party returned
bringing with them as proof of victory, Gen. M. G. Vallejo,
Col. S. Vallejo, Col. Victor Prud'homme, a Frenchman, &
J. P. Leese, an American. I have them at present under my
charge. The next move of the insurgents (for they had it all
to themselves, our camp laying by as mere spectators) was to
issue a proclamation from Headquarters at Sonoma signed
by said Ide, calling on the people who loved their liberty to
fly to arms &c., &c. This produced a counter one from Castro
ordering the people to arm themselves in defence of their
firesides, which were about to be invaded by a party of Bar-
barians . . .

Later in his letter, Kern set down a translation of Castro's
proclamation calling on the Mexicans to join him in expel-
ling the Frémont party from the province. This message—
which Kern termed "as pretty a piece of bombast as was ever
written"—read as follows:

> *Fellow Citizans: A band of robbers commanded by a Captain of the U.S. Army, J. C. Frémont, have without respect to the laws and authority of the Department, daringly introduced themselves into the country and disobeyed both the orders of your Commander-in-Chief and of the Prefect of the District by which he was required to march forthwith out of the limits of our Territory, and without answering their letters he remains encamped at the farm "Natividad" from which he sallies forth committing depredation, and making scandalous skirmishes.*
>
> *In the name of our native country I invite you to place yourselves under my immediate orders at headquarters, where we will prepare to lance the ulcer which (should it not be done) would destroy our liberties and independence, for which you ought to sacrifice yourselves as will your friend and fellow-citizen*
>
> *José Castro*

Matters turning out as they have [continued Kern] it will be almost impossible for us to reach home this winter, as it will be so late before we get through here that the snows will have set in, & though we could cross the Cal. Mts., the R [ocky] Mts. will be unpassable . . . I am in hopes of getting a furlough when I am relieved and may have a chance of seeing something more of the settlements. I am so far away from any place at this fort that it is only now & then when an express comes that I am enabled [to] know what is going on . . .

There is a large emigration expected this fall from the states, led by Hastings, author of the Emigrant's Guide . . . There is a party of Mormons reported to be on their way from N.Y. by way of the [Hawaiian] Islands. The lord knows where they will settle, as there are so many rumors of their doings that the people are opposed to their entrance . . .

Thus was set up the short-lived Bear Flag Republic, which
had existed only a short time before word arrived of the out-
break of war between Mexico and the United States. This
was followed by the capture of Monterey by Commodore
Sloat and the defeat of the Mexican forces in the south by
United States troops under Stephen W. Kearney. Then, by
the Treaty of Guadalupe Hidalgo in 1848, Mexico formally
ceded the territory to the United States, and the Bear Flag
that had flown over Sonoma was permanently lowered.

ii

Although the taking over of the province by the United
States was accomplished with a minimum of violence and
bloodshed, yet there is evidence that certain segments of
the population found it difficult to accustom themselves to
the new order of things. One amusing instance of this can be
cited. Before the coming of the Yankees, the Spanish and
Mexican residents had been inveterate gamblers, and during the early period of the American occupation little effort
was made to stamp out the practice. "During the pastoral
days of California," wrote the historian H. H. Bancroft, "men
were free, and might gamble if they chose. It came rather
hard on them, therefore, when the straight-laced Yankee
alcalde of Monterey [Walter E. Colton, former chaplain of
the warship *Congress*] placed a veto on the pastime." Under date of October 18, 1846, Colton wrote in his diary:

I issued, a few days since, an ordinance against gambling—a
vice which shows itself here more on the sabbath than any
other day of the week. The effect has been to drive the gamblers from the town into the bushes. I have been informed
this evening, that in a ravine, at a short distance, some thirty

individuals have been engaged through the day in this desperate play. They selected a spot deeply embowered in shade, and escaped the eye of my constables.

> Later the gamblers seem to have moved back into the town, for on May 12 of the following year Colton thus reported a raid on one of their hideaways:

A nest of gamblers arrived in town yesterday, and last evening opened a monte game at the hotel honored with the name of the Astor House. I took a file of soldiers, and under cover of night reached the hotel unsuspected, where I stationed them at the two doors which afforded the only egress from the building. In a moment I was on the stairs which led to the apartment where the gamesters were congregated. I heard a whistle and then footsteps flying into every part of the edifice. On entering the great chamber, not a being was visible save one Sonoranian reclining against a large table, and composedly smoking a cigarito. I passed the compliments of the evening with him, and desired the honor of an introduction to his companions. At the moment a feigned snore broke on my ear from a bed in the corner of the apartment—"Ha! Dutre, is that you? Come, tumble up and aid me in stirring out the rest." He pointed under the bed, where I discovered, just within the drop of the vallance a multitude of feet and legs radiating as from a common center. "Hallo, there, friends—turn out," and out came some half-dozen or more, covered with dust and feathers. Their plight and discovery threw them into a laugh at each other. From this apartment, accompanied by my secretary, I proceeded to others, where I found the sleepers stowed away in every imaginable position—some in the beds, some under them, several in closets, two in a hogshead, and one up a chimney.

Mr. R. from Missouri—known under the sobriquet of the

"prairie wolf"—I found between two bedsticks, with his coat and boots on, and half smothered with feathers. He was the ringleader, and raises a monte table wherever he goes . . . All shouted as he tumbled out from his ticks. Among the rest I found the alcalde of San Francisco, a gentleman of education and refinement, who never plays himself, but who, on this occasion, had come to witness the excitement. I gathered them all, some fifty in number, into the large saloon, and told them the only speech I had to make was in the shape of a fine of twenty dollars each. The more astute began to demur on the plea of not guilty, as no cards and no money had been discovered; and as for the beds, a man had as good a right to sleep under one as in it. I told them that was a matter of taste, misfortune often made strange bedfellows, and the only way to get out of the scrape was to pay up. Dr. S. was the first to plank down. "Come, my good fellows," said the doctor, "pay up, and no grumbling, this money goes to build a schoolhouse, where I hope our children will be taught better principles than they gather from the examples of their fathers." The "prairie wolf," planked down next, and in ten minutes the whole Chillanos, Sonoranians, Oregonians, Californians, Englices, Americanos, delivered their fines. These, with the hundred dollar fine of the keeper of the hotel, filled quite a bag. With this I bade them goodnight, and took my departure.

iii

Although California's existence had been known for more than three centuries before it became a part of the United States in 1846, during all that period it had been looked on as a remote frontier land, far removed from the centers of civilization and consequently of no outstanding importance to the world's great powers. It continued to be so regarded after it passed under the control of the United States—but not for long.

The event that first focused the eyes of the world on that far-distant land, and brought about the settlement of the entire West Coast far earlier than would otherwise have been the case, was, of course, Jim Marshall's discovery, in late January, 1848, of flakes of gold in the tailrace of Captain Sutter's new sawmill in the Sierra foothills. While during the century and more that has passed since that historic day, the story of the discovery has been told and retold times without number, none of these accounts is more graphic than that of the discoverer himself. How Marshall's version of the event came to be preserved is thus explained by an artist named Charles B. Gillespie, who reached California during the early months of the rush that followed.

One day while I was taking a pencil sketch of the mill and its surroundings [wrote Gillespie], Marshall came along and seated himself beside me; and there, sitting on the high bank with our feet dangling over the race, he pointed out the very spot where his eye had caught the glimmer of the first bit of gold. He was very communicative, but somewhat soured, and spoke rather freely of the heartlessness of the Government at Washington because it had not protected him in his rights as a settler . . . He had made nothing from his discovery, and now all this land surrounding his mill, which was his by right of settlement, was gathered up and taken from him little by little "without leave or license." He had nothing left but the fame, which, as he naïvely remarked, was "neither victuals nor clothes to any one."

I fully sympathized with him in his tribulations, and finally obtained what I so much desired, a full statement of the causes which impelled him to come so far from Sutter's Fort, together with all the incidents pertaining to his great discovery. This narrative, which I penciled down at the time, I believe was the first he ever gave to anyone. And it is written just as it fell from his lips, without correction or addition of any kind.

Then followed Marshall's narrative:

In May, 1847, with my rifle, blanket, and a few crackers to eat with the venison (for the deer then were awful plenty), I ascended the American River, according to Mr. Sutter's wish, as he wanted to find a good site for a saw-mill, where we could have plenty of timber, and where wagons would be able to ascend and descend the river hills. Many fellows had been out before me, but they could not find any place to suit; so when I left I told Mr. Sutter I would go along the river to its very head and find the place, if such a place existed anywhere along the river or any of its forks. I traveled along the river the whole way. Many places would suit very well for the erection of the mill, with plenty of timber everywhere, but then nothing but a mule could climb the hills; and when I would find a spot where the hills were not steep, there was no timber to be had; and so it went until I had been out several days and reached this place, which, after first sight, looked like the exact spot we were hunting.

I passed a couple of days examining the hills, and found a place where the wagons could ascend and descend with all ease. On my return to the fort I went out through the country examining the cañons and gulches, and picking out the easiest places for crossing them with loaded wagons.

You may be sure Mr. Sutter was pleased when I reported my success. We entered into partnership; I was to build the mill, and he was to find provisions, teams, tools, and to pay a portion of the men's wages. I believe I was at the time the only millwright in the whole country. In August, everything being ready, we freighted two wagons with tools and provi-

sions, and accompanied by six men I left the fort, and after
a good deal of difficulty reached the place one beautiful afternoon and formed our camp on yon little rise of ground
right above the town.

Our first business was to put up log houses, as we intended
remaining here all winter. This was done in less than no
time, for my men were great with the ax. We then cut timber and fell to work hewing it for the framework of the mill.
The Indians gathered about us in great numbers. I employed about fifty of them to assist us with the dam, which
we put up in a kind of way in about four weeks. In digging
the foundation of the mill we cut some distance into the soft
granite; we opened the forebay and then I left for the fort,
giving orders to Mr. Weimar to have a ditch cut through the
bar to the rear of the mill, and after quitting work in the
evening to raise the gate and let the water run all night, as
it would assist us very much in deepening and widening the
tail-race.

I returned in a few days, and found everything favorable,
all the men being at work in the ditch. When the channel
was opened it was my custom every evening to raise the gate
and let the water wash out as much sand and gravel through
the night as possible; and in the morning, when the men
were getting breakfast, I would walk down, and, shutting off
the water, look along the race and see what was to be done,
so that I might tell Mr. Weimar, who had charge of the Indians, at what particular point to set them to work for the
day . . .

One morning in January,—it was a clear, cold morning;
I shall never forget that morning—as I was taking my usual
walk along the race after shutting off the water, my eye was
caught with the glimpse of something shining in the bottom
of the ditch. There was about a foot of water running then.
I reached my hand down and picked it up; it made my heart
thump, for I was certain it was gold. The piece was about

half the size and of the shape of a pea. Then I saw another piece in the water. After taking it out I sat down and began to think right hard. I thought it was gold, and yet it did not seem to be of the right color: all the gold coin I had seen was of a reddish tinge; this looked more like brass. I recalled to mind all the metals I had ever seen or heard of, but could find none that resembled this. Suddenly the idea flashed across my mind that it might be iron pyrites. I trembled to think of it! This question could soon be determined. Putting one of the pieces on a hard river stone, I took another and commenced hammering it. It was soft, and didn't break: it therefore must be gold, but largely mixed with some other metal, very likely silver, for pure gold, I thought, would certainly have a brighter color.

When I returned to our cabin for breakfast I showed the two pieces to my men. They were all a good deal excited, and had they not thought that the gold only existed in small quantities they would have abandoned everything and left me to finish my job alone. However, to satisfy them, I told them that as soon as we had the mill finished we would devote a week or two to gold hunting and see what we could make out of it.

While we were working in the race after this discovery we always kept a sharp lookout, and in the course of three or four days we had picked up about three ounces—our work still progressing as lively as ever, for none of us imagined at that time that the whole country was sowed with gold.

In about a week's time after the discovery I had to take another trip to the fort; and, to gain what information I could respecting the real value of the metal, took all that we had collected with me and showed it to Mr. Sutter, who at once declared it was gold, but thought with me that it was greatly mixed with some other metal. It puzzled me a good deal to hit upon the means of telling the exact quantity of gold contained in the alloy; however, we at last stumbled on an old American cyclopedia, where we saw the specific gravity of all the metals, and rules given to find the quantity of each in a given bulk. After hunting over the whole fort and borrowing from some of the men, we got three dollars and a half in silver, and with a small pair of scales we soon ciphered it out that there was no silver nor copper in the gold, but that it was entirely pure.

This fact being ascertained, we thought it our best policy to keep it as quiet as possible till we should have finished our mill. But there was a great number of disbanded Mormon soldiers in and about the fort, and when they came to hear of it, why it just spread like wildfire, and soon the whole country was in a bustle. I had scarcely arrived at the mill again till several persons appeared with pans, shovels, and hoes, and those that had not iron picks had wooden ones, all anxious to fall to work and dig up our mill; but this we would not permit. As fast as one party disappeared another would arrive, and sometimes I had the greatest kind of trouble to get rid of them. I sent them all off in different directions, telling them about such and such places, where I was certain there was plenty of gold if they would only take the trouble of looking for it. At that time I never imagined that the gold was so abundant. I told them to go to such and such places, because it appeared that they would dig nowhere but in such places as I pointed out, and I believe such was their confidence in me that they would have dug on the very top of yon mountain if I had told them to do so.

The second place where gold was discovered was in a gulch near the Mountaineer House, on the road to Sacramento. The third place was on a bar on the South Fork of the American River a little above the junction of the Middle and South forks. The diggings at Hangtown were discovered next by myself, for we all went out for a while as soon as our job was finished. The Indians next discovered the diggings at Kelsay's, and thus in a very short time we discovered that the whole country was but one bed of gold. So there, stranger, is the entire history of the gold discovery in California—a discovery that hasn't as yet been of much benefit to me.

iv

The man who is credited with having first heralded Marshall's discovery to the outer world was Edward C. Kemble, pioneer California newspaper editor, whose journal, the weekly *California Star*, published in the village of Yerba Buena, announced the news in its issue of May 6, 1848. Here is Kemble's own story, written more than four decades later, telling of his visit to the scene of the find.

Sometime in March, 1848, vague rumors of the gold discovery at Sutter's Mill found their way to Yerba Buena, now San Francisco, at that time a town of three or four hundred inhabitants. The writer of this was editing and printing with his own hands a small weekly paper in the town, the first that had been started there, and when the reports of gold on the Rio de los Americanos began to multiply he deemed it to be in the line of his duty to go and investigate the wonder.

It was a seven days' journey by sloop or "launch," as the Sacramento River carrier of that day was called, from San Francisco to Sutter's Fort, and the party, consisting of the editor and two friends, reached the "embarcadero" of Sutter's Fort,—that is to say, the river landing,—where Sacramento now stands, in the early part of April. One of Sutter's Indians, apprized the captain of our coming, and, as was his invariable custom, on the arrival of strangers, he caused saddled horses in charge of vaqueros to be sent to convey the new-comers to the fort. Its proprietor met us at the entrance, hat in hand, and gave his usual whole-hearted welcome . . . After seeing us made comfortable, he set before us a hearty meal of the beef and frijoles of the country, and we announced that we had come to see the gold-mine which it was reported he and Marshall had opened on the American River.

He not only readily assented, but offered to provide horses, provisions, and attendants for our journey, and also to go with us in person to the spot. It may have been that he had not the faith of his partner Marshall in the extent and permanency of the newly discovered "diggings," but those who knew Sutter well will see in the incident the overflowing kindliness of heart and the unselfish generosity that characterized his whole life.

At sunrise the next morning we took the road to the lumber camp, distant a good day's ride from the fort. Captain Sutter's two Indian body-servants preceded us with extra saddle-horses and a pack-animal carrying provisions and camp equipage. Our party, consisting of the captain, mounted on a favorite riding-mule, and my two friends and myself, on native horses, followed at a good gait, though at this period of his life Captain Sutter was not an overbold rider, and in fording streams and crossing marshy places was careful almost to timidity. I remember well his appearance under his broad-brimmed hat, and carrying under his arm his gold-headed cane. At one point on the road, where it led through a stony bog, his mule made a misstep, and I heard her rider expostulate in a low tone: "God bless me, Katy! Now den, child! De oder foot. So!"

We reached the fork of the American, on which the sawmill was being erected, early in the afternoon. During our ride we had not seen a human being, and had passed but one house. The camp of the millwright and lumbermen was in a beautiful grove of pines on the side of a long hill sloping to

the river. This "long hill of Coloma" became memorable
not many months afterward, when freight wagons and stages
came into use, for its wearisomeness, occasionally relieved by
a runaway among the half-trained bronco teams. The mill,
now so famous in history, was at the foot of this hill, on the
edge of the stony bar that stretched out to the river. The
race, in which the first gold was found, ran along the bank
just above the level of the bar, both bar and race were
flooded now from the sudden and unusual rise of the river;
work had stopped at the mill, and the lumbermen were idle
in the camp.

Riding up to the camp, Captain Sutter saluted the men with
his characteristic politeness and cordiality, and introduced
our party to Marshall. "These gentlemen have come to see
der gole-mines, Mr. Marshall," he said; and then, seeing the
vexed and disappointed look that came into the latter's face,
he added that we were his friends, and showed by his open
manner that so far as we were concerned, at least, there need
be no secrecy about the gold. But Marshall would not be
propitiated, and gave us only gruff and evasive replies to our
inquiries about the locality where it was to be found.

"You'll find it anywhere you're a mind to dig for it down
there," said he, half extending his arm in the direction of
the river. Some months later this proved to be literally true,
but it was very misleading to our unpractised party at that
time, and we searched diligently until near sundown in most
impracticable places. Only one of us was rewarded by the
"color"; Major P. B. Reading washed out a few grains with
an Indian basket and thought himself very poorly paid for
his labor.

After supper we gathered about the camp-fire, and the
Indians of the neighborhood, having heard of Captain Sutter's arrival, came, as was their custom, to see him, dropping
in by twos and threes until we had nearly all the principal
men of the Coloma bands before us. Then an old chief arose

and began to harangue the captain, warning him against looking for the gold, which he declared was very "bad medicine." He said his ancestors had known all about it; that it existed all through the mountains, but that it belonged to a demon, who devoured all who searched for it. The demon inhabited a lake in the mountains the shores of which were lined with gold. All our dusky friends agreed with the speaker that it was a very awful thing to meddle with the gold. We afterward came to the conclusion that the early Mission fathers had learned of the existence of gold, and, wishing to keep the knowledge secret and prevent its value becoming known among their Indian catechumens, had invented the fable of the demon to work upon their superstitious fears. But the old chief was a true prophet as to the disastrous effects of the newly discovered gold on the fortunes of poor Sutter and of the simple-minded and hospitable Spanish rancheros who had dwelt at ease on the land.

We returned to the fort the next day. On our way through the foothills we had another illustration of Captain Sutter's unbounded generosity. Crossing the beautiful little valley through which Weber Creek flowed, one of our party expressed his admiration of the spot in such warm terms that our host offered to present a deed of the land to him. From the fort we returned to San Francisco, and in the columns of the "California Star" of the following Saturday appeared the first veritable announcement of the discovery of gold, coupled with half a column of serious advice to farmers, mechanics, and all who were plying their trade successfully to stick to their calling and let the gold-mines severely alone. This was the first investigation of the gold-mines in California, and the first visit by Captain Sutter to the scene of the discovery which laid open the wonders of the region to the world.

V

In California as elsewhere, news of Marshall's discovery was
at first greeted with skepticism. Gold found in the Sierra
foothills? Most residents of the province shook their heads in
unbelief. If it existed, demanded many, why had it not been
found earlier? Permanent settlements had been in existence
in California for more than three-quarters of a century, and
the region where the purported discovery had been made
was familiar ground to hundreds of white men: hunters,
trappers, explorers, even members of scientific expeditions.
Surely, they argued, the presence of the glittering metal
could hardly have been overlooked by all of these.

An interesting—and entertaining—account of how the first
rumors of the find were received at Monterey, then the capital of the province, is to be found in the previously quoted
recollections of Walter Colton, *Three Years in California,*
first published in 1852. Colton, who, as recorded earlier, was
serving as alcalde of the town, related that when, toward
the end of May, travelers from the north brought word of
the discovery, none believed them. However, when the
rumors persisted and daily grew stronger, Colton took steps
to end the uncertainty. Under date of June 6, he wrote in
his diary:

I determined to put an end to the suspense and dispatched a
messenger this morning to the American Fork. He will have
to ride, going and returning, some four hundred miles, but
his report will be reliable. We shall then know whether this
gold is a fact or a fiction—a tangible reality on the earth or a
fanciful treasure at the base of some rainbow . . .

Later diary entries read thus:

Monday, June 12: A straggler came in today from the American Fork, bringing a piece of yellow ore weighing an ounce.

The young dashed the dirt from their eyes, the old from their spectacles. One brought a spyglass, another an iron ladle; some wanted to melt it, others to hammer it, and a few were satisfied with smelling it. All were full of tests, and many who could not be gratified in making their experiments declared it a humbug. One lady sent me a huge gold ring in the hope of reaching the truth by comparison, while a gentleman placed the specimen on top of his gold-headed cane and held it up, challenging the sharpest eye to detect a difference. But doubts still hovered in the minds of the great mass. They could not conceive that such a treasure could have lain so long undiscovered. The idea seemed to convict them of stupidity.

Tuesday, June 20: My messenger, sent to the mines, has returned with specimens of the gold; he dismounted in a sea of upturned faces. He drew forth the yellow lumps from his pockets and passed them around among the eager crowd, and the doubts, which had lingered till now, fled. All admitted they were gold except one old man who still persisted they were some Yankee invention, got up to reconcile the people to the change of flag. The excitement produced was intense, and many were soon busy in their hasty preparations for a departure to the mines. The family who had kept house for me caught the infection. Husband and wife were both packing up; the blacksmith dropped his hammer, the carpenter his plane, the mason his trowel, the farmer his sickle, the baker his loaf, and the tapster his bottle . . . An American woman who had recently established a boarding-house here pulled up stakes and was off before her lodgers had even time to pay their bills. Debtors ran, of course. I have only a community of women left and a gang of prisoners, with here and there a soldier who will give his captain the slip at the first chance. I don't blame the fellow a whit; seven dollars a month, while others are making two or three hundred a day! That is too much for human nature to stand.

Saturday, July 15: The gold fever has reached every serv-ant in Monterey; none are to be trusted in their engage-ment beyond a week, and as for compulsion, it is like at-tempting to drive fish into a net with the whole ocean before them. General Mason, Lieutenant Lanman, and myself form a mess; we have a house and all the table furniture and cu-linary apparatus requisite, but our servants have run, one af-ter another, till we are almost in despair; even Sambo, whom we thought would stick by from laziness, if no other cause, ran last night; and this morning, for the fortieth time, we had to take to the kitchen and cook our own breakfast. A general of the United States army, the commander of a man-of-war, and the alcalde of Monterey, in a smoking kitchen, grinding coffee, toasting a herring, and peeling onions! . . . Well, it is an ill wind that blows nobody any good; the na-bobs have had their time, and now comes that of the "nig-gers." We shall all live just as long and be quite as fit to die.

Tuesday, July 18: Another bag of gold from the mines and another spasm in the community. It was brought down by a sailor from the Yuba River and contains three hundred and thirty-six ounces . . . My carpenters, at work on the schoolhouse, on seeing it, threw down their saws and planes, shouldered their picks, and are off for the Yuba. Three sea-men ran from the *Warren,* forfeiting their four years' pay; and a whole platoon of soldiers from the fort left only their colors behind. One old woman declared she would never again break an egg or kill a chicken without examining yoke and gizzard.

Commenting further on the social upheaval that took place in Monterey as a result of the exodus, Colton wrote on Au-gust 28:

The gold mines have upset all social and domestic arrangements in Monterey; the master has become his own servant, and the servant his own lord. The millionaire is obliged to groom his own horse and roll his wheelbarrow, and the *hidalgo*—in whose veins flows the blood of all the Cortes—to clean his own boots! Here is Lady L——, who has lived here seventeen years, the pride and ornament of the place, with a broomstick in her jeweled hand! And here is Lady B——, with her daughter—all the way from old Virginia, where they graced society with their varied accomplishments—now floating between the parlor and kitchen, and as much at home in the one as the other! And here is Lady S——, whose cattle are on a thousand hills, lifting, like Rachel of old, her bucket of water from the deep well! And here is Lady M. L——, whose honeymoon is still full of soft seraphic light, unhouseling a potato and hunting the hen that laid the last egg. And here am I, who have been a man of some note in my day, loafing on the hospitality of the good citizens and grateful for a meal though in an Indian's wigwam. Why, is not this enough to make one wish the gold mines were in the earth's flaming center from which they sprung? Out on this yellow dust! It is worse than the cinders which buried Pompeii, for there high and low shared the same fate!

vi

How tremendous was the impact the discovery had on the economy of California—indeed of the entire West Coast—is made clear by a letter of the future Civil War general, William T. Sherman, written from Monterey on August 5, 1848, and addressed to a superior in Washington, D.C. Sherman, then a lieutenant attached to the U.S. Third Artillery, began thus:

Some months ago I addressed you a letter upon the subject of the most economical mode of subsisting the troops in California. I then gave it as my opinion that for many years to come articles of subsistence should be sent from the United States save those of beef & flour.

A most extraordinary state of things now exists here and will continue for a long time, making it a very doubtful question whether troops can be kept here at all; but if garrisons can be kept from desertion, it is a matter of absolute certainty that they will have to draw their supplies even of flour from other countries.

Colonel Mason in his official Reports will give the Department a full account of the discovery of certain Gold Mines in the Sacramento District, of the effect of it upon the citizens of the country, as well as his personal observations whilst on a tour of the mines themselves. Being his staff officer here, it would be very improper for me to touch upon those subjects, and I will only mention that the mines are extensive, more rich than I could have credited had I not seen them, and that they have changed the entire character of the Country.

It never was an agricultural land, and accident has shown to what use nature designed it. Rich in Gold and Mercury, it will attract a large population, who must depend upon commerce for food & clothing. At present those articles are very scarce, and no man would sit down and make a pair of shoes or coat or any other garment for ten times its value in the United States. A Gold ounce a day is a small yield at the mines and of course . . . in San Francisco or Monterey no man will work at a trade or at common labor at less than a dollar an hour. Even this price freely offered has restrained very few men in San Francisco and none at all in Monterey; both may be said to be deserted save by the officers, a few soldiers and some women.

The aged have called for their crutches & children have

caught the common infection. A very large fraction of the Garrisons of Sonoma, San Francisco and Monterey have gone, including the best men. Every exertion has been made to stop it, but the facilities for escape and concealment have thus far made the effort fruitless. When it is to stop no one knows. The fever is going south, and if it operates, as it surely will, on the Garrisons of Santa Barbara, Los Angeles and San Diego, not more than one or two hundred men will be left to maintain our authority in this country and to guard the immense amount of property in our warehouses. No man except those who are earning from 50 to 300 dollars a day can now afford to employ a servant. No less a personage than the Governor himself has had to cook his own breakfast . . .

At present there is not a man-of-war on the coast . . . Nor will they come here if they [can] possibly avoid it, on account of the danger of desertion. The crews of Merchant vessels desert as fast as they arrive; two are now at anchor in the Bay of San Francisco without a sailor on board and unable to go to sea. Others have left port with hardly enough men to spread a sail. Yet the profits of trade are so great that they can afford to run these risks.

Even in the short period of four months since the Gold mines first began to yield, the Commerce of San Francisco has increased four fold, whilst that of Monterey and leeward ports is completely destroyed.

At present English merchants in the Sandwich Islands are reaping the chief fruits of this lucrative trade, because they have their deposit of goods near at hand and are by the Tariff placed upon the same footing with American Merchants. They likewise have a greater command of Specie, will carry to Chile and other Countries a large quantity of this Gold, which for cash is selling readily at 11 or 12 dollars the ounce.

As the Government has been to heavy expense in acquiring this Country they should devise some means to return a small stream of the Golden Current into the National Coffers, instead of letting it go to enrich foreigners.

The amount of Gold already obtained cannot fall much short of a million dollars' worth, and the lowest calculation is that from $30,000 to $50,000 are daily obtained and yet not an impression has been made on the whole. The largest piece I have heard of weighed 7 lbs. but the largest I have seen weighed six ounces—very many were of one or two ounces. I abstain from giving particulars as they will be treated by Colonel Mason . . .

vii

When news of the discovery spread eastward to the Atlantic seaboard it aroused a degree of interest no less keen than on the Pacific Coast. There too it was greeted with skepticism in many quarters, some branding it as a clever scheme to promote emigration to the new possession. One of the first to hasten west to verify the truth of the purported find was Bayard Taylor, correspondent for the *New York Tribune*, who reached California, via Panama, in the summer of 1849, visited places of interest both on the coast and in the interior, and wrote of what he saw with the fluency and interest of a trained reporter. His dispatches, later collected in a book entitled *Eldorado*, made highly rewarding reading to residents of the East Coast. Here are the newly landed journalist's first impressions of San Francisco:

Crossing the shoulder of the hill, the view extended around the curve of the bay, and hundreds of tents and houses appeared, scattered all over the heights, and along the shore for more than a mile. A furious wind was blowing down through a gap in the hills, filling the streets with clouds of dust. On every side stood buildings of all kinds, begun or half-finished, and the greater part of them were mere canvas sheds, open in front, and covered with all kinds of signs, in all languages. Great quantities of goods were piled up in the open air, for want of a place to store them. The streets were full of people, hurrying to and fro, and of as diverse and bizarre a character as the houses . . . We came at last into the plaza, now dignified by the name of Portsmouth Square. It lies on the slant side of the hill, and from a high pole in front of a long, one-story adobe building used as the Custom House, the American flag was flying. On the other side stood the Parker House—an ordinary frame house of about sixty feet front—and towards its entrance we directed our course.

Our luggage was deposited on one of the rear porticos, and we discharged the porters, after paying them two dollars each—a sum so immense in comparison to the service rendered that there was no longer any doubt of our having actually landed in California . . . There were no lodgings to be had at the Parker House—not even a place to unroll our blankets; but one of the proprietors accompanied us across the plaza at the City Hotel, where we obtained a room with two beds at $25 per week, meals being an additional $20 per week. I asked the landlord whether he could send a porter for our trunks. "There is none belonging to the house," said he, "every man is his own porter here." I returned to the Parker House, shouldered a heavy trunk, took a valise in my hand, and carried them to my quarters, in the teeth of the wind. Our room was in a sort of garret over the only story of the hotel; two cots, evidently of California manufacture, and covered only with a pair of blankets, two chairs, a rough table, and a small looking-glass constituted the furniture. There was not space enough between the bed and the bare rafters overhead to sit upright, and I gave my-

self a severe blow on rising the next morning without the
proper heed . . .

> A bit farther on, Taylor stated that the environment in which
> he found himself was quite unlike any he had previously
> known. "Never," he wrote, "have I had so much difficulty in
> establishing, satisfactorily to my own senses, the reality of
> what I saw and heard." He continued thus:

I was forced to believe many things which in my communi-
cations to the *Tribune* I was almost afraid to write with any
hope of their obtaining credence. It may be interesting to
give here a few instances of the enormous and unnatural
value put upon property at the time of my arrival. The Parker House rented for $110,000 yearly, at least $60,000 of
which was paid by gamblers, who held nearly all the second
story. Adjoining it on the right was a canvas tent fifteen by
twenty-five feet, called "Eldorado," and occupied likewise by
gamblers, which brought $40,000 . . . A mercantile house
paid $40,000 rent for a one story building of twenty feet
front; the United States Hotel, $36,000; the Post Office,
$7,000, and so on to the end of the chapter. A friend of
mine who wished to find a place for a law office, was shown
a cellar in the earth, about twelve feet square and six deep,
which he could have for $250 a month. One of the common
soldiers at the battle of San Pasquale was reputed to be
among the millionaires of the place, with an income of
$50,000 *monthly*. A citizen of San Francisco died insolvent
to the amount of $41,000 the previous autumn. His adminis-
trators were delayed in settling his affairs, and his real estate
advanced so rapidly in value that after his debts were paid
his heirs had a yearly income of $40,000 . . .

viii

The California gold rush is admittedly one of the most thoroughly documented mass movements in history, with not only a vast amount of material in print from the pens of trained observers, but also a plenitude of letters, diaries, and reminiscences of participants. In view of the extraordinary volume of writing on the subject that has been preserved—and of the eminence of many of the writers—it is interesting, and more than a little surprising, to learn that what has come to be regarded by many as the most revealing picture of life in the Sierra gold towns was from the hand of a busy housewife, set down in the form of letters to a stay-at-home sister on the East Coast.

Their writer, known to her intimates as Dame Shirley, was Louise Amelia Knapp Smith, born in New Jersey in 1819 and educated in New England at the Amherst Academy, where one of her fellow students was the poet Emily Dickinson. She married Dr. Fayette Clappe and with him sailed round the Horn in 1849. After some months in San Francisco, where the climate proved bad for the doctor, the pair made their way to Rich Bar, an isolated settlement deep in the gorge of the Feather River. It was from that outpost that she penned the first of the two dozen epistles that have become known as "The Shirley Letters." These were written at intervals during the fourteen months from September, 1851, to November, 1852, the first six from Rich Bar (which she described as being on the "East Branch of the North Fork of the American River") and the balance from nearby Indian Bar, to which the couple moved toward the end of 1851.

The Shirley Letters have been preserved for later generations mainly through the efforts of Ferdinand G. Ewer, a friend of their writer, who recognized both their literary quality and historical importance and obtained her permission to publish them in his newly launched San Francisco magazine, *The Pioneer*, where they appeared in successive numbers from January, 1854, to February, 1855. Years later they were exhumed from the files of that long-defunct journal and issued in book form.

The second letter, dated September 15, 1851, thus describes the hotel where she and the doctor put up on their arrival at Rich Bar:

The Empire is the only two-story building in town, and absolutely has a live "up-stairs." Here you will find two or three glass windows, an unknown luxury in all the other dwellings. It is built of planks of the roughest possible description; the roof, of course, is covered with canvas, which also forms the entire front of the house, on which is painted in immense capitals, the following imposing letters: "The Empire!" I will describe, as exactly as possible, this grand establishment. You first enter a large apartment, level with the street, part of which is fitted up as a bar-room, with that eternal crimson calico, which flushes the whole social life of the "Golden State," with its everlasting red—in the center of a fluted mass of which gleams a really elegant mirror, set off by a background of decanters, cigar cases and jars of brandied fruit; the whole forming a *tout ensemble* of dazzling splendor. A table covered with green cloth—upon which lies a pack of monte cards, a backgammon board, and a sickening pile of "yellow kivered" literature—with several uncomfortable looking benches, complete the furniture of this most important portion of such a place as "The Empire."

The remainder of the room does duty as a shop; where velveteen and leather, flannel shirts and calico ditto—the latter starched to an appalling state of stiffness—lie cheek by jowl with hams, preserved meats, oysters and other groceries, in hopeless confusion. From the bar-room you ascend by four steps into the parlor, the floor of which is covered by a straw carpet. This room contains quite a decent looking-glass, a sofa fourteen feet long, and a foot and a half wide, painfully suggestive of an aching back—of course covered with red calico (the sofa, *not* the back),—a round table with a green cloth, six cane-bottom chairs, red calico curtains, a cooking stove, a rocking chair, *and* a woman and a baby . . . , the latter wearing a scarlet frock, to match the sofa and curtains. A flight of four steps leads from the parlor to the upper story; where, on each side of a narrow entry, are four eight feet by ten bed-rooms, the floors of which are covered by straw matting. Here your eyes are again refreshed with a glittering vision of red calico curtains, gracefully festooned above wooden windows, picturesquely lattice-like.

These tiny chambers are furnished with little tables covered with oil-cloth, and bedsteads so heavy that nothing short of a giant's strength could move them. Indeed, I am convinced that they were built, piece by piece, on the spot where they now stand. The entire building is lined with purple calico, alternating with a delicate blue . . . The floors are so very uneven that you are always ascending a hill or descending into a valley. The doors consist of a slight frame, covered with dark blue drilling, and are hung on hinges of leather. As to the kitchen and dining-room, I leave to your vivid imagination to picture their primitiveness . . .

Dame Shirley's third letter, dated September 20, 1851, begins thus:

I intend today, dear M., to be as disagreeably statistical and as praiseworthy matter-of-fact as the most dogged utilitarian could desire. I shall give you a full, true and particular account of the discovery, rise and progress of this place [Rich Bar], and with a religious adherence to *dates,* which will rather astonish your unmathematical mind. But let me first describe the spot, as it looked to my wondering and

unaccustomed mind. Remember, I had never seen a mining
district before; and had just left San Francisco, amid whose
flashy-looking shops and showy houses the most of my time
had been spent, since my arrival into the Golden State. Of
course, to me, the *coup d'oeil* of Rich Bar was charmingly
fresh and original. Imagine a tiny valley, about eight hundred yards in length and, perhaps, thirty in widst (it was
measured for my especial information), apparently hemmed
in by lofty hills, almost perpendicular, draperied to their
very summits with beautiful fir trees; the blue-bosomed
"Plumas," or Feather River I suppose I must call it, undulating along their base, and you have as good an idea as I
can give you of the *locale* of "Barra Rica," as the Spaniards
so prettily term it . . .

   Through the middle of Rich Bar runs the street, thickly
planted with about forty tenements; among which figure round tents, square tents, plank hovels, log cabins, &c,—
the residences, varying in elegance and convenience from
the palatial splendor of "The Empire," down to a "local
habitation," formed of pine boughs, and covered with old
calico shirts.

   Then followed this description of the office presided over
   by her physician husband:

I had heard so much about it from others, as well as from F.,
that I really *did* expect something extra. When I entered
this imposing place, the shock to my optic nerves was so
great that I sank, helplessly, upon one of the benches which
ran, divan-like, the whole length (ten feet!) of the building
. . . There was, of course, no floor; a rude nondescript in
one corner, on which was ranged the medical library, consisting of half a dozen volumes, did duty as a table. The
shelves, which looked like sticks snatched hastily from the
wood-pile . . . , contained quite a respectable array of

medicines. The white canvas window stared everybody in the face, with the interesting information painted on it, in perfect grenadiers of capitals, that this was Dr. ——'s office.

Letter Six, written on September 30, has this to say of one of the peculiarities of the miners:

I think I have never spoken to you of the mournful extent to which profanity prevails in California. You know that at home it is considered *vulgar* for a gentleman to swear; but I am told that here, it is absolutely the fashion, and that people who never uttered an oath in their lives while in the "States," now "clothe themselves with curses as with a garment." Some try to excuse themselves by saying that it is a careless habit, into which they have glided imperceptibly, from having been compelled to associate so long with the vulgar and the profane; that it is a mere slip of the tongue, which means absolutely nothing, etc. . . . Whether there is more profanity in the mines than elsewhere, I know not; but during the short time I have been at Rich Bar, I have *heard* more of it than in all my life before. Of course, the most vulgar blackguard will abstain from swearing in the *presence* of a lady; but in this rag and card-board house, one is *compelled* to hear the most sacred of names constantly profaned by the drinkers and gamblers who haunt the bar-room at all hours . . .

Some of these expressions, were they not so fearfully blasphemous, would be grotesquely sublime. For instance; not five minutes ago, I heard two men quarreling in the street, and one said to the other, "only let me get hold of your beggarly carcass once, and I will use you up so small that God Almighty himself cannot see your *ghost!*"

In early October, 1851, the letter-writer and the doctor moved from Rich Bar to an even smaller settlement a bit

farther up the river. In her next letter Dame Shirley, after
describing the log cabin in which she and her husband were
to pass their first Sierra winter, continued thus:

There, my dainty Lady Molly, I have given you, I fear, a
wearisomely minute description of my new home. How
would you like to winter in such an abode? in a place where
there are no newspapers, no churches, lectures, concerts or
theaters; no fresh books, no shopping, calling nor gossiping
little tea-drinkers; no parties, no balls, no picnics, no *tab-
leaux*, no charades, no latest fashions, no daily mail (we
have an express once a month), no promenades, no rides
nor drives; no vegetables but potatoes and onions, no milk,
no eggs, no *nothing*. Now I expect to be very happy here.
This strange, odd life fascinates me. As for the churches,
"the groves were God's first temples," "and for the strength
of the hills, the Swiss mountains bless him;" and as to books,
I read Shakespeare, David, Spencer, Paul, Coleridge, Burns
and Shelley, which are never old. In good sooth I fancy that
nature intended me for an Arab or some other Nomadic
barbarian, and by mistake my soul got packed up in a chris-
tianized set of bones and muscles . . .

ix

That in the democracy of the gold camps all men were
equal, regardless of their standing at home, is evident from
this passage in L. M. Schaeffer's record of his experiences
in the Mother Lode during the winter of 1849.

Hawkins' Bar [he wrote], afterwards dignified by the ap-
pellation of Hawkinsville, was beautifully situated on the
Tuolumne river, a narrow stream which gently flowed

along, its course about as straight as a Virginia fence. Hawkinsville contained a population of about one thousand
men; not a single woman or child within fifty miles of the
place. The hearty miners "dwelt not in marble halls," but
under the fragile covering of 10-cent muslin. Preachers, doc-
tors, lawyers, mechanics and laboring-men cooked their provisions, mended and washed their clothing, and not infre-
quently a man who had been classically educated, and perhaps had been a professor of belles lettres in some college
might be seen turning his "slap jacks" dexterously in the
frying pan, or sitting on an old stump mending his
britches . . .

The writer continued thus:

A neighbor offered me the use of his tent and board at nine
dollars a week . . . , the bill of fare to consist of salt pork
of questionable age, musty crackers and tip-top coffee, provided somebody knew how to make it. However, I relished
the food and never enjoyed better health . . .
   With only a knife, broken pick and pan, did I, day after
day, search for the glittering metal, secreted amid rocks,
crevices and dirt. The general custom was to dig down until
a stratum of earth was reached, which indicated the presence
of gold. The earth was then shoveled into the box on top
the rocker, water was constantly poured upon it, whilst
the rocker was shaken to and fro; at night that left in the
bottom of the cradle was carefully scooped up, and the profits of the day's labor soon known.

Another picture of the methods employed by the first to mine
the foothill streams is given by one Ciriaco Molina, who arrived in California during the early days of the rush, having
been one of a group that had driven a herd of 2000 sheep
from his native village of Belen, New Mexico, to the pueblo

of San José. Incidentally, during that long trek, which included hundreds of miles of waterless desert, only a few of
the animals were lost. At San José the sheep were sold and
the party disbanded, Molina going first to the Napa Valley
and then to the diggings in the vicinity of Placerville.

The mines around Placerville [he later recalled] were what
we called placer mines. I considered them very rich, for almost every day I cleared fifty or sixty dollars by simply carrying my rocker near a place where water was abundant. Besides the rocker I owned a tin pan, and every morning I
scraped the surface dirt with a bone or some sharp instru-
ment, piled up a good quantity of dirt, say from ten to fifteen plates full, and then placed the dirt in a rocker and
threw water over it. Afterwards I kept on shaking the rocker
and pouring water over the dirt. After the dirt had been
duly washed I searched the bottom of the rocker, and there
invariably a few ounces of gold could be seen. The gold
around Placerville was rather fine, and I believe that the rest
of the miners and I lost about one-half of our gold by working in such a loose manner. A year or so after my arrival in
Placerville some Americans in partnership with four French-
men built sluices and with the help of quicksilver and a
great quantity of water succeeded in effecting quite an improvement in the manner of working the mines. As soon
as the advantages of the new system began to be known
and appreciated, the primitive rockers were thrown away
and sluicing was all the go . . .

Typical of the uncertainties of life in the diggings during
the early days were the experiences of Jean Antonio Sánchez,
a Yaqui Indian, who, having joined a large party of fellow
New Mexicans, reached Los Angeles in the spring of 1848.
Although he looked on himself as a jeweler, having become
adept at fashioning the silver ornaments admired by his

tribe, Sánchez had not been long in California before he, like virtually everyone else, decided to try his luck at the mines. The story of his adventures there, set down some years later, reads thus:

Having saved sufficient to defray my expenses . . . , I proceeded to the placers of Agua Fría near Mariposa. There I contracted to work for an American company that owned a good claim on the Tuolumne river; these people fed me and besides allowed me ten dollars per diem. The food was coarse, generally consisting of wild game, then very abundant in every mining camp, bacon and slapjacks. Once in a while we managed to purchase a few vegetables. The vegetables were not raised in the mines but were brought from Sacramento by large teams usually of six or eight mules. They . . . were mostly potatoes, onions and cabbages. They sold for a high price, onions generally for seventy-five cents or even one dollar a pound. After remaining three months with my American masters, I jumped a claim in the vicinity . . .

In this business I had four partners and on the average we made sixty dollars each, every day. Besides my company, there were in Agua Fría ten other Mexican companies, every one of them doing as well as we. Indeed we were full of hopes and on the road to fortune when an unfortunate event dashed our cup of bliss from our lips. A set of heartless Missourians, having found that we had a rich claim, mustered in force, drove us away, and destroyed our houses, [the latter] a matter of no great consequence, for . . . our dwellings consisted of four poles planted on the ground, four smaller ones fastened on the sides, and branches spread over them. The Americans came so unexpectedly upon us that we were not even allowed time to dig out the gold we had buried in the vicinity of our camp.

Not wishing to run the risk of being outraged a second

time, I resolved to forsake the wilderness . . . I therefore
directed my steps towards Sonora, a middle-sized town that
contained boarding-houses, gambling dens, and even a Cath-
olic Church. A week after my arrival . . . the town caught
fire and the whole center was destroyed. The people, however, were not disheartened and the day following . . .
they began to build finer houses than the ones destroyed . . .

As soon as the town began to flourish a second time, I
opened a jewelry store. My stock in trade consisted of several *chispitas* [i.e., small diamonds], a pound or more of
gold, and the implements of my trade. I did a good business and made many breast pins, finger rings, and earrings
for the female portion of the inhabitants. American women
were then a rare thing, but Mexican and California girls
were quite abundant. After a while the mines began to pay
but poorly; my business began to dwindle and, having many
idle hours on my hands . . . , I began to gamble, and in
less than two weeks I lost every dollar I possessed . . .

> At the time he dictated his reminiscence—that is, in the
> early 1870's—Sanchez was eking out a precarious livelihood
> as a woodchopper. This too was typical of the California of
> the day.

x

Jean Sánchez's disastrous experience at the gaming tables
was a by no means uncommon one, for the recollections of
the miners make it clear that during the first years of the
rush the most widely patronized gathering places were the
gambling houses. Indeed, in most localities, these were the
only spots to which the hard-working forty-niners could turn

for recreation, for it was not until later that more conventional forms of entertainment became available.

In order to entice patrons into their own gaming houses, and away from those of their rivals, it was the custom of owners to provide such attractions as the time and place afforded. Usually these consisted of no more than a single musician, who, seated on a platform at one end of the room, spent the hours from sundown to long after midnight industriously thrumming a banjo or scraping a fiddle. Sometimes, however, more elaborate musical fare was provided. One such group of entertainers, consisting of a German emigrant named Frank Oettl, his wife, sister, and brother-in-law, landed in San Francisco in the fall of 1850 and promptly found a berth in a gambling saloon on Pacific Street, at an honorarium of $100 a night.

While so engaged [Oettl later recalled] I had a fine opportunity of studying the tricks of the gamblers at the expense of the many fools who visited that resort of amusement. I can assure you that hundreds of hard working men daily lost their money, some allured by the shining piles of glittering gold nicely arranged on the tables at which sat pretty, fair-looking Frenchwomen who, with a smile upon their lips and poison in their hearts, used to allure the unwary miners and induce them to stake their last dollar. Of course, honesty was out of the question and tricks of all sorts were played upon the unfortunates . . . I have often seen men who had entered Barriolet's house with pockets full of glittering bags of gold leave it penniless, and I may say ruined in purse and mind . . .

After playing a couple of weeks in San Francisco, I removed to Sacramento with my family . . . , under contract with a Mr. Butler . . . He then kept a gambling house in the city of the plains, and having heard of our fine playing was anxious to have us help him in getting fools within the meshes of his hired ruffians . . . I admit that I was engaged in a nefarious work. I cannot deny that my family and I were no better than the aiders and abettors of robbers, blacklegs, and swindlers, yet our poverty did not allow us to argue with conscience. We had come to California bent on making money, and when Mr. Butler offered us one hundred dollars per night and free board and lodgings with drinks and cigars thrown in, provided we would play at least six hours every night in his gambling hell, I could not resist the temptation, so I accepted his proposal, signed a contract for six months, and removed to Sacramento.

That city . . . was then no better than a sixth-class town, thickly settled in the winter season but almost deserted in the summer. Her population was mostly composed of miners who came down from the mountains to recruit their health, or to run away from the inclemency of the weather. Nearly the whole of them on the approach of spring would pack their traps and return to their mountain homes . . . The house during the six months in which I played for its benefit was always crowded. Thousands of fools visited it daily, and I am pretty certain that the profits must have been enormous, for the *honest* landlord dabbled in every known game. By his direction and under his supervision every trick known to the fraternity was resorted to, so as to give the dealers of the games a sure advantage over the unhappy miner. For example, if a miner played a game of monte, sure enough the cards were greased or scraped with sandpaper, and as the dealer when shuffling the pack always kept track of every one of the forty cards used in the game, he was always in a position to pull the winning card and win the money staked on the result.

After residing six months in Sacramento the health of my family required a change of climate, and I accepted an engagement for Nevada City, where I repaired in August 1851. The price paid my troupe was something like one hundred and twenty dollars per night. The scenes I had witnessed in San Francisco and Sacramento were repeated . . . My new employer was a kindhearted man, and whenever the miners, having lost the contents of their purses, wished to pawn either their watches, chains, or revolvers, he always kindly loaned them a good sum with which they could again try their luck. The result of this little transaction was always the same, namely that the dealers of the games gained the money, and the landlord obtained for about one-fourth of their real value costly watches and pistols . . .

After performing several months in Nevada, I removed to Marysville where pay was not so large but living cheaper and society more refined. I noticed nothing worth mentioning while living in Marysville, but I might as well observe that in that town everyone gambled. I firmly believe that it would have been an impossibility to pick out ten persons out of the whole town who did not invest in cards or dice. The game of dice was peculiar to the town . . . I had not seen it played in San Francisco, Sacramento, or Nevada. I was told that the game had been introduced in California by a lot of Peruvian gamblers who first took up their residence in Marysville. They were great swindlers, invariably played with loaded dice, and sure enough every greenhorn who happened to fall into their clutches was stripped of everything he staked on the throw of the "square bones."

xi

Among the most revealing pictures of life in the diggings are those contained in letters written by the miners themselves and sent to relatives or friends at home. For these hastily scrawled messages were designed only to tell their recipients something of how the writers were faring in their

quest for the precious metal in far-off California. A goodly
number of these have fortunately been preserved, and from
them have been selected the three examples that follow.
The first, written by a '49er named Jacob Engle and addressed to a brother in Virginia, was headed "Weaver
Creek, Feb. 7th, 1850."

I take my pen in hand again to inform you that I am well [it
begins], and I hope these few lines will find you all enjoy-
ing the same blessing . . . We have not done much in the
way of mining this winter on account of the rainy season
which commenced about the middle of November . . . The
newly sprung up Citty of Sacramento has bin inundated with
water and to its inhabitants the los is great in the way of
goods . . . We expect to leave here in a few days if the
weather will permit and go to the middle fork of the Ameri-
canus River or in the vicinity of Hangtown which is north
west of this place . . .

I spoke of not making much this winter and I expect you
would like to know how much we have made. We have bin
working on a branch of Weaver creek where we found a
place about fifty feet long and three wide, wich we got one
thousand of the pure stuff, and I think we will have clear
besides what we paid for our winter provisions from ten to
twelve hundred and we have on hand some provisions yet
and we have a team and wagon wich we use to hawl our
provisions. We have not used much salt provisions this winter, we used principly deer meat. We have killed some
twenty deer this winter between the rains . . . This is a
great country for game, there has bin nearly a hundred deer
killed in this neighborhood this winter; there is phesants,
hairs, squirrels, wolves, wild cats, panthers and grisly bears.
There was a general fight come a few months ago between a
grisly and two brothers. They shot some five or six bawls
into him when the bear closed in on them. Then they had it

rough and tumble. The bear would jump on one of them
and nock him down and the other would hit him with the
brich of his gun, then he would turn on him and nock him
down—so they kept this up for some time when the bear
made his escape. The two was verry much chawed and
clawed up but principly their arms which they would thrust
into his mouth while laying on the ground to keep him out
of their faces. One has since recovered and the other is
mending . . .

> The next, written by C. A. Branett, a native of Logansport,
> Indiana, tells of life in the northernmost of the diggings, in
> and about the town of Shasta Butte City, now Yreka.

If there was plenty of water so that a man could run a
long tom [he commented] he could make from 15 to 30 dols
per day, but water is scarce. The dirt that the gold is in is a
redish or yellow clay somewhat sandy, the dirt is two or
three feet deep to the bed rock, the most of the gold lays on
the bed rock. The dirt pays from 3 to 5 cents per pan or
bucket, a man can work from 1 to 2 hundred buckets per
day in a rocker. It is a mistake that a man can't make his
board in the gold mines for if he will work he can make
wages as above stated. The gold is in particles from the size
of the finest sand up to pieces worth 500 dollars. The largest
piece that I have found was 7 dollars and the next 1 dollar . . .

Shasta Butte City is a city of dram shops and music and
houses with good old earthen floors and canvas doors; the
houses are plastered with muslin and look splendid by candle light. All the lumber they use here is made by whip
saws and sells for 25¢ per foot! They weather-board with
clapboards. The city is now 10 months old and is composed
of two streets, one running north and the other east and
west and each ½ mile long which makes a mile of town built

just as close it can be and has no alleys. I will now give you
the price of some more articles, sugar 45¢, salt 75¢!! coffee
50¢. T[obacco] $2.00, butter one dollar and 25 cents,
cheese one dollar, blankets 16 dollars per pair, shovels 8 to
12, picks 6 to 10, gold pans 3 dollars, small frying pans
2½, &c. Sunday is the great business day, they have auction
to sell horses and other things; most of the folks work on
Sunday in the mines, every fellow trying to make his pile.
There is a large number of gambling houses that have 7 or
8 monte tables and splendid music all the time to allure
miners so they can win their hard earned gold . . . There
is gold on Rogue river in Oregon where the miners make 6
to 8 dollars per day; when we came through that country
we had to stand guard every night the Indians being very
bad. They had killed a man only a few days before us but
we kept our eyes peeled and was on the lookout for them
but they did not attack us . . .

> The third epistle, written from "Weaver Creek, El Dorado
> Co.," and dated September 15, 1850, is by William R. Rock-
> well, a Missourian, who had arrived a few months earlier.
> That the trials of his journey were still fresh in mind is in-
> dicated by this passage from his letter to his father at home.

No man knows or can know what has to be undergone when
he undertakes the trip to California by the Overland Route.
The suffering of emigrants this year has been immense.
Thousands of teams failed and their owners had to trudge
through with pack upon the back. Many almost died of starvation and nearly everyone suffered to some extent with sickness. From the Mo. frontier to Sacramento City the emigrant
has no peace of mind or rest of body. It is unhealthy and unpleasant except to those who come for the sake of travel. I
have never had an hour's sickness since I left home. My health
now is perfectly good—just such as I never enjoyed before

. . . I do not regret but rather feel pleased that I have taken the trip—am moderately well pleased with so much of the country as I have seen . . .

All our train got through safe and sound and all are doing something in the way of mining though the profits are far less than they had reason to expect when they left Mo. Instead of 16$ per day it requires hard labor to make 4$ and many that I am acquainted with are making nothing more than a living —some not that. We have had a very fair streak of luck in mining. Will Price, Capt. P., Dr. S. & myself working together have averaged since the 28th of August fourteen dollars and a half to the hand per day; our smallest day's work was $6.75 and the largest was $143.25. Last week ending yesterday our average was 25$ each per day. Our claim which has so well paid us is now however about worked out and when I write again it is probable I shall not be making over 4$ per day—possibly not that. Mining is the hardest work imaginable and an occupation which very much endangers the health. A weakly man might about as well go to digging his grave as to dig for gold.

The greater portion of those who expected to make a fortune in a day have given it over and that part of them who have the means have already taken passage for the states. Dissatisfaction is almost universal. More than half the emigration will return on "first money." . . .

While in this western world far from the land I love to call Home I design to exert myself to the best purpose possible and eventually I shall again fill my place among you, Providence permit. I undertook this enterprise with the design of carrying it to its ultimate and so I am yet determined . . .

This section can appropriately close with the following, from the pen of Major William Downie, founder of the present town of Downieville, on the north fork of the Yuba River, high in the Sierra foothills:

It was the 10th of December, 1849, when we moved into our new quarters, and then came Christmas. We were determined to make the best of the festive season, even though we were in the midst of the wilds, far away from friends and relations. Our greatest trouble was, that we had but one bottle of brandy in camp, and it took us some time to decide whether we would drink it on Christmas or New Year Day. The discussion, pro and con, was very animated and resulted in the drawing of the cork on Christmas morning. It was quite early, when this important event took place, and we made punch with the liquor, using hot water and nutmeg. We drank to absent friends, to wives and sweethearts and to the great American Nation. Gradually, as the sun rose higher in the heavens and the brandy got lower in the bottle, we became more enthusiastic. I had a small representation of the stars and stripes in my possession, and we determined that on this day it should adorn our house. So I climbed upon the roof with the flag in one hand, a pistol in the other. I made a short speech, waved the flag and fired a few shots and finished up by giving three cheers for the American Constitution. Then I fixed the flag on the gable point, and we all shouted for joy when we saw it unfurled to the breeze for the first time in the fastnesses of the Sierras.

VII
The Rush by Land

i

That the months-long ordeal of the overland trail was a severe strain on the stamina of all who took part in it, and that many were at the point of complete exhaustion when they reached their promised land, is made clear by the following, the recollections of A. C. Ferris, who in the fall of 1849 was working a claim high on the western slope of the Sierra.

The "Long Bar" mining claim on Bear Creek [wrote he], where I was located, lay in the route of arriving immigrants, on the Sutter's Fort trail, a hundred miles from the fort. I shall never forget the sight presented by the tired, starved, sick, and discouraged travelers, with their bony and foot-sore cattle and teams. Men, women, and children, and animals were in every state of distress and emaciation. Some had left everything along the way, abandoning wagons and worn-out cattle to the wolves—leaving even supplies of clothing, flour, and food—and in utter desperation and extremity had packed their own backs with flour and bacon; some had utilized the backs of surviving oxen for the same purpose; and a few of

the immigrants had thus made the last 600 miles on foot, exhausted, foot-sore, and starving. . . .

I remember well the arrival of a once stalwart man, reduced almost to a skeleton. His comrades had perished on
the way with cholera, his cattle had given out, and, selecting
what he could carry that was most essential, he had finished
the journey on foot. Reaching the place where we were digging and washing out the gold, he threw himself on the
ground, and said:

"And now I've reached at last where you dig out the gold.
For this I have sacrificed everything. I had a comfortable
home, but I got 'the fever.' Everything is gone, my comrades
are dead, and this is all there is left of me. I thought I would
be glad to get here, but I am not. I don't feel the least desire
to dig gold now. All I ask for is rest—rest—rest. It seems to
me as if I never could get rested again. I want to find home—
home—and there is no home here."

He inquired how far it was to Sutter's Fort, and refusing
proffered food or a look at the gold, he staggered feebly on
again to look for "rest" and "home."

In September the swarm of immigrants became so continuous and their condition so wretched, that I obtained one of
their mules that seemed able to carry me, and giving up my
business of gold-digging for a time started with a comrade up
the Truckee River route to advise and encourage the new-
comers. Here I witnessed many sorrowful scenes among sick
and hungry women and children just ready to die, and dead
and dying cattle. The cattle were usually reduced to skeletons. There was no grass, and they were fed solely by cutting
down trees for them to browse on. But the cattle were too
many for this supply of food along the trail. I once counted as
many as thirty yoke hitched together to pull an almost empty
wagon up a hillside, while to descend an incline it was necessary to chain a large tree to the back of the wagon, with all
its limbs attached that they might impede the descent of the

wagon, for the cattle were entirely too weak to offer the necessary resistance. One after another the wagons would follow, and thus slowly work their way up and down the mountain sides of the Sierra pass, while the women and children wearily plodded along in the deep, dry, and exceedingly dusty trail. Some fared better, but I apprehend few would ever care to pass twice through the hardships of the overland journey in '49.

As an instance of courage and suffering: A preacher, of the Methodist Church in Indiana, accompanied by his wife (a delicate little woman) and three children, started overland with ox-teams. On the way he was suddenly attacked with dysentery and had to lie helpless in the bottom of his wagon, vibrating between life and death. His brave little wife took his place, walked by the side of the team and guided them; but she lost her way, and for two weeks, with husband and children to care for, trudged along alone until by good fortune or a good Providence she found the trail again . . .

At first we tried to give the new-comers employment on our mining claims, but in every case but one their strength was not equal to the labor of digging gold, and on they swept, all eager to reach a "settlement." Some in their enthusiasm had, at great sacrifice, dragged along strange, heavy, and wonderful patent devices to work out the gold. Often they had thrown away their flour and bacon, thus reducing themselves to starvation, to make room for their pet machine, which on trial was found utterly worthless, and was left to rust or rot in the mines.

Special relief parties were also sent up the trail with supplies of food, medicine, and other necessaries, as well as with fresh animals, and many immigrants were safely brought in, before the snows fell in the mountains, who otherwise might have perished in the storms of early fall.

ii

Among the many hazards faced by the early emigrant parties
was that of straying off the main traveled trails and, before
they realized their error, finding themselves deep in the unexplored country that lay to the north or south. This was a by
no means infrequent occurrence, for the early roadways were
often difficult to follow; moreover, should a party lose its way
in the arid country that lay to the west of the Rocky Mountains, a lack of food or water for man and beast could
speedily bring disaster.

Such was the plight in which one such group found themselves in the fall of 1849. California bound, they were crossing what is now western Nevada. Traveling at night to
avoid the desert heat, in the darkness they missed a turn in
the trail, and when daylight came they found themselves
"miles out on the desert without a mouthful of food for the
cattle and only two or three quarts of water in a little cask."

What followed is told in the words of a woman member of
the party, Sarah Royce (mother of the philosopher Josiah
Royce, and herself a writer of distinction), who made the
journey in company with her husband and two-year-old
daughter.

What could be done [she wrote]? Halt we must, for the oxen
were nearly worn out and night was coming on. The animals
must at least rest, if they could not be fed; and that they
might rest, they were chained securely to the wagon, for,
hungry and thirsty as they were, they would, if loose, start off
frantically in search of water and food and soon drop down
exhausted. Having fastened them in such a way that they
could lie down, we took a few mouthfuls of food, and then,
we in our wagon and the men not far off upon the sand, fell
wearily to sleep—a forlorn little company wrecked upon the
desert.

The first question in the morning was, "How can the oxen be kept from starving?" A happy thought occurred. We had thus far on our journey managed to keep something in the shape of a bed to sleep on. It was a mattress tick, and just before leaving Salt Lake we had put into it some fresh hay—not very much, for our load must be as light as possible; but the old gentleman traveling with us also had a small straw mattress; the two together might keep the poor things from starving for a few hours. At once a small portion was dealt out to them, and for the present they were saved. For ourselves we had food which we believed would about last us till we reached the gold mines if we could go right on; if we were much delayed anywhere, it was doubtful. The two or three quarts of water would last only a few hours, to give moderate drinks to each of the party . . .

Should we try to go on? . . . No, it would be madness to go further out in the desert under such conditions. Should we turn back and try to reach the meadows with their wells? But as near as we could calculate, it could be not less than ten or fifteen miles to them. Would it be possible for our poor cattle to reach there? Their only food would be the pitiful mess still left in our mattresses. It might be divided into two portions, giving them each a few mouthfuls more at noon, and then, if they kept on their feet long enough to reach the holes at the Sink, we might possibly find enough water to give them each a little drink, which with the remainder of the fodder might keep them up till the meadows were reached. It was a forlorn hope, but it was all we had.

The morning was wearing away while these things were talked over. Precious time was being wasted, but the truth was the situation was so new and unexpected that it seemed for a while to confuse—almost to stupefy—most of the little party . . . But this would never do. So the more hopeful ones proposed that we should all eat something and as soon as the noon heat abated prepare for a move. So we took some lunch, and soon the men were lying upon the sand, a short distance from each other, fast asleep. Soon some of the party awoke and after a little talk concluded that two of them would walk to a bald ridge that rose out of the flat waste about a mile and a half distant and take a view from thence in the faint hope that we might yet be mistaken and the forking road and the meadows might still be in advance . . .

When the explorers returned from their walk to the ridge, it was only to report no discovery, nothing to be seen on all sides but sand and scattered sagebrush interspersed with the carcasses of dead cattle. So there was nothing to be done but turn back and try to find the meadows. Turn back! What a chill the words sent through one. Turn back, on a journey like that, in which every mile had been gained by the most earnest labor, growing more and more intense until of late it had seemed that the certainty of advance with every step was all that made the next step possible. And now for miles we were to go back. In all that long journey no steps ever seemed so heavy, so hard to take, as those with which I turned my back to the sun that afternoon . . .

We had not been long on the move when we saw dust rising in the road at a distance and soon perceived that we were about to meet a little caravan of wagons. Then a bright gleam of hope stole in. They had doubtless stopped at the meadows and were supplied with grass and water. Might it not be possible that they would have enough to spare for us? Then we could go on with them. My heart bounded at the thought. But the hope was short-lived. We met, and some of the men gathered round our wagon with eager inquiries, while those who could not leave their teams stood looking with wonder at a solitary wagon headed the wrong way.

Our story was soon told . . . But when the question was asked whether they could spare sufficient grass and water to get our team over the desert, they shook their heads and unanimously agreed that it was out of the question. Their

own cattle, they said, were weak from long travel and too
often scant supplies. They had only been able to load up
barely enough to get to the Carson River. The season was
far advanced, and the clouds hanging of late round the
mountain tops looked threatening. It would be like throwing away their own lives without any certainty of saving ours,
for, once out on the desert without food, we would all be
helpless together . . .

The next morning we resumed our backward march after
feeding out the last mouthful of fodder. The water in the
little cask was used up in making coffee for supper and
breakfast . . . We had lately had but few chances for cooking, and only a little boiled rice with dried fruit and a few
bits of biscuit remained after we had done breakfast. If we
could only reach the meadows by noon! But that we could
hardly hope for; the animals were so weak and tired. There
was no alternative, however; the only thing to be done was to
go steadily on, determined to do and endure to the utmost.

I found no difficulty this morning in keeping up with the
team. They went so slowly and I was so preternaturally stimulated by anxiety to get forward that before I was aware of
it I would be some rods ahead of the cattle, straining my gaze
as if expecting to see a land of promise, long before I had
any rational hope of the kind. My imagination acted intensely. I seemed eager to see Hagar in the wilderness walking wearily away from her fainting child among the dried-up
bushes and seating herself in the hot sand. I seemed to become Hagar myself, and when my little one from the wagon
behind me called out, "Mamma, I want a drink," I stopped,
gave her some, noted that there were but a few swallows left,
then mechanically pressed onward again, alone, repeating
over and over the words, "Let me not see the death of the
child."

Wearily passed the hottest noonday hour, with many an
anxious look at the horned heads which seemed to me to bow

lower and lower, while the poor tired hoofs almost refused to move. The two young men [who had gone on ahead] had been out of sight for some time when all at once we heard a shout and saw, a few hundred yards in advance, a couple of hats thrown into the air and four hands waving triumphantly. As soon as we got near enough, we heard them call out, "Grass and water! Grass and water!" and shortly we were at the meadows.

iii

Of the many thousands who trekked westward during '49 and '50, the majority chose what became known as the Northern Route; that is, they proceeded up the Missouri and North Platte rivers to Fort Laramie, in present-day Wyoming, crossed the continental divide to Fort Hall, headed southwest through the plains of Nevada, climbed the steep trails over the Sierra, and so gained what they hoped would be their Promised Land.

A reading of the diaries, letters, and reminiscences of those who undertook that journey makes it clear that, while no part of the route was free from trials and tribulations, that which involved the greatest hardships was the section described above by Sarah Royce—a sandy, waterless region in west central Nevada that became known as the Sink of the Humboldt.

Here are excerpts from the diary of a thirty-year-old Missourian who also made the crossing in 1849:

July 23: Drove 6 or 8 miles this morning & camped for the day as it was important to rest and graze our stock. Every other train is reduced to the same necessity . . .

24: No vegetation to be seen on the hills and mountains except the wild sage, a growth which has become most sickening to us.

25: A dusty barren bottom covered with the eternal dust from 6 to 8 inches deep. Passed another grave today. These are melancholy sights to the traveller as they serve to remind him that he too may die far away from home & kindred . . . During the night the wolves were quite noisy & alarmed our mules.

26: Nothing but the sterile lands and dust immediately around us & naught in the distance to relieve the eye but the bare rugged hills of basalt. Our feelings just now are that if we once get safely out of this great Basin we will not again be caught here in a hurry.

27: We are beginning to feel alarmed lest our stock will not take us through.

29: A continuance of yesterday's hard work & poor fare for our stock. We were struck with the contrast between our appearance now & when we left home. Then we had gay outriders prancing along proudly on their fiery steeds & our teams pressing forward with fierce resolution. Now what a scene—the teams crossing along slowly, their gaunt sides marked with many a whip cut & their rigging defaced with dust—a sorry show. And where are all these gay outriders? Look before the train & you see them strung along the road for a mile on foot, their faces and clothes covered with dust and looking worn and livid . . .

August 1: The mules were by this time so hungry that they greedily devoured the leaves of the willow. Fortunately we have found some grass—although of an inferior quality. This is a more trying time than any we have yet encountered & as we have yet some 71 miles to go over the same kind of fare, we feel altogether uncertain about the result. We think, however, that at the worst we can walk the balance of the way.

2: Started early and drove 10 miles to the slough without water. The stock look very badly.

4: A general panic now seized upon all & doubt & fear prevailed every where. There is yet a stretch of 45 miles ahead of us without grass or water except at the boiling spring 25 miles from this point.

We left here at 4 o'clock this evening & taking the right hand or old route travelled all night & reached the Hot Spring at daylight.

This is the most dreary, desolate looking place we ever saw. It is on the top of a mountain & the water bubbles & boils up from the fissures in the rocks & forms into a small lake quite clear but so hot that it scalds. We dipped up the water & poured it into some holes in the earth & cooled it & then watered our animals, mixed flour with it. The mules were so hungry that they ate dust & gravel & chewed up whatever came in their way—gearing, wagon covers or any thing they could reach.

5: We had 20 miles to accomplish & the heat of the day to make it. About 2 oclock we struck the heavy sand 10 miles from Truckee river & had the utmost difficulty in getting our stock thro—stopping every few yards to rest. A little before night we reached the river. We all felt greatly relieved. We found grass very abundant and the water very fine.

All along the desert road from the very start even the wayside was strewed with the dead bodies of oxen, mules & horses & the stench was horrible. All our traveling experience furnishes no parallel for this. Many persons suffered greatly for water during the last 8 or 10 miles, and many instances of noble generosity were developed on these occasions. Some trains that got over before us sent water back in kegs & left them on the road marked for the benefit of the feeble. We slept here for the first time in four nights.

iv

As we have seen, one of the major problems faced during
the crossing of the plains and deserts to the west of Salt
Lake was that of finding sufficient food to enable the animals to keep up their strength. How one group solved
that difficulty is described in the diary of a youth named
Lemuel Clarke McKeeby, who made the crossing in the
summer of 1850.

For the last few days [wrote he] we have adopted a plan to
get feed for our horses; it is this; while we are nooning and
our horses are picking up the scant feed and resting, we go a
mile or two from the road where we find here and there a
bunch of what is called bunch grass; this we gather in quite a
little armful and return to camp; this we do regularly while
others of our party throw a blanket over a sage bush to keep
off the scorching hot sun and lie down under it . . . When
we start on the road we mount our ponies (we have only
one each) with this armful of bunch grass which we feed to
them as we ride along . . . While other horses look starved
our ponies are in pretty fair condition; in fact my pony is in
good condition, but they are both leg-weary . . .

July 16th, 1850. We pack up and start at midnight and at
sunrise we find we have traveled ten miles and then rest on
a very barren spot; almost no feed at all; however, we wander
from the road and our horses and cut or pull an armful each
of bunch grass for them. After a rest of two hours we saddle
up and start on. We carry this grass under our arms and
while we ride along we feed it to our horses, a handful at a
time. It is wonderful how intelligently the horse reaches his
head up for this mouthful of grass as he travels along. This
manner of helping our horses to feed has kept them in good
heart while the travel keeps them weary. We travel some

twenty miles further over the most God-forsaken country
I ever saw . . .

> Six days later, having progressed down the dry bed of the
> Humboldt to the point where it disappeared into the sandy
> plain called the Humboldt Sink, the party started across
> that level expanse which McKeeby described as a "much-
> dreaded desert waste of 45 miles without water and entirely
> destitute of vegetation."

At 2 P.M. [he wrote on July 23] all being in readiness we
saddled up and, adjusting my boots, filled with hay, across
my saddle, one boot on each side, I rode my horse out into
the slough of water and with my tin cup filled each boot full
. . . Our horses though weary as they must have been, yet
were in comparatively good condition for the journey. We
let them take their own gait and did not urge them; we favored them by walking much of the way by their side . . .
The road is mostly a coarse white sand in which man and
beast will sink up to the ankle. As the sun set in the west,
relieving us of its scorching heat, the moon in its full arose
in the east to light our pathway across this desolation. We
continued on without a stop until 10 P.M.; for the past few
miles we had noticed quite a number of abandoned wagons
and some animals . . . We partake of our coffee and "Pinola"
(parched cornmeal mixed with sugar), feed our horses
and rest . . .

After resting for two hours we saddled up and started on
our way. I want to mention that in lifting my long boots
from the horse I found that they must have weighed all of
thirty pounds each. The rest of our way for some miles the
roadside was strewn with dead animals and deserted wagons.
We passed many teams and men on horseback and many on
foot. At 5 A.M. on the morning of July 24th, 1850, we
arrived at . . . the sink of the Carson. The last 15 miles of

desert was a fearful road; the sand was so very deep. Within
five miles of the river we were met by men with loads of
water, crying out at the top of their voices, "Here is water!
Ten cents a pint." I thought then that gold diggings must
be scarce when men could resort to this mode of making
money. We were not over thirsty, neither man or beast, so
we did not buy water at ten cents a pint, but we journeyed
on until we came to the river and camped on its bank, ending that day's travel with 45 miles.

V

Having made their way across the parched Nevada plains to
the borders of California, the emigrants faced a hardly less
formidable obstacle. For the lofty ridges of the Sierra had
yet to be surmounted before the weary parties arrived at the
goldfields.
    William Warner, a young Philadelphian who made the
crossing in the early 1850's, thus described the passage in a
letter to his mother:

The latter end of our journey [he wrote] proved to be the
most interesting. When within six days of California we ran
out of provisions. We had nothing to eat but a little dried
fruit and tea. We concluded to stop until we could obtain
something from some of the emigrants as they passed along, I
tried all day in vain; they all let on to be nearly in my own
condition (that is, as they would say, short of provisions).
Night came and I for the first time in my life, had want to
stare me in the face. However, after a little further inquiry
I found a man who had a few onions and potatoes. He was a
trader from California who had gone east of the Nevada
Mountains for the purpose of buying lame cattle from emi-

grants. He was out of all kinds of provisions but onions and potatoes. I obtained a hat full of them for $2.12 which sufficed for supper and breakfast. The next day one of the men shouldered his rifle and went up the mountains in pursuit of game and I placed myself on the roadside and renewed my energies to buy something to eat. Finally I succeeded in obtaining 25 lbs of flour for which I paid $12.50. My man returned from his hunting expedition without success.

The next day we resumed our journey. After traveling three days our meal bag again had the consumption and we were once more out of provisions. We concluded that we would drive all night and crowd our team, so we overhauled our load and threw away everything only what we had on our backs, in order to lighten our load, after which we started, expecting to eat our next meal in California. When night came we overtook an emigrant who spared us from his scanty supply a few pounds of hard bread at 50¢ a pound —in addition to this I killed two sage hens . . .

The next morning we were again on our winding way through and over the mountains. When night came we were minus the wherewithal to satisfy hunger—when lo! and behold!! we discovered at a short distance from us an old She Bear with three cubs—drinking at a brook. We snatched our rifles and commenced an attack. After a short battle of ten or fifteen minutes we had the old bear stretched out before us . . . By and by a man came along and I exchanged some bear meat for flour . . . That night we had a supper—such a one as people in this country seldom sit down to. We had bear meat roasted; we had some fried and some boiled—besides fried liver and sundry pieces of meat that we stuck on sharp sticks and roasted before the fire. We also had biscuits, slap jacks and stewed fruit—together with tea . . . Two days from this we landed in Nevada City where we are all well and have plenty to eat, wear and drink . . .

vi

Not all the throngs who crossed the plains in the late '40's and early '50's were drawn westward by the lure of gold. Among their number were many who were heading toward the Northwest, where they planned to begin life anew in the fertile valleys of the Oregon country.

In the introduction to his book, *Traits of American Indian Life and Character*, first published in London in 1853, the anonymous author thus commented on the influences that had led these people to undertake their long journey:

A word on . . . the toils and privations which must necessarily be undergone by those who seek a home beyond the Rocky Mountains, may not be out of place [he began]. It is hard to conceive by what inducement so many thousands of reasonable men could have been prevailed on to leave their comfortable homes and fertile lands for this wild adventure; except, indeed, the spirit of enterprise, which seems to be inherent in the Anglo-American race, and which rejoices to meet and overcome every kind of difficulty, is sufficient to account for it. But whatever hope induced them to undertake this distant pilgrimage, it is sad to think of the disappointment that awaits the lately happy family whose homestead is broken up, and their little all conveyed into these deserts by the poor animals which had heretofore rendered such useful service on their farms;—sad to picture them, herding together for mutual protection, as they advance slowly, while the months roll on, through a country teeming with warlike marauders, and often surprised by the treacherous bands . . .

In course of time the waters of the Missouri roll behind them, and the river of their hopes may be seen glancing in the distance. Now, however, the dreary wastes of burning sand and scrubby wormwood, unrelieved by any nobler veg-

etation and affording a scanty pasture to the tired quadru-
peds at wide intervals only, begin to dissipate the sanguine
hopes in which they had so lately indulged. Provisions fail;
hunger, thirst, privation in every form are endured; till,
weary and way-worn, the travellers at length reach the banks
of the Columbia. If fortunate, they effect various exchanges
with the Indians for fresh horses, to replace their own tired
animals no longer able to proceed. Their little hoards of
ready money are expended to procure the necessaries of
existence, and they arrive at length in the settlements de-
nuded of everything—in short, destitute—to begin the world
anew . . .

> An account of what befell one such party which set out for
> the Columbia River country in the early 1850's is related in
> *Crossing the Plains,* the autobiography of Isaac Van Dorsey
> Mossman. From it the following excerpts have been taken.

Our train [he wrote] was known as the Miller's train. We
crossed the Missouri River at Council Bluffs on the third
day of May, 1853. We passed over the site of the present
town of Omaha, there being no human habitations there at
the time, but a few Indian tepees. Nothing of extraordinary
interest transpired with us until we reached the Loup Fork
of the Platte River, where we had our first experience with
ferrying a stream in our wagon boxes. We first drove our
horses and cattle over, then a man swam the river, taking one
end of a small line, to the other of which was attached one
end of a large . . . cable. The cable being hauled across the
stream and fastened on one end to a tree on each side, the
crossing began. First the women and children, then the
camping outfit, then the running gear of the wagons were
transported across. There was brandy in the train for medicinal purposes. This some of the men indulged too freely in,
and on the last trip over upset the wagon box and were

drowned, the swift water carrying their bodies beyond the possibility of recovery.

Mossman's narrative continues thus:

We travelled on without other incident worthy of mention until, reaching some sand hills . . . we encountered a terrific sand storm. We were in whirling, drifting sand for over three hours. It cut our faces and hands like knives. Proceeding to the Platte River, we travelled up the north bank of it, being in sight of Chimney Rock, the tall "Sentinel of the Plains," for eight or ten days. We were generally entertained at night with coyote concerts (admission free), but as a usual thing we were so fatigued that we said our prayers backwards, turned over on the other side, and went to sleep, when the music began.

We passed myriads of graves of the emigrants of the year before, 1852, who had died of the cholera. The wolves had dug up their bodies . . . We were often compelled to halt our teams and form a circle with our wagons around our stock to keep it from being stampeded by the buffalo, which crossed our track at intervals in herds of thousands, sounding like distant thunder as they rushed on with tremendous speed.

We were often deluded by mirage, sometimes seeing ahead of us the most beautiful lakes . . . which always seemed but a little pace ahead of us. We would hurry on, and when we imagined ourselves almost in reach of the water, the lake would disappear completely. This is no fairy tale, but too advanced a subject for me to attempt an explanation. The rarefied air on the desert was another curious thing, a raven at a distance would look as tall as a man.

On our journey we passed the celebrated Independence Rock on the Sweetwater, whereupon thousands of emigrants had carved their names. Independence Rock is near the

Devil's Gate, where the Sweetwater runs for many miles under a mountain. It took us two nights and a day to cross the Great American Desert, and when we came in sight of Green River we imagined we had reached Paradise at last. When still a mile from the river we were compelled to un-hitch our cattle from the wagons, so frantic was our stock for lack of water . . .

One of the curiosities of our journey was the celebrated "Steamboat Springs," near Bear River, one hot enough to boil an egg in the allotted four minutes, and the other not a hundred feet away, with water of ice-cold temperature, each of them puffing and blowing like a steamboat.

From Steamboat Springs we went to Port Nueff River, near old Fort Hall, arriving there July 4th. At this point the mosquitoes were so bad we were compelled to build smudges, or smothered fires, for our cattle. Otherwise they could not have withstood the torture of the little pests. Our way from this point lay past the American and Shoshone Falls of Snake River, on to Burnt River, and thence over into the River Valley.

> Having at this point met two former Illinois schoolmates, "who had come out from the Willamette Valley to purchase cattle from the emigrants," Mossman joined forces with them and pushed on westward. During this part of his jour-ney he thus records two contacts with the Indians of the region:

One day while camped at this point [that is, beside the Powder River], being in possession of a Hudson's Bay Com-pany salmon hook, I rode about fifteen miles up the river to do some fishing. I soon caught three fine large salmon. The fourth one I hooked fell off into the edge of the water, and I threw myself after it. In the ensuing scuffle we both rolled into the river. I received a good ducking and my pistol got wet, but I saved my salmon. Just as the four salmon had been secured to the saddle-bow, and I was on the eve of mounting, four Snake Indians rode up, and, without ceremony, compelled me, at the point of their arrows, to deliver up my piscatorial catch to them. Badly chagrined at losing my fish, I mounted my mule and started off, when the Indians started after me; but I bluffed them off with my wet pistol, wandered on and reached home late, fully promising never to fish so far from home again.

About the first of October the cattle which my friends had purchased were started for the Willamette Valley. We crossed the Blue Mountains on the old Lee encampment road, and camped near where the City of Pendleton now stands. While here the Indians drove off some of our cattle at night, and the next morning came to us looking as innocent as doves and asked: "Conchi chick-a-mon mika pot-latch spose nika iscum moos moos?" (which liberally interpreted means: How much money will you give if I get your cattle?) Five dollars was the price agreed on, and the cattle was soon in our possession again. It was an old trick of the Indians to steal horses and cattle and hold them in hiding until ransomed by the emigrants.

Excerpts from Mossman's recollections of his adventures as a pioneer express rider in the Northwest appear in a later chapter.

VIII

The Rush by Sea

i

To carry the throngs who believed that a passage by water would be the quickest and easiest means of reaching the goldfields, vessels of virtually every type, age, and degree of serviceability were called up. These were hastily refitted, and, loaded to the gunnels with men and goods, they sailed forth for the new Eldorado. Some headed for ports on the east coast of Mexico; others for Nicaragua or Panama, from all of which points the Argonauts proceeded overland to the Pacific side, where if they were lucky they boarded other vessels which took them on the final leg of their journey. Still others—and at the outset these were in the majority— embarked on the tedious, months-long passage 'round the Horn.

Throughout the early period the owners of sailing vessels had a virtual monopoly on this highly profitable trade. As time passed, however, an ever greater number of steamers were put on the run on both oceans, thereby enabling those passing to or from California to make the journey in a far shorter time than had been possible aboard the windjam- mers. A graphic picture of the types of accommodation offered aboard these pioneer steamers is given by L. M. Schaeffer, who made the trip from San Francisco to Panama aboard the *Winfield Scott* early in 1852:

Our vessel [wrote he] carried at least two hundred more passengers than she could comfortably accommodate, and the decks were so crowded that a man really had not a place *to spit* . . . The vessel was expressly built for the California trade, and even the smallest space was adapted to some use; down, "way down in the hold" forward, several feet below the surface of the water, where usually in other vessels the ropes, chains, ship's riggings, &c., are stored, berths were fitted up from floor to ceiling, and hardly room enough left for a passenger to pass along. The place was dark; daylight rarely penetrated there; but at least fifty men occupied this apartment, for which the charge was seventy-five dollars each. Then there were the steerage passengers, who paid one hundred dollars each, who were allowed the second deck to sleep in—much more comfortable than the "hold" below, and where they enjoyed a little more daylight, and above these, on the third deck, were still higher-paying passengers, who had comfortable berths and bedding, and then we reach another class, who sleep on this deck, but eat in the cabin, "after the third table." Then still another class, by paying fifty dollars more, sleep on "standee berths aft," having the privilege of the "quarter deck," and can promenade "abaft the wheel house," but are required to eat at Table No. 2; that is, after first cabin passengers have eaten, and at last, but the first class aboard, were the first cabin passengers, first table, choice of state-rooms, and the privileges and hospitalities of the whole vessel. This class (and, by the way, every one who can afford it, should always take a first cabin ticket), had to pay over a hundred dollars more than anybody else on board . . .

ii

Steamers, however, did not begin to operate on the Pacific
side until some eight months after the gold discovery;
consequently, the first to embark for the far side of the continent had of necessity to take the sailing vessels, the majority of which made the long, slow passage via Cape Horn.
This proved an ordeal that few who experienced it would
willingly have repeated.

One of many discomforts of life aboard the tiny, over-
crowded windjammers was that, before the voyage had well
begun, supplies of fresh fruits, meats, and vegetables were
all consumed, whereupon for the balance of the trip passengers and crew subsisted on a diet made up exclusively
of dried or smoked fish, beans, and salt meats—the latter
often on the borderline of spoiling and occasionally well
over it. That was bad enough, but frequently the supply of
water ran so low that strict rationing became necessary. In
such diaries and journals as have been preserved this is likely
to be the source of their writers' bitterest complaints, especially when their ships were passing through the tropics. Thus
one of their number, a passenger aboard the brig *Canton* on
one of its 'round-the-Horn voyages, commented:

We receive half a pint of stinking, rusty, brackish fluid twice
a day and each man disposes of it as he sees fit . . . The
thoughtless gulp it down at once and a few hours later they
are to be seen with parched tongues and dry lips cursing the
ship, the captain, and the day they left their comfortable
homes. The prudent husband their supply like misers, now
and then permitting themselves a tiny sip and smacking
their lips with satisfaction. They guard their remaining supply of the warm, obnoxious liquid with the utmost care, and
woe to anyone who thoughtlessly approached so close as to
run the risk of upsetting their precious cup of nectar . . .

The fastidious adds to his portion a dram of brandy, or, if he cannot obtain that, he mixes in a spoonful of molasses and a few drops of vinegar. This makes the concoction drinkable; I will not go so far as to call it palatable . . .

> During the rounding of the Horn, the passengers, huddled below decks, had two further problems to cope with: that of keeping warm and—in stormy weather—of eating such food as was furnished them. Of the second of these, J. Lamson, a traveler aboard the *James W. Page*, wrote:

The gale became furious last night, and seemed increasing in force this morning. We had no little difficulty in eating . . . A pan of fried pork and boiled beef, another pan of hardbread, and a pot of coffee, were set on the table, but how to keep it there required a greater degree of skill than we possessed. We could not sit, and we were in danger every moment of being pitched over the table, and across the cabin. To avoid such a catastrophe, we were obliged to hold by the berths with both hands. We made an effort, however, to eat, but had hardly made a beginning when a violent lurch of the ship sent our pork, bread, coffee, and all, in an instant upon the floor and into a neighboring berth. The scene was rather ludicrous, and we managed to extract a laugh from it as we picked up the fragments . . .

iii

On the whole, those who chose to make a combined sea-and-land journey fared somewhat better than the 'round-the-Horners. For the crossing—whether at Panama, Nicaragua, or elsewhere—made a welcome break in the long sea voyage, and besides, since the distance was far shorter, it promised to land them at the goldfields weeks ahead of those who went the whole way by sea.

Moreover, those who traveled via Panama found that the crossing of the Isthmus, notwithstanding its inconveniences, was profoundly novel; for, to all but a few, this was their first contact with a foreign land and foreign customs. Even Bayard Taylor, seasoned globe-trotter though he was, pronounced the 60-mile passage from Chagres to Panama City "decidedly more novel, grotesque and adventurous than any trip of similar length in the world . . . It was rough enough, but had nothing I could exactly call hardship, so much was the fatigue balanced by the enjoyment of unsurpassed scenery and the continual sensation of novelty."

On his journey from the Atlantic to the Pacific, Taylor's first overnight stop was at the village of Gatun. By the good offices of a boatman, who was carrying him and his belongings up the river, he was able to rent a hammock in the hut of a native. This he described as "a single room, in which all the household operations were carried on." He continued thus:

A notched pole, serving as a ladder, led to a sleeping loft, under the pyramidal roof of thatch. Here a number of the emigrants who arrived late were stowed away on a rattling floor of cane, covered with hides. After a supper of pork and coffee, I made my day's notes by the light of a miserable, starveling candle, stuck in an empty bottle, but had not written far before my paper was covered with fleas. The owner of the hut swung my hammock meanwhile, and I turned in to secure it for the night. To lie there was one thing, to sleep was another. A dozen natives crowded round the table, drinking their aguardiente and disputing vehemently; the cooking fire was on one side of me, and every one who passed to and fro was sure to give me a thump, while my weight swung the hammock so low, that all the dogs on the premises were constantly rubbing their backs under me . . .

iv

As time passed and the westward migration by sea grew in volume from month to month, several booklets appeared offering information and advice to those contemplating the journey. One of the most curious of these is a little pamphlet entitled *Gregory's Guide for California Travellers via the Isthmus of Panama,* published in New York early in 1850 and, in the words of its author, "containing all the requisite information needed by persons taking this route." The *Guide,* now extremely rare, was compiled by Joseph W. Gregory, proprietor of Gregory's California and New York Express, which from 1850 to 1853 did a large business carrying merchandise, mail, and gold dust between the Sacramento Valley and certain of the more populous towns and camps of the Mother Lode.

As such a large proportion of the "Universal Yankee Nation" have a migratory tendency towards California at the present time [he began], it has become a matter of no small interest to those persons about undertaking so important an affair as a journey thither, to ascertain not only that which will most conduce to their welfare on the route, but also what measures are needful to guard against imposition and unnecessary delay . . .

From New York to Chagres, the route may be considered plain sailing, and we will commence with the anchorage off Chagres, which is usually from one to two miles distant. The Steam Ship Company provide for the landing of the passengers and their baggage, using the ship's quarter-boats for the former, and the launch of the Steamer Orus for the latter, conveying the whole to the Orus, which vessel lands the passengers on what is called the American side of the river. The captain of the Orus is paid by the Steam Ship for landing both passengers and baggage. Three or four taverns are kept at this landing by white men, one or two of whom are Americans.

After seeing your baggage safely landed from the Orus, your first object should be to secure a good canoe—one holding four or five persons is the most preferable.

Then make your contract to convey yourself and baggage to Cruces, which will cost from thirty to forty dollars the trip, (six to eight dollars each person) usually occupying three days, during which time your pleasure will be greatly enhanced if you have been provident in supplying yourself with a sufficient stock of provisions . . .

The great secret of getting well up the river during the day is to get off early in the morning, and be liberal with the men that work the canoe. You can coax, better than drive them. At the end of about two days you will reach Gorgona, where it is tempting to stay, but should you go on shore there, you will experience great difficulty when you are ready for a start, in getting your boatmen into their canoe again . . . At Gorgona, interested persons will advise you to take the road to Panama from that point. *Pay no attention to such advice,* for that road is totally impassable for nine months in the year.

Push on without delay to Cruces, and if you arrive there in the morning, you will hardly be able to get on the Panama road before the next morning. Meanwhile you can call at Funk's and Pleise's houses.

They forward baggage by mules to Panama. Ascertain their charge for sending it next morning, *but let no promises induce you to leave your baggage to be forwarded after you, but see it start at least.*

The above persons may ask ten or twelve dollars per hundred pounds, but plenty of natives can be had to carry it at the rate of seven to eight dollars per one hundred pounds. If you employ a native, it is necessary for you to have him sign an agreement, to fulfil his contract.

This you can get drawn in Spanish for twenty-five cents, to which you must make him sign his mark, binding him to deliver the baggage for the stipulated price at Zacharisson Nelson & Co.'s office, Panama.

In two days you can walk to Panama and if desirable, keep your trunk and baggage in view the whole time, but I consider that quite unnecessary. Should you prefer riding, a mule would cost you from ten to sixteen dollars.

On arrival at Panama, your first business is to ascertain from the Agents when the Steamer is to leave, and if you are to be delayed a week or more, it is advisable for four or five persons to engage a room, with a cot in it for each, and arrange for a supply of drinking water. This will cost a dime a day for each person. Taking meals at restaurants or Eating houses, a person may lodge in a good room, and thus live moderately at about three and a half dollars a week.

The day before the Steamer leaves, notice is posted up by the Agents of the hour that passengers are required to be at the Mole, in front of the Custom House.

Passengers are required to pay the expense of conveying themselves and their baggage to the Steamer.

Travellers in the Steamships between New York and Chagres are of course much better provided than on the Pacific Steamers. Having the New York Markets to resort to, once in each month, makes a very essential difference. The Pacific Steamers are supplied with stores from New York, via Cape Horn, with the exception of such as are obtained on the Pacific coast.

Steerage passengers will find one or two jars of preserves, and one or two pecks of dried fruit (peaches or apples) very acceptable. A few jars of pickles, and a few pounds of Milk, Soda, or Butter crackers, some Bologna Sausages and Cheese, a Ham and a piece of Smoked Beef, would not only prove very palatable and comfortable, but more agreeable in case of sea-sickness than Ship's fare . . .

Take sufficient of coffee, tea, loaf sugar, &c., for five days' consumption in crossing the Isthmus, and should there be anything left of your stores on arriving at Panama, *anything you have is preferable to tropical fruit, which should be avoided* by all means.

A similar outfit of provisions is desirable for the steerage on the Pacific, and more so, for reasons before stated; each steerage passenger is provided with his own *plate, knife and fork, spoon, drinking-cup, mattress and pillow* . . .

In consequence of the great and bitter disappointment incurred by many persons in being delayed for weeks and months in Panama, *it has become indispensably necessary* for each person to be provided with a ticket for the Pacific Steamer, before leaving New York, which can be procured thus, at the office of the Company, 54 South street, New York.

For want of this precaution, many have been compelled to wait at Panama until they could send for a ticket to the above office . . . The expense of landing at San Francisco is borne by each passenger; the Steamer coming to anchor as near the city as the landing is safe and practicable.

This route to California, although more expensive than that by way of Cape Horn, is by far the most desirable for those who can afford the additional outlay . . . , not the least of which is, the very great saving in time in making the trip, and the avoiding of a tedious and monotonous life on shipboard. The voyage by way of Cape Horn will occupy on an average five or six months, while by the Isthmus route, the trip is accomplished in as many weeks, and to most persons presents varied scenes of no ordinary pleasure. The

voyage up the Chagres River has been by some persons
execrated in tolerably strong terms, not to say diabolical. As
far as my own feelings were concerned, I must assert that I
received the greatest pleasure and never beheld more magnificent scenery, or luxuriant vegetation, than I witnessed
while upon this river . . .

After a perusal of the foregoing, any practical man can,
before leaving home, estimate very nearly what his expenses
will amount by the time he lands in San Francisco. Some
allowance for detention at Panama should be made, which
you can easily estimate after learning from the Steam Ship
Company in New York on what day the Steamer will leave
Panama.

As a matter of course, no prudent person will undertake
so long a journey without making some provision in his calculations for unforeseen events that may require some outlay beyond the estimate of his entire expenses. Any surplus
of funds he may have on hand on his arrival at San Francisco,
will not be found very burthensome, and he may feel quite
sure that his money will not trouble him long, if he remains,
even for a little while, in a state of *masterly inactivity.*

Hoping that the foregoing remarks may prove servicable,
and a useful guide to the travelling public—

> I remain,
>> Their Humble Servant,
>> *Joseph W. Gregory,*
>> Proprietor of Gregory's California
>> and New York Express.

V

Throughout the early days fire was one of the prime dangers
faced by those going out to the West Coast by sea. The sail-

ing ships of the period were all constructed of wood and, should a fire break out, the result was likely to be tragic unless it could be promptly extinguished. Accordingly, during the long voyages a close watch was kept to guard against that menace. However, the annals of the period make it clear that, despite these precautions, fires were by no means infrequent aboard the gold ships, some of which resulted in a heavy loss of life.

Here is an account of one such disaster—one that, fortunately, involved no fatalities. The narrator was a Mrs. D. B. Bates, who, with her husband, set sail from Baltimore in the summer of 1850, bound for San Francisco. So far as fires were concerned, hers was a singularly unfortunate voyage, for during the nine months at sea the passengers experienced no less than three. The first took place during the passage down the east coast of South America, and, although the ship was destroyed, it remained afloat long enough to permit all hands to land on the Falkland Islands. After a month's delay, the marooned group embarked again, this time on a Scotch vessel bound for Valparaiso. Then, during a stormy rounding of Cape Horn, disaster struck again.

That night [recalled Mrs. Bates] it came on to blow tremendously. Next morning, we found ourselves eighty miles from land, and, horror of horror, the ship on fire! My heart refused to give credence to the startling report until my eyes beheld it. Our worst fears were too soon confirmed by the flames darting upwards, and igniting the hatch the men were vainly endeavoring to caulk . . . When that burnt and fell in, the flames shot upward almost to the top-masthead. The combustible nature of the cargo [coal, tar, and liquors] caused the fire to increase with wonderful rapidity. The long-boat was launched, and I was placed therein, with my pet-goat; for I would not leave her behind . . . After sev-

eral ineffectual attempts to get at some bread and water, the
fire and smoke drove them all in confusion to the boat. They
pulled off a short distance, and we gazed in silence and sad-
ness upon what had so recently been our happy home, now a
burning wreck. The calmness of despair pervaded my whole
being: all was comprehended at a glance—eighty miles from
land, and that an inhospitable coast, inhabited only by savages, without bread or water; in an open boat, exposed to
the . . . Cape Horn weather!

> All was not lost, however. For although the hapless group
> were unaware of it, help was close at hand. Mrs. Bates' nar-
> rative continues:

All at once the joyful cry of "Sail, ho!" was shouted from our
midst; and, far away, I could descry a speck upon the ocean.
Nearer and nearer it came, until, when within about a mile
of us, she "hove to," and lowered away a boat, which came
bounding over the water to our relief. This ship proved to
be the *Symmetry*, of Liverpool, Captain Thompson, bound
for Acapulco, and laden with coal. How that word rang in
my ears! It seemed to me that every ship that floated was
coal-laden . . .

> Two weeks later the nomads were transferred at sea to a
> third ship, the *Fanchon,* Captain Lunt, outward bound
> from Baltimore to San Francisco—and likewise laden with
> coal.

Our fancied security [she wrote], our sanguine expectations
that our troubles from fire at sea were over . . . were sustained and strengthened by reiterated assurances from Captain Lunt that there was no danger whatever of the *Fan-
chon's* burning, she was so well ventilated. In fact, he attrib-
uted the destruction of the other ships to want of proper

ventilation. Besides, he argued, if there had been the least
probability of its taking fire, it would have done so long ago.
We all conceded his arguments were conclusive; and, for a
few days, anxiety, fear, suspense, and all the attendant train
of harrowing reflections, were strangers to my bosom.

> But not for long. "Less than a week later," wrote Mrs. Bates,
> "a puff of air was wafted into the cabin, so strongly impreg-
> nated with gas as to render the conviction certain in my
> mind that the coal was on fire . . ." At first her fears and
> warnings fell on deaf ears.

Things remained in this state for two or three days [she con-
tinued]. I cannot affirm that the minds of *all* were perfectly
free from apprehension; yet, as strict watch was kept, and
nothing except that disagreeable smell of gas was apparent to
confirm my fears, I felt a little more at rest. The third day,
as Captain Lunt was watching one of the large ventilators on
deck, he saw something having the appearance of smoke escaping therefrom. He sprang down between decks—there
was no appearance of smoke or fire whatever; raised the
lower hatch—all appeared as usual. He then ordered the
second mate to dig down into the coal, and soon proofs be-
yound a doubt were too apparent. The coal was so hot it
could not be taken in the hand. The whole body of coal,
two or three feet below the surface, was red hot. The same
preparations for a life on board a burning ship were again
repeated . . . In this instance, we had not to contend with
the elements of wind and water as well as fire; for the ocean,
at times, was as smooth and transparent as a glass . . . The
ship would be lying listlessly upon the surface of the unbroken waste of waters, while our minds were constantly
agitated between hope and fear, hope . . . that some welcome sail would come to the rescue; and fear, as each returning day numbered disappointed hopes, and increased the

heat on shipboard, that we were indeed a doomed crew . . .

Daily convincing proofs appeared to warn us of the slow but sure destruction of the ship, in the form of gas and smoke, which were escaping through every seam. The beautiful paint-work and gilding of the cabin assumed the darkest hue; everything on board seemed shrouded in the sable habiliments of mourning. Slowly and gradually we neared the land; and, after three weeks of intense suspense . . . the exulting cry of "Land, ho!" was echoed far and near. It was an uninhabited part of the coast of Peru—a small bay or, rather, indenture made in at this place, called the Bay of Sechura . . .

Long before we reached our anchorage, the roaring of the surf, as it dashed upon the lonely beach, sounded like a mournful dirge to our ears. There appeared to be a short stretch of sandy beach, circumscribed by high and jutting rocks. Around us, on either side, were innumerable breakers; threatening destruction as we approached nearer . . . but the noble ship bounded gayly over the waters, unmindful of the destiny awaiting the doomed . . .

Immediately upon bringing the ship to anchor, preparations were made to effect a landing in the boats. Captain Lunt and my husband deposited their nautical instruments and charts, and some few articles of clothing, in a chest which they had rendered as nearly water-proof as possible, and consigned it to one of the boats. We threw overboard all the spare spars upon deck, and everything that would float. We had no provisions or water to take on shore, and had been refreshed with none through the day . . .

I recollect distinctly my sensations on leaving the ship in a boat; how intently I watched the foaming surf we were fast approaching, and which had already engulfed the boat in advance; then an indistinct recollection of roaring and splashing of water—of voices heard above the din of all, giving directions—of being dragged, minus bonnet and shawl, through the surf upon the sandy beach . . . After removing everything off the ship's deck, they ran her still nearer in, and scuttled her; but the fire had made such progress, it was impossible to save her. In two hours after we left her deck, she burst into a sheet of flame . . .

It is quite impossible to convey by language an adequate conception of the solemn magnificence of this midnight scene. The burning ship in the foreground, the light from which revealed the sublime altitude of the mountains in the background, whose barren heads seemed to pierce the sky, every object distinctly daguerrotyped; the rocks on either hand; the bald and inaccessible cliffs in close proximity, in the rear; and twenty-six human beings (myself the only female) standing upon the narrow beach, viewing silently the work of destruction, rapidly progressing, which deprived us of a home, and the necessary sustenance required to support life . . . By three o'clock that night, nought remained to mark the spot—where, a few hours before, lay the gallant ship . . .

> The first problem facing the stranded group was that of finding some means of sustenance, for they had been able to bring no food from the doomed ship. Fortunately for them, however, the glare of the burning vessel had attracted a tribe of Indians who lived farther down the coast, and on the following morning two raftloads of them paddled into view. Being friendly, they readily agreed—in Mrs. Bates' words—"to furnish us with water and sweet potatoes while we remained upon the beach."
>
> The next problem they faced was how to effect their escape from this lonely beach. After discussion, it was decided to send the mate and four sailors up the coast in the small boat, in the hope that they could reach the seaport town of Payte, report their plight to the American consul there, and ask his help. Following the departure of the

little craft those who remained behind kept a close watch to sea, eager to catch sight of the rescue vessel. However, when a week had passed without a single sail appearing on the horizon, their hopes began to wane. Then, one night, after the party had gone disconsolately to bed, rescue finally came.

All at once [wrote Mrs. Bates] we heard the clanking of chains letting go anchor. All rushed out, and there lay a dark object in the offing. Soon we heard the splashing of oars; and in a short time Mr. McCrellis [the mate], his countenance beaming with smiles, stood in our midst. He was accompanied by Captain Hillman, originally of New Bedford. His bark had been chartered by the American consul to come to our rescue. The next morning we bade farewell to the rocks, and sand, and fleas, and repaired on board the bark . . .

vi

The menace of fire was by no means confined to the early-day sailing ships; it also constituted an ever-present threat to those aboard the wooden steamers of the period.

One of the most destructive of such catastrophes was that which befell the Pacific Mail Steamship Company's side-wheeler, *Golden Gate*, in July of 1862. That 2200-ton vessel, having accommodations for 300 passengers, had left San Francisco on July 21. Six days later, while some fifteen miles to the northwest of the Mexican port of Manzanillo—where a stop was to be made—fire broke out in the ship's galley and spread so rapidly that within a few minutes it became clear that the vessel was doomed. One of the survivors of the tragedy that followed was André Chavanne, California mine owner, who was bound for a visit to his native France.

Soon after his rescue, Chavanne wrote an account of the
disaster, from which the following has been taken.

The fire had spread to every part of the ship from the engine
room aft. The flames were driven back upon us by the speed
of the vessel and by a strong breeze blowing from shore. All
avenues of escape were cut off; no longer was it possible to
reach the top deck, the flames were sweeping over it, extending twelve or fifteen feet beyond the stern; they whirled over
my head. The boats were gone, and in a few minutes the
passengers about me, dazed, hemmed in on all sides and
driven away by the conflagration, were huddling together
and banging on the sides of the steamer; then, one after
another, they were forced to jump into the water . . .

Soon, I was almost alone on that part of the boat. The
swirling flames were over me and all around me; I could
hardly breathe, the smoke hurt my eyes, the heat was becoming intolerable, the fire was already reaching me. I pulled
my broad brimmed hat over my eyes to protect them. Still I
hesitated! I could not make up my mind to add another victim to those I could see struggling before me . . .

But the time for hesitation had passed! I also was going to
jump overboard. At that supreme moment, I saw ropes, that
had been used to lower the boats, dangling a short distance
from me. Clinging to the side of the vessel, at the risk of
falling into the water, I leaped upon one of them with a precision and ability of which I would have been quite incapable
at any other time. I hoped to be able to hang there for a
while, and in this manner, get closer to the shore, toward
which the ship had been rapidly steaming since the beginning of the fire.

But the smoke, and flames, bits of canvas and other burning debris, driven by the wind, were falling upon me and
soon forced me to slide down closer to the water . . . I was

exposed for a few seconds to a shower of burning tar and was compelled to get into the water. Endeavoring to take advantage of anything that would postpone my abandoning the vessel, I hoped I could be towed by tying around my body the rope to which I was hanging. I had already begun to carry out that idea, but had barely touched the water when its resistance, so much the greater that the ship was going faster, snatched the rope violently out of my hands, spinning me around several times.

Then began Chavanne's struggle to reach shore, an ordeal that was to last for nearly twenty-four hours.

As soon as I was clear of the ship [he recalled] and had recovered from the shock I had experienced, I proceeded to fasten around me the belt I had on my shoulders and used it to float more easily. Then, I looked around and was frightened to see that I was surrounded by a hundred or more people. To describe that sight, and the death scenes that were being enacted, is impossible. . . . Frantic and crazed men and women, frightful to behold and hear, were struggling in every direction, grappling with one another, drowning one another in ferocious embraces. I understood I was lost if I remained within reach of my poor fellow companions . . .

For an hour or so, I swam here and there with no other aim than to isolate myself. I succeeded, but I had lost precious time, and instead of getting nearer shore, I noticed that I had gone materially away from it . . .

While I was swimming, trying to avoid people, I had come across another life preserver. I succeeded in securing it and was, from then on, able to float more easily and take some rest, of which I was in great need . . . Night was approaching. I could but faintly see the coast. While thus anx-

iously watching the boats that were going away from me and
vanishing in the darkness, I could hear the voices of the
drowning, now few in number, dying out with the day . . .

> Throughout the night, Chavanne paddled in what he be-
> lieved to be the direction of shore, only to discover when
> dawn came that land was nowhere to be seen.

Now I could see for a considerable distance [he wrote], but
there was nothing around me. It was strange to me that I
should be so far from shore. The day before, when I had
been forced to leave the ship, it was but a few miles away,
and now nothing could be seen as far as my eyes could reach
. . . Rising as high as I could, several times, I scanned the
horizon. Finally, far off in the morning mist, I perceived a
darker line. My heart beat violently, a frightful apprehension
that had taken hold of my mind was being dispelled, I could
see land! I could not realize I was at such a distance from it—
I looked all around, but in every other direction I could see
only the immense ocean, eternally in motion . . .

> All that day until late afternoon he continued his struggle
> toward the distant shore.

I kept swimming without looking about me any more [he con-
tinued]. I stopped only to catch my breath; but I could not
remain long without moving. It seemed to me that by resting, my limbs lost their suppleness and became numbed. So
I moved almost continuously and mechanically. My head was
sound, my ideas clear; but my heart ached at the idea that
very soon I would have no strength left to make headway.
During one of the short periods of rest, I fancied I heard a
noise in the water. Turning my head around quickly, I saw
two boats coming toward me . . . The men in the first boat
stretched out an oar to me; I seized it with both hands and

they pulled me towards them. It required several men to pull me in. I could hardly help myself. I tried to hold on to the side of the boat, but my hands would slip, and had no strength. Once out of the water, it seemed my weight was enormous. I slid to the bottom of the boat, and in the midst of confused ideas, muttered the words, "At last."

The little craft that had rescued him was manned by a party of Mexicans. It was one of a number of vessels that had put out from Manzanillo when news of the disaster had reached that port. On being picked up, Chavanne had been astonished to learn that during his twenty-three hours in the water he had drifted a distance of forty miles. His narrative concludes thus:

On July 29, in the evening, we landed at Manzanillo. It was with joy that I met on the beach the survivors . . . But among the people who had been saved, many were in deep despair. Husbands, wives, children, brothers were missing. The number of victims exceeded two hundred—about two hundred and sixty-five. We had lost two-thirds of the passengers and a third of the crew.

vii

As the California-bound ships, after many weeks at sea, finally neared the end of their voyages, a new spirit of excitement and animation began to pervade one and all. Passengers shook off their lethargy, and while the vessels were still far off-shore, crowded the rails, eagerly scanning the horizon ahead.

Rarely did the scene that greeted them measure up to their expectations. For as the succession of bare hills that comprise much of the California coastline came into view, the reaction of by far the greater number of Argonauts was one of sharp disappointment. Thus Richard Hale—whose ship, the *General Worth,* neared the journey's end in May of 1849—after describing the wild excitement on board when land was first sighted, added dolefully: "But with all the glamor our wildest enthusiasm can paint it, it is yet only an uninviting stretch of waste land." And in a letter written by Enos Christman, who reached California on board the sailing ship, *Europe,* in early February, 1850, we read:

About nine o'clock in the morning the joyful cry of "Land, ho!" was heard and by going aloft to the fore-topsail guard, I was able to see the dim outline of several ridges of land . . . The water had changed in appearance from the dark blue of the wide ocean to the dirty green always found near shore. By noon we could discern several specks in the distance, which we supposed to be vessels, but subsequently they proved to be three clusters of rugged rocks about 25 miles distant . . . The land became plainer and plainer as we approached, and at sunset we were so near that we could discern the trees on top of the distant hills.

On the other hand, John Linville Hall, diarist aboard the barque *Henry Lee,* painted the scene in less gloomy colors. His entry for September 12, 1849, reads:

As we near the land a more accurate view of its surface is discernible, which is altogether more inviting than any we have seen since leaving our homes. It rises into gentle slopes and is covered with verdure, upon which hundreds of horses and cattle can be distinctly seen feeding. But few trees, and these scattered near the summit in clumps, are in view.

THE RUSH BY SEA

However, little time was spent viewing the scenery, for as the ships neared their destinations, preparations for landing got promptly under way.

The passengers are all engaged in packing up [wrote J. M. Letts, who arrived at San Francisco in the summer of 1849 aboard the *Niantic*]. The retorts, crucibles, gold tests, pickaxes, shovels, and tin-pans, are put into a separate bag, and laid on the *top;* each determined to be the first off for the mines. Each one having conceived a different mode of keeping his gold, one would exhibit an ingenious box with a secret lock, another, a false bottom to his trunk, a third a huge belt, while a fourth was at work on a fifteenth buckskin bag, each of 20 lbs. capacity . . .

But the safe storage of their gold was not the only concern of the about-to-land miners. Soon, they knew, they would find themselves in a primitive frontier land, and it seemed the part of prudence to be prepared for any emergency. E. I. Barra, who had made the trip aboard the *Urania,* wrote in his diary:

We now have the prospect of arriving . . . in a short time, and the passengers are now preparing to invade an unknown country, where they expect to encounter Indians and wild beasts. The deck is looking like a veritable arsenal. Guns, pistols, bowie-knives, powder flasks, and other death-dealing apparatus that a man may need in a new, unexplored country, can be seen in the process of being cleaned and prepared for action when needed.

IX
The Northwest

i

The magnet that drew the first trading ships to the shores of the Northwest Coast was furs, namely, the pelts of the sea otter, beaver, marten, and other animals that then abounded throughout the region. This trade—which was to flourish for the next half century—had its beginning in the late 1770's, when the master of a British vessel, having dropped anchor in one of the coastal inlets and bartered with the Indians for a quantity of furs, proceeded to China, where he found a ready market for his cargo, at many times its original cost. When word of this profitable enterprise became known, others made haste to join in. During the first few years, this lucrative trans-Pacific trade was largely in the hands of the British, but as time passed an ever-growing number of Yankees entered into competition. Thus during the year 1799 the fleet of trading ships that appeared off the coast included twelve from Boston alone.

One of the most interesting of the first-hand accounts of this trade with the Northwest Indians that has come down to us is that of Richard J. Cleveland, the 26-year-old master of a Salem, Massachusetts, vessel which arrived off the coast in April of 1799. Cleveland's narrative, having told of anchoring in the Norfolk Sound, "in latitude fifty-seven degrees north," continues thus:

The following day was very clear and pleasant. At the first dawn of the morning we discharged a cannon to apprize the natives who might be near of our arrival. We then loaded the cannon and a number of muskets and pistols, which were placed where they could be most readily laid hold of. The only accessible part of the vessel was the stern, and thus was exclusively used . . . as the gangway. As it was over the stern that we meant to trade, I had mounted there two four-pound cannon and on the tafferel a pair of blunder busses on swivels, which were also loaded. Soon after the discharge of our cannon several Indians came to us, and before dark some hundreds had arrived, who encamped on the beach near which the vessel was anchored. As we observed them to be loaded with skins, we supposed that we were the first who had arrived this season.

With a view to our own security as well as convenience, I directed my interpreter to explain to the chiefs, and through them to the tribe, that after dark no canoe would be allowed to come near the vessel, and that if I perceived any one approaching I should fire at it; that only three or four canoes must come at a time to trade, and that they must always appear under the stern, avoiding the sides of the vessel. With my own men I neglected no precaution to make escape impossible but at the imminent risk of life. While at anchor they were divided into three watches. One of these I took charge of, and stationed them in such parts of the vessel that no movement could be made undiscovered, obliged them to strike the gong every half hour throughout the night and to call out from each end of the vessel and amidships, "All's well." This practice so amused the Indians that they imitated it by striking a tin kettle and repeating the words as near as they were able.

But a more hideous set of beings in the form of men and women I had never before seen. The fantastic manner in which many of the faces of the men were painted was probably intended to give them a ferocious appearance, and some groups looked really as if they had escaped from the dominions of Satan himself.

One had a perpendicular line dividing the two sides of his face, one side of which was painted red, the other black, with the head daubed with grease and red ocher and filled with the white down of birds. Another had the face divided with a horizontal line in the middle and painted black and white. The visage of a third was painted in checkers, etc. Most of them had little mirrors, before the acquisition of which they must have been dependent on each other for those correct touches of the pencil which are so much in vogue and which daily require more time than the toilet of a Parisian belle . . .

It was quite noon before we could agree upon the rate of barter, but when once arranged with one of the chiefs and the exchange made, they all hurried to dispose of their skins at the same rate; and before night we had purchased upwards of a hundred, at the rate of two yards of blue broadcloth each. The Indians assured us that a vessel with three masts had been there a month before, from which they had received four yards of cloth for a skin, but this story was rendered improbable by the number they had on hand, and I considered it as a maneuver to raise the price. As soon as it became dark they retired in an orderly manner to their encampment, abreast the vessel; and some of them appeared to be on the watch all night, as we never proclaimed the hour on board without hearing a repetition of it on shore.

The following morning the natives came off soon after daylight and began without hesitation to dispose of their furs to us at the price fixed upon the day before, and such was their activity in trading that, by night, we had purchased from them more than two hundred sea-otter skins, besides one hundred and twenty tails. Our barter consisted of blue cloth, greatcoats, Chinese trunks, with beads, China cash, and knives as presents. Canoes were arriving occasionally throughout the day, so that at night there was a very perceptible augmentation of their numbers.

Having observed on the 4th and 5th that their store of furs was nearly exhausted, we weighed anchor the next morning, and parting on good terms with the natives, steered up a narrow passage in an easterly direction till we arrived at that extensive sound which Vancouver has called Chatham's Straits. Several women came off and told us there were no skins in the village; that the men were gone in pursuit of them; and that, if we came there again in twice ten days, they should have plenty. Here we passed a day in filling up our empty water casks and getting a supply of wood.

In the afternoon of the 9th we put out of the snug cover in which we were lying, having been informed by the Indians that there was a ship in sight. This we found to be true, as on opening the sound we saw her not more than a mile distant from us. Soon after, we were boarded by Captain Rowan of the ship *Eliza*, of Boston, who had arrived on the coast at least a month before us, and who, having been very successful, was now on his way to the southward to complete his cargo and then leave the coast.

ii

The movement of early-day settlers into the Northwest, which had been under way for some time, reached its high point in 1843. For in that year there set forth for the Oregon country a band of emigrants of unprecedented size, the party numbering more than 1000 men, women, and children. These traveled in 120 ox-drawn wagons, and drove with them some 5000 horses and cattle, the latter to be used to stock the farms and ranches they planned to establish in the wilderness. Years later one of the leaders of the expedition, Jesse Applegate, published a lively account of their adventures en route.

The emigrants first . . . attempted to travel in one body [wrote he] but it was soon found that no progress could be made with a body so cumbrous and yet so averse to all discipline. And at the crossing of the Big Blue it divided into two columns, which traveled in supporting distance of each other as far as Independence Rock on the Sweet River.

From this point, all danger from Indians being over, the emigrants separated into small parties better suited to the narrow mountain paths and small pastures on their front. Some of the emigrants had only their teams, while others had large herds in addition which must share the pastures and be guarded and driven by the whole body. Those not encumbered with, or having but few loose cattle, attached themselves to the light column; those having more than four or five cows had of necessity to join the heavy or cow column. Hence the cow column, being much larger than the other and encumbered with its large herds, had to use greater exertion and observe a more rigid discipline to keep pace with the more agile consort. It is with the cow or more clumsy column that I propose to journey with the reader for a single day.

It is 4 A.M.; the sentinels on duty have discharged their rifles—the signal that the hours of sleep are over; and every wagon and tent is pouring forth its night tenants, and slow-kindling smokes begin . . . to float away on the morning air. . . .

The herders pass to the extreme verge and carefully examine for trails beyond, to see that none of the animals have strayed or been stolen during the night.

This morning no trails lead beyond the outside animals in sight, and by five o'clock the herders begin to contract the great moving circle and the well-trained animals move slowly toward camp, clipping here and there a thistle or tempting bunch of grass on the way.

In about an hour five thousand animals are close up to the encampment, and the teamsters are busy selecting their teams and driving them inside the "corral" to be yoked. The corral is a circle one hundred yards deep, formed with wagons connected strongly with each other, the wagon in the rear being connected with the wagon in front by its tongue and oxchains. It is a strong barrier that the most vicious ox cannot break, and in case of an attack of the Sioux would be no contemptible entrenchment. From six to seven o'clock is a busy time; breakfast is to be eaten, the tents struck, the wagon loaded, and the teams yoked and brought in readiness to be attached to their respective wagons. All know that when, at seven o'clock, the signal to march sounds, those who are not ready to take their proper places in the line of march must fall into the dusty rear for the day.

There are sixty wagons. They have been divided into fifteen divisions or platoons of four wagons each, and each platoon is entitled to lead in its turn. The leading platoon of today will be the rear one tomorrow . . . It is within ten minutes of seven; the corral, but now a strong barricade, is everywhere broken, the teams being attached to the wagons. The women and children have taken their places in them. The pilot (a borderer who has passed his life on the verge of civilization and has been chosen to the post of leader from his knowledge of the savage and his experience in travel through roadless wastes) stands ready . . . to mount and lead the way.

Ten or fifteen young men, not today on duty, form another cluster. They are ready to start on a buffalo hunt, are
well mounted and well armed, as they need be, for the un-
friendly Sioux have driven the buffalo out of the Platte, and
the hunters must ride fifteen or twenty miles to reach them.
The cow drivers are hastening, as they get ready, to the rear
of their charges, to collect and prepare them for the day's
march.

It is on the stroke of seven: the rushing to and fro, the
cracking of the whips, the loud command to oxen, and what
seems to be the inextricable confusion of the last ten minutes has ceased. Fortunately every one has been found and
every teamster is at his post. The clear notes of the trumpet
sound in the front; the pilot and his guards mount their
horses, the leading division of wagons moves out of the encampment and takes up the line of march, the rest fall into
their places with the precision of clockwork, until the spot
so lately full of life sinks back into the solitude . . . as the
caravan draws its lazy length toward the distant El
Dorado . . .

They [the wagons] form a line three quarters of a mile
in length; some of the teamsters ride upon the front of their
wagons, some walk beside their teams; scattered along the
line companies of women and children are taking exercise
on foot; they gather bouquets of . . . flowers that line the
way; near them stalks a stately greyhound or an Irish wolf
dog, apparently proud of keeping watch over his master's
wife and children . . .

The company's midday stop is thus described:

The pilot, by measuring the ground and timing the speed
of the wagons and the walk of his horse, has determined the
rate of each, so as to enable him to select the nooning place
as near as the requisite grass and water can be had at the

end of five hours' travel of the wagons. Today, the ground being favorable, little time is lost in preparing the road, so that he and his pioneers are at the nooning place an hour in advance of the wagons; which time is spent in preparing convenient watering places for the animals and digging little wells near the bank of the Platte. As the teams are not unyoked but simply turned loose from the wagons, a corral is not formed at noon, but the wagons are drawn up in columns, four abreast, the leading wagon of each platoon on the left . . . This brings friends together at noon as well as at night.

> With the approach of nightfall the wagons were formed into a closely knit circle at a spot selected by the advance party, the teams unyoked, and, under the watchful eyes of guards, turned out to graze.

Meanwhile [continues Applegate's account] everyone is busy preparing fires of buffalo chips to cook the evening meal, pitching tents, and otherwise preparing for the night . . . All able to bear arms in the party have been formed into three companies, and each of these into four watches. Every third night it is the duty of one of these companies to keep watch and ward over the camp, and it is so arranged that each watch takes its turn of guard duty through the different watches of the night . . .

It is now eight o'clock when the first watch is to be set; the evening meal is just over, and the corral now free from the intrusion of the cattle or horses, groups of children are scattered over it. The larger are taking a game of romps . . . Before a tent near the river a violin makes lively music, and some youths and maidens have improvised a dance upon the green; in another quarter a flute gives its mellow and melancholy notes to the still air . . .

But time passes; the watch is set for the night . . . and

each has turned to his own quarters. The flute has whispered its last lament; the violin is silent, and the dancers have dispersed . . . All are hushed and repose from the fatigue of the day save the valiant guard and the wakeful leader . . .

iii

One of the most perceptive observers of the early westward movement was the frail young New Englander, Francis Parkman, who at the age of twenty-three joined a party bound for the Pacific Northwest, his purpose both to study the Indians encountered along the way and to regain his health. Throughout that months-long trip he kept a diary, which he later used as the basis for his best-known book, his memorable *The Oregon Trail*. Here is his picture of Independence, Missouri, the jumping-off place for many of the parties heading west, which he reached on May 7, 1846:

Rode by vile roads, through the woods, to Independence. The clouds in this region are afflicted with an incontinence of water—constant alternations of showers and sunshine— everything wet, bright, and fresh. Plenty of small game and gorgeous birds.

At Independence, every store is adapted to furnish outfits —the public houses were full of Santa Fe men and emigrants. Mules, horses, and waggons at every corner. Groups of hardy-looking men about the stores, and Santa Fe and emigrant waggons standing in the fields around.

While I was at the Noland House, the last arrival of emigrants came down the street with about twenty waggons, having just broken up their camp near Independence and set out for the great rendezvous about 15 miles beyond Westport.

What is remarkable, this body, as well as a very large portion of the emigrants, were from the extreme western states —N. England sends but a small proportion, but they are better furnished than the rest. Some of these ox-waggons contained large families of children, peeping from under the covering. One remarkably pretty girl was seated on horseback, holding a parasol over her head to keep off the rain. All looked well—but what a journey before them!

The men were hardy and good-looking. As I passed the waggons, I observed three old men, with their whips in their hands, discussing some point of theology—though this is hardly the disposition of the mass of the emigrants.

I rode to Westport with that singular character, Lieut. Woodworth . . . Woodworth parades a revolver in his belt, which he insists is necessary—and it may be a prudent precaution, for this place seems full of desperadoes—all arms are loaded, as I have had occasion to observe. Life is held in little esteem.

This place, Westport, is the extreme frontier, and bears all its characteristics.

As we rode home, we met a man itching for Oregon, but restrained by his wife—at McGee's at Westport, there was a restless fellow who had wandered westwards from N.Y. in search of work, which he had not found; and now he was for Oregon, working his passage, as he could not supply himself with provisions.

Pleny of vagabond Indians are about here, trading at the different stores, and getting drunk.

I saw many at the store of Mr. Boone, a grandson of Daniel . . .

A keen observer and wielding a ready pen, Parkman set down much of interest during the course of his westward journey. Here is his description of Fort Laramie, in present-day Wyoming, which his party reached on June 15, 1846:

Laramie appeared, as the prospect opened among the hills. Rode past the fort, reconnoitered from the walls, and passing the highest ford of the Laramie Fork River, were received at the gate by Boudeau, the *bourgeois*. Leading our horses into the area, we found Inds.—men, women, and children—standing around, voyageurs and trappers—the surrounding apartments occupied by the squaws and children of the traders.

Fort divided into two areas—one used as a *corale*—two bastions or clay blockhouses—another blockhouse over main entrance. They gave us a large apartment, where we spread our blankets on the floor. From a sort of balcony we saw our horses and carts brought in, and witnessed a picturesque frontier scene. Conversed and smoked in the windy court. Horses made a great row in the *corale*. At night the Inds. set up their songs. At the burial place are several Inds. laid on scaffolds, and a circle of buffalo skulls below.

> The following day, June 16, a group of Indians appeared on the bank of the river opposite the fort and, in Parkman's words, "crossed over on their wild, thin little horses."

Men and boys [he continued], naked and dashing eagerly through the water, horses with lodge poles dragging through squaws and children, and sometimes a litter of puppies—gaily attired squaws, leading the horses of their lords—dogs with their burdens attached swimming among the horses and mules—dogs barking, horses breaking loose, children laughing and shouting—squaws thrusting into the ground the lance and shield of the master of the lodge—naked and splendidly formed men passing and repassing through the swift water.

They held a kind of council in the fort. Smoke [their chief] presided, but he had another man to speak for him, and ask for presents, and when they were placed on the floor before him, they were distributed under his eyes, by one of the "soldiers." Several of the warriors had their faces blackened, in token of having killed Pawnees, or at least of having been on the warpath when they were killed.

Some who visited us kept looking, with great curiosity, at the circus pictures that Finch has nailed up in the room.

At their camp in the evening, the girls and children, with a couple of young men, amused themselves with a dance, where there was as much merriment and fooling as could be desired . . .

iv

In the introduction to a book called *Traits of American Indian Life*, published in London in 1853, the author, "A Fur Trader" (believed to have been Peter Skeene Ogden, an official of the Hudson's Bay Company), had this to say of the "great and rapid changes" taking place throughout the western frontier:

Not the least of these [he wrote] is the extended organization of the great Fur Company, which has now penetrated the remotest districts, and sends its emissaries into the most secluded glens. Next to this, perhaps, may be reckoned the rivalry of the English and American adventurers, and the recent influx of immigrants from the United States. . . .

The author goes on to state that "while the hazards these adventurers must undergo, and the savage life of the wilderness for which they are bound" are depicted in his book, these were not his prime purpose in writing it. He then added that "the occurrences he has described were spread over many years, and have a different kind of interest. Im-

pressed by them at the time as an eye-witness, he has here
recorded them . . . in the hope that they may serve for the
amusement of others who feel an interest in tales of adventure, and to add to the stock of authentic anecdotes
from which alone a true judgment of the Indian character
can be formed."

Having [he continued] had frequent opportunities of observing the customs and traits of character by which the various tribes of Indians are distinguished, and more particularly
of those who inhabit the western part of North America beyond the Rocky Mountains, I have been surprised to remark
how falsely their character is estimated in the recently published journals of certain travellers. The gentlemen have
been delighted to represent the aborigines . . . as quiet,
peaceable souls, meriting nothing so much as the most delicate attention on the part of their European visitors . . .
The author of the first, it is observed, scarcely left the confines
of civilization; and the second had merely an opportunity
of communicating with a few Indians who had resided from
their infancy in the vicinity of long established trading posts,
where they had learned the art of comporting themselves
with some degree of propriety, in order the more readily to
gain a livelihood and to acquire the means of satisfying their
fictitious wants.

The forefathers of these people, being independent of
the traders, made no scruple of exhibiting the vices which
their sons are studious to conceal. Their wants were comparatively few; the bow and arrow supplied the means of
procuring large animals; from the bark of the willow they
made fishing nets; the skin of the hare or the beaver sufficed
them for clothing; and fire was always at their command by
resort to friction . . . It cannot be said that the present gen-
eration is really improved by the change they have undergone in some of these respects. The trader, having in view

his own sole benefit, has taught them to use European clothing, with the addition of much superfluous finery; and their
modern virtues become them about as well as these garments,
and are just as consistent with their real character. In a word,
those very Indians whose quiet demeanor has been so much
lauded, only conceal, under this specious mask, all the vices
which their fathers displayed more openly: unprovoked murder and habitual theft are committed by them whenever the
opportunity offers; and their character, generally, is of a
description to afford a constant source of anxiety to those who
reside among them.

Such being the treacherous disposition of those Indians
who, residing in the immediate vicinity of the trading-posts,
are in a great measure restrained by fear . . . , what must
he be destined to experience who wanders among the lawless
tribes that are strangers to the faces of Europeans?

By way of answering that question, the author related the
following incident, drawn, he said, from his own experience:

In 1829 I was appointed to explore the tract lying south of
the Columbia, between that river and California . . . It was
in the month of September that I set out . . . , with a party
of thirty men, well appointed, to overcome the obstacles
and encounter the perils which long experience had taught
me to anticipate . . . After leaving the Columbia, we journeyed a month through a sterile country, before we came
upon the trace of any human inhabitants, which then appeared more numerous than I had expected. On the day following their first appearance, a party consisting of ten men,
who had been sent in advance as scouts, came in sight of
about fifty Indians, who fled on their approach, but not soon
enough to prevent the capture of two of their number. These
were fully sufficient to answer all my views, which were to

obtain, if possible, some information of the country before us
. . . Having secured the two strangers, we treated them with
all possible kindness, and by signs endeavored to express our
wishes . . .

Having succeeded in gaining some partial information of
the country in advance of us, I dismissed my informants, first
presenting them with a few baubles in return. Wild as deer,
they were soon out of sight, but the kind reception they had
met with being, as I suppose, duly represented to their countrymen, they returned on the morrow, accompanied by a
large body of men, who soon became very troublesome.
Everything about us attracted their curious attention; our
horses, if possible, still more than ourselves. It was with
evident reluctance that our numerous visitors left us in the
evening, a few of them, indeed, hinting a wish to remain.
This, I doubt not, was with the double view of observing how
we secured our horses, and the precautions we took to guard
against surprise . . . I gave orders to clear the camp, and
for the night watch to turn out, upon which they went away.

At the dawn of day, according to my invariable custom, I
had all the men aroused, the fires lighted, and the horses
collected in the camp; this being the hour that Indians always fix upon for making their predatory attacks, it being
then, as they say, that men sleep most soundly. In this, as in
other calculations of a savage cunning, they are not far wrong.
They would certainly have found it so in our case, had the
precaution alluded to not have been adopted . . . Thanks
to the method we observed, every one was awake and stirring
—preparing, in fact, for a start—when I perceived, in the
gray dawn, a large body of Indians drawing near. When
within a short distance of the camp, they hesitated to advance,
as if dubious of the reception that awaited them. This had a
suspicious appearance, nothing having occurred on the previous day to give rise to any doubt that it would be otherwise
than friendly. We were not long left in uncertainty of their

hostile intentions, for a shower of arrows were presently discharged into the camp. This was too much for our forbear-
ance; I considered it high time to convince them that we
would resent the unprovoked attack. Three of our horses
were already wounded, and if we ourselves had escaped, it
was probably owing to the poor beasts having sheltered us
from the arrows. I therefore ordered a rifle to be discharged
at them. The ball was true to its aim, and a man fell. This was
sufficient as a first lesson, for on witnessing it they at once
took to flight, leaving their companion dead on the field,
as a mark of their evil design and its punishment. I trust they
were not only duly impressed with our superiority over
them, but likewise with a sense of the lenient treatment they
had received, although, from past experience, I could have
little hope at the time that the effect of either would be very
durable.

v

The hazards to life and limb faced by the first whites to
reach the Far West were not alone those posed by hostile
Indians; indeed in some parts of that area a more immediate
threat to safety lay in the danger of attack by wild animals.
This was particularly true in the mountainous regions of the
Pacific slope, a favorite haunt of the grizzly bear. For while
the grizzly would rarely attack man unless the latter came
upon him unexpectedly, or made the first hostile move,
once the beast's ire was aroused, his ferocity, plus his great
size—specimens frequently weighed upwards of a thousand
pounds—made him a formidable foe.

The story of one such encounter—and a thrilling tale it is
—has been preserved in the diary of Lewis Keysor Wood, a
thirty-year-old Kentuckian who, in the fall of 1849, joined

a party of prospectors and headed for the newly discovered diggings in the Trinity River country bordering the Pacific near the present California-Oregon line. Early in January of the following year, while Wood and two companions were following the course of the heavily wooded Eel River, they sighted a group of the animals. What transpired is told in his own words.

We continued our course up the river as best we could, sometimes aided by an Indian or elk trail, at others literally cutting our way along. Upon passing from the forest into a small opening we came suddenly upon five grizzly bears. Willson and myself immediately went in pursuit of them, but unfortunately met with no further success than to wound one of them severely. The day following this, while travelling over a piece of mountain prairie and passing a small ravine or gulch, we espied a group of no less than eight more of these animals. Although exhausted from fatigue and so reduced in strength that we were scarcely able to drag ourselves along, we yet determined to attack these grim customers.

For several days all we had or could obtain to subsist upon was the deer skin which we had saved and a few buckeyes. The former we cut up and boiled in water and afterwards drank the water in which it had been boiled and chewed the hide.

Willson, Sebring and myself prepared for the conflict, which it was altogether probable that we should have before the matter could be ended, and advanced toward them. While yet a long distance from them, Sebring sought shelter for himself by climbing a tree, not wishing to hazard the chance of a hand to hand contest with bruin. Willson and myself advanced until within about a hundred yards of the nearest of them when a consultation was again made in reference to the mode of making the attack.

It was arranged that I should approach as near as possible and fire: then make my way to some tree for safety. The latter part of the arrangement I did not assent to for one very good reason—I was so completely prostrated that had I the will to run, my limbs would scarcely have been able to execute their functions. We continued to approach our antagonists until within about fifty paces when I levelled my rifle at the one nearest me and after careful aim fired. The shot was to all appearances a fatal one, for the huge monster fell, biting and tearing the earth with all the fury of one struggling in death. So as soon as I had fired Willson said to me in a low tone of voice, Run! run! Instead, however, of yielding to his advice, I immediately commenced reloading my rifle. Willson now discharged his gun at another with equal success.

When I fired, five of the bears started up the mountain. Two now lay upon the ground before us and a third yet remained, deliberately sitting back on her haunches and evidently determined not to yield the ground without a contest, looking first upon her fallen companions and then upon us.

Willson thought it about time to retreat and accordingly made the best of his way to a tree. Unfortunately I could not get the ball down upon the powder and in this predicament as soon as Willson started to run, the bear came dashing at me with fury. I succeeded, however, in getting beyond her reach in a small buckeye tree. I now made another effort to force the ball down my rifle but with no better success than at first and was therefore compelled to use it to beat the bear off as she attacked the tree, for the purpose of breaking it down or shaking me out of it. She kept me busy at this for two or three minutes when to my astonishment the bear I had shot down, having recovered sufficiently from the effects of the wound, came bounding towards me with all the violence and ferocity that agony and revenge could engender. No blow that I could inflict with my gun upon the head of the maddened monster could resist or even check her.

The first spring she made upon the tree broke it down. I had the good fortune to gain my feet before they could get hold of me and ran down the mountain in the direction of a small tree standing about thirty yards distant. Every jump I made I thought must be my last as I could distinctly feel the breath of the wounded bear as she grabbed at my heels. I kept clear of her while running but the race was a short one. On reaching the tree or bush I seized hold of the trunk of it and swung my body around so as to afford the bear room to pass me, which she did and went headlong down the hill some twenty paces before she could turn back. I exerted all my energies to climb the tree but before I could get six feet from the ground the hindmost bear caught me by the right ankle and dragged me down again.

By this time the wounded bear had returned and as I fell grabbed at my face. I, however, dodged and she caught me by the left shoulder. The moments that followed were the most critical and perilous of my life. Here then, thought I, was the end of all things for me! That I must perish—be mangled and torn to pieces—seemed inevitable. During all the time I was thus situated my presence of mind did not forsake me. Immediately after the second bear caught me by the shoulder, the other still having hold of my ankle, the two pulled against each other as if to drag me in pieces; but my clothes and their grip giving away occasionally saved me. In this way they continued until they had stripped me of my clothes except a part of my coat and shirt, dislocated my hip and inflicted many flesh wounds—none of the latter, however, being very serious. They seemed unwilling to take hold of my flesh, for after they had divested me of my clothes, they both left me—one going away entirely and the other (the wounded bear) walking slowly up the hill about a hundred yards and there she deliberately seated herself and fastened her gaze upon me, as I lay upon the ground perfectly still. After remaining thus several minutes I ventured to move. Which I suppose she must have seen, for the first motion brought her pell-mell upon me again, roaring at every jump . . . At this moment, I must confess, my presence of mind entirely forsook me. I knew that if she again attacked or took hold of me it must be upon my naked flesh. The moment left me was one of fearful suspense. No sooner had she reached me than she placed her nose violently against my side and then raised her head and gave vent to two or three of the most frightful, hideous and unearthly yells that were ever heard by mortal man. I remained perfectly quiet, hoping that by so doing she would leave me, and in this hope I was not disappointed, for after standing over me a short time she again walked away. I now thought she had left for good and determined to place myself beyond her reach should she, however, make up her mind to return again and continue the attack.

Up to this time I was unconscious of the extent of the injury I had received; that an accident had befallen my leg I was well aware, but not until I attempted to get up was my true condition manifest to me. I then found that I could not use my right leg and supposed it was broken.

Turning to look about to assure myself that my enemy had retired, imagine my surprise on seeing her again not more than one hundred yards distant, sitting back upon her haunches and her eyes glaring full at me. With my leg in the condition I have related I dragged myself to the buckeye bush from which I had been pulled down by the bear, and after much difficulty succeeded in climbing up about eight feet. As soon as Willson had discovered me up the tree he left his tree and came to me. The bear, seeing him, came bounding towards us with the greatest ferocity. Willson remarked: "What in the name of God shall I do." I replied that he could come up the limb of the adjoining tree and he was barely able to get beyond reach before she arrived. She deliberately seated herself immediately beneath us and kept her eyes steadily upon us, and as either one or the other of us happened to move, she would utter an angry growl. I observed Willson present his rifle at her and not shooting immediately. I remarked, "Shoot her—for God's sake, shoot her . . ." He watched her for a moment with his aim still fixed upon her and when I again repeated my request for him to shoot, he replied, "No sir; let her go—let her go, if she will."

After having detained us in this situation for a few moments she went away and disappeared altogether, much to our joy and relief—thereby giving me an opportunity to get down from the tree . . .

> Although the immediate danger was then past, Wood's narrative makes it clear that a lengthy ordeal still awaited him. Once it had grown apparent that the bears had permanently withdrawn, the injured man's companions carried him down the mountainside and made camp beside a stream. There they remained twelve days, "subsisting entirely upon the meat afforded by the bear Willson had shot in the late encounter." Then, Wood's condition having shown no improvement, and all suffering from cold and hunger and with their supply of ammunition dangerously low, it was decided that they must at all costs make their way out of the wilderness. Accordingly, the sufferer was lifted on to a horse and the group slowly made their way southward, headed toward what they believed to be the nearest settlement, an outpost Northern California farm which was reached at the end of the tenth day.

vi

Over much of the West during the early days roamed great
herds of buffalo, the ungainly beasts serving a useful purpose
to both the Indians and the whites by providing them not
only with food but with clothing and shelter. Their hides
were fashioned into shoes, tents, britches, and other garments and their fleeces into "buffalo robes"—the latter
highly prized for their warmth and durability. Moving north
in the springtime and turning southward with the advent of
winter, the animals traveled in such numbers that, according to one observer, as far as the eye could see the entire
landscape appeared to be "one unbroken mass of moving
backs and bobbing heads." However, with the wholesale
slaughter that followed the coming of the white hunters
and trappers, their number suffered a rapid decline. That
they were still far from extinct as late as the opening of the
1870's is, none the less, made clear by this recollection of
one Peter Koch, an early-day resident of Montana Territory:

In March 1870 [wrote he], I traveled from Muscleshell to
Fort Browning on Milk River, and for a distance of forty
miles I do not think we were out of easy rifle shot of buffalo . . . We could see many miles on either side; but . . .
the eye met only herd and herd of grazing and slowly moving buffalo . . . Three days later I passed over the same
trail on my return trip, and the vast herds had disappeared
as if by magic. Only two or three old bulls were still wandering over the prairie . . .

That more than a decade later great numbers were still to
be seen in remote sections of eastern Montana is, however,
testified to by another old-timer, James McNaney, who,
while on a hunting trip in that area late in 1882, reported
that "an immense herd" of them had appeared from out of
the north.

It reached our vicinity one night, about 10 o'clock, in a mass that seemed to spread everywhere [wrote McNaney]. As the hunters sat in their tents, loading cartridges and cleaning their rifles, a low rumble was heard, which gradually increased to "a thundering noise," and some one exclaimed, "There! that's a big herd of buffalo coming in!" All ran out immediately, and hallooed and discharged their rifles to keep the buffaloes from running over their tents . . . The herd came at a jog trot and moved quite rapidly. In the morning the whole country was black with buffalo.

> The animals presently disappeared into the south and for several weeks not one was to be seen. Then the hunting party had a second visitation, this time in even greater numbers than before.

One morning about daybreak [the account goes on] . . . a long line of moving forms was seen advancing from the northwest, coming in the direction of the hunters' camp. It disappeared in the creek valley for a few moments, and presently the leaders came in sight again at the top of "a rise" a few hundred yards away, and came down the intervening slope at full speed, within 50 yards of the two tents. After them came a living stream of followers, all going at . . . "a long lope," from four to ten buffaloes abreast. Sometimes there would be a break in the column of a minute's duration, then more buffaloes would appear at the brow of the hill, and the column went rushing by as before . . . For about four hours did this column gallop past the camp over a course no wider than a village street.

vii

The discovery, in the early 1860's, of rich deposits of gold
and silver in the Owyhee region of southwestern Idaho,
and the founding of several populous towns within the area,
was responsible for one of the most picturesque enterprises
in the annals of the pioneer West. This was a series of
"cattle drives" by which great herds of Texas livestock were
driven over hundreds of miles of prairies and mountains
to provide beef for the horde of miners working the
Owyhee claims.

A spirited account of the trials and rewards of such drives
has been preserved in the recollections of a young Indianian
named David L. Shirk, who participated in two of them.
Here are excerpts from Shirk's story of the first of these,
that of 1871:

On the morning of March 17th [he wrote], we mounted and
started for Belton, Bell County, Texas, where we landed
March 23rd. Here, we began making inquiries and soon
learned that T. E. Vanness had the selling of all the cattle
of Bell and Johnson counties. We were not long in getting
in touch with him, and as a result, by twelve o'clock, March
24th, had closed a contract for 1500 head of cattle. For
four year old cows, the contract price was $4.50, and for five
year old cows $5.75 per head . . .

The reader may be curious to know the number of men
necessary to handle and drive 1500 head of cattle. We always figure on one man for every one hundred head of cattle, up to 500 head, and then one man for every 200 head.
Thus it will be seen that to handle 1500 head required ap-
proximately ten men. This force does not include the fore-
man, the party whose duty it was to look up the camping
places, or the night guard. For the first two weeks of the
drive, it generally requires eight men to hold the cattle of

nights, four in the first part and four during the after part of the night. After the cattle are thoroughly broken to being held, and accustomed to being rounded up for the night, two men are sufficient on each guard, save during a storm and then it takes all the force to hold them, especially if the storm is accompanied by hail. In that event, you can only let them drift with the storm, holding them so as to prevent scattering and consequent loss of cattle. In handling a large herd when it is storming, or when a stampede occurs, the rear cattle crowd the others, forcing the leaders ahead, and compelling the herders to give way. Therefore, all you can do is to travel with the storm, and hold the herd together as well as you can. This is especially a difficult task on a dark night.

On the morning of April 15, as per contract, Mr. Vanness's men began branding the cattle with our road iron "T", and by ten o'clock, our 1500 head of cattle were branded and ready to start. The branding is done in a chute, fifty feet long and about two feet wide, from twenty to twenty-five being branded at a time. . . .

We were on hand when the branding was completed and at once took charge of the herd, and that day drove six miles. And here our troubles began, and we were forcibly reminded of what was in store for us, as we were compelled to experience the worst storm encountered on the entire trip. All but three of our force were green hands, unused to handling cattle, and the result was that we found it impossible to hold the herd, and hence turned them loose. The following day, we succeeded in finding all but six head, and these were later recovered . . .

The day following the stampede, we moved three miles and camped in order to dry our clothes, which were rain-soaked. In fact, we had been in the saddle practically two days and one night, our clothes soaked to the skin, and the only rack upon which to dry them being our frames. This was, indeed, an unfavorable beginning, but it was not to be our last, as many such experiences awaited us before our journey should be ended.

The weather was not the only—or indeed the most serious —hazard with which Shirk and his fellows had to contend. For cattle thieves, both Indians and whites, lay in wait along the trail, and a constant watch had to be maintained to ward off their raids. Despite constant vigilance, however, the party had several brushes with the outlaws, one of which Shirk thus described:

On July 28th, we camped on a small stream called Hood Rock and found some difficulty in getting a level bed ground for the herd. We were now in the hostile Indian country and great prudence was necessary if we would save our stock as well as our scalps. Finally selecting a spot, we rounded up the herd about four hundred yards from our camp. The ground sloped gently toward a small stream or canyon, and not being deemed very safe, great caution had to be exercised. Those not on guard rolled up in their blankets to sleep and rest, both being badly needed. The moon went down about three o'clock in the morning, and it was so dark that an animal could not be seen even at a short distance.

Just as the moon disappeared, a band of Indians, or white men, we could not determine which, came up out of the canyon, and with shots and yells stampeded the herd. The guards extended themselves to hold the cattle, but handicapped by the darkness, about one hundred head were cut off and driven away. Roused by the noise, all of us at the camp quickly mounted our horses and rode for the herd at a breakneck speed.

We finally rounded up all we could find and held them until daylight, when Miller, Walters and myself took the

226 of the thieves

trail of the thieves . . . and followed with all possible speed. We were not long in coming in sight of the fugitives. Seeing they were pursued, they began shooting and killing the cattle, but soon sought safety in flight. Two head of cattle were killed and four wounded. Our horses being far spent by the rapid pursuit, it was out of the question to overtake them, and we contented ourselves with gathering up the cattle and returning to camp . . .

For several days following the incidents noted above, the cattle were very restless and gave us no end of worry, but with care, they again settled down and gave us a much needed rest.

Again days slipped into weeks with the ever interminable grind. Hailstorms were frequent, some of the hailstones being as large as marbles. On August 7th, we passed Ft. Hallock and crossed the summit of the great Rocky Mountains. Game was still abundant, consisting of deer, antelope, elk, and sage hens, and afforded an abundance of fresh meat, and of the finest quality . . .

On September 10th, we crossed over the line of Utah into Idaho and entered upon the last lap of our long, tedious and dangerous journey. We had in the herd at this time 1650 head of cattle, and considering the length of the drive, its dangers and many hardships, had been most successful, in fact, all we could wish.

On September 12th, we went into camp on the head of Bruno Valley where Mr. Miller and Mr. Walters expected to remain. Here, we made a careful count of the cattle. We left Bell County, Texas, on April 25, 1871, being occupied with the drive five months and seventeen days . . .

> Young Shirk, who owned one-sixth of the herd, took his animals—numbering some 225 head—into winter quarters and the next spring drove them to Silver City, where he sold the entire lot at a price of $35 a head.

After settling all my expenses incurred in the drive from Texas [his account concludes], I found that my investment had netted me $2,160. . . . "A very fair profit," you will say. But when one considers the risk, dangers of the drive, and the risk of losing every dollar you had in the world, not to mention life itself, the profits were not unreasonable.

viii

As in other stock-raising districts throughout the West, the coming of the first bands of sheep was resented by the cattlemen of the Northwest, who well knew with what speed a herd of these animals could reduce once bountiful ranges to barrenness. The story of how one of the first droves of "woolies" were driven into Montana has been told by John F. Bishop, a resident of the town of Dillon, who, with a neighbor, Richard A. Reynolds, set off for Oregon in the late 1860's, their purpose being to buy horses.

Portland in 1869 [Bishop later recalled] was a small town with little more than one street along the river. Loading our team and wagon on the boat we took passage up the Columbia River to The Dalles. Having changed our minds about buying horses we looked about for a band of sheep. I sold my gold dust and took greenbacks in return, getting a dollar in paper for 75 cents in gold. On a ranch three miles from The Dalles we found sheep that suited us belonging to a man named Beasley. I got eleven hundred head of ewes and Dick four hundred. I paid $2.75 per head in greenbacks for my sheep.

It was about the first of August, 1869, that we started back for Montana. A man who had gone broke gambling offered to help drive the sheep to work his passage. We crossed the

Deschutes River on a toll bridge and paid $40 toll on the out-
fit. From the Deschutes we took the old road by Fort Wat-
son. Here three goats joined the sheep. We told a soldier
about them and he said to let them follow if they wanted to
and they came all the way to Montana.

We crossed the Blue Mountains by a toll road, paying out
another $40, and came to Canyon City. We staid over a day
here and bot bolts of heavy muslin or drill and cut some
stakes. We fastened a stake to the cloth about every ten
feet so that we could use it for a corral at night. In the morning we rolled it up and put it in the wagon.

From here we struck across to the Malheur River and
followed it down to the Snake. When we came to a small
stream the sheep would usually swim but sometimes we
had to throw a crude bridge across the water. We crossed the
Snake River at Keene's Ferry. Again it cost $40 . . .

Soon we reached the Boise River and were back on the
road we came out on. We forded the river and had a very
hard time getting the sheep across as they wouldn't go into
the water. Back in Boise City again we had a 400 mile drive
ahead of us without a settlement. But the only mishap we
had was when I tipped the wagon over and lost most of our
pail of molasses. There was small chance of getting any more.

On Lost River we came to a place where some Chinamen
were camped for the night. First we knew they had a fire
which was fast getting out of hand. All of us worked like mad
and got it put out before it burned up the sheep and the
Chinese outfit. Soon they began to cook their supper. I went
over to their fire to watch them and found they had dressed
off a skunk. They put it on the fire to boil and stirred in some
dumplings. Each man pinched off a lump of dough and
marching around the pot dropped it into the stew. What
this ceremony meant I did not learn. Their supper looked
good and they asked me to eat with them but I went back to
our own sour dough bread and beans, and molasses.

Finally we got back to Junction, Idaho, crossed over the Main Range of the Rockies by Bannack Pass into Horse Prairie and reached Bannack on Grasshopper Creek Nov. 7th, 1869. We estimated the trip from The Dalles with the sheep at 800 miles and we made it in 80 days of travel. Ten miles a day to the tune of blatting sheep.

We drove the sheep to John Selway's ranch on the Black Tail Deer Creek for a month and then to Birch Creek where Dick herded them for the winter. He lived in a wickiup and did not suffer from cold as it was a mild winter. The sheep came through in fine shape . . .

ix

The invasion of their ranges by hordes of sheep was, however, not the major trial faced by the Montana cattlemen during pioneer days. Far more serious were the activities of the rustlers: organized gangs of ruffians who raided the herds, spirited off the stolen cattle to places of concealment, and, after their brands had been altered, drove them to distant points where they sold them. The efforts of regularly appointed law-enforcement agencies to cope with this evil having failed, the ranchers took matters into their own hands and organized bands of vigilantes. These proceeded to round up the culprites and, to those adjudged guilty, dealt out summary justice—usually at the end of a rope.

Although the operations of the vigilantes were conducted in strict secrecy, with each member sworn not to divulge the names of his companions, we have, fortunately, an eye-witness account of the result of one of their exploits. In the fall of 1882, a steamship plying the upper Missouri stopped to take on wood at a spot a short distance above the settle-ment of Bates Point—where a few hours earlier the vigilantes had staged one of their punitive raids against a gang of rustlers. On board was an artist named Rufus F. Zogbaum; later he thus described what he saw:

Smoke has been seen rising over the trees down the river, vague rumors of a fight below seems to fill the air, and the feeling of excitement communicates itself to our little group of passengers, and as the boat swings out again into the swift yellow current . . . we gather at her low rails, looking out curiously and anxiously ahead . . . Rounding a long point of land running out into the river, a call from the pilot house attracts our attention to a blackened, smoking heap of ashes on the left bank—all that is left of a ranch house that had stood there—and a short distance further we slow up a little at the still burning ruins of another house. "It's the Jones boy's ranch," says the mate. "By Jiminy, the cow-boys is making a terrible clean sweep of the kentry!" That they have not been long gone is evident. Two half-charred wagons stand in the "corral," the flames licking the edge of a great woodpile, that even as we pass bursts into flames . . . Near a pile of debris, which may have been a kitchen or other out-house . . . , a few chickens, shrilly cackling, are huddled together. No other sign of life is visible . . .

Suddenly there is a movement . . . on the deck below; they are gazing with bated breath and blanched faces at something on the river's bank . . . Almost hidden from our sight by the tangle of underbrush and low trees, something is hanging there motionless . . . something formless and shadowy in the gloom of the jungle, something indistinct, but fearful in its mystery and silence . . .

"Look! Look! down thar by them cotton-woods! that's them! that's the cow-boys!" Half hidden in a mass of wild rose-bushes . . . a group of men and horses is standing . . . As the current takes the boat inshore, and we approach nearer and nearer, they present an interesting tableau. Most of them have dismounted and are standing at their horses' heads waist-deep in weeds and flowers, bronze-faced, resolute looking men, unconsciously picturesque in costume and attitude; bright-barreled Winchesters swing across their high pommelled saddles, on which is bound the scanty baggage of the cowboy, while a few pack-mules quietly crop the grass a few paces in their rear . . . They are evidently under some discipline for no one else moves as a tall, handsome, blond-bearded man, flannel-shirted, high-booted, with crimson silk kerchief tied loosely, sailor fashion, around his sunburnt neck, advances to the water's edge; and with courteous wave of broad-brimmed hat hails the boat. Clang! goes the gong; the big wheel stops. The stranger politely requests information about the purchase of some supplies, and inquires as to the news up the river. Many on board recognize him as a man of wealth and education well-known in the territory, but nothing is said as to the errand of himself and his men in this distant, wild region. During our parley his men remain quietly at their posts, and when their leader, his questions answered, returns toward them, and we move on again, we see them mount and ride off over the hills in a straggling, dust-enveloped little column.

X

From the close of the Civil War onward, the cattle industry of the Northwest had flourished, with each year ever larger herds roaming the unfenced ranges and, in good seasons, yielding substantial profits to their owners. During the late 1860's and early 1870's the "cattle kings," as they came to be called, wielded almost unlimited power throughout the territory and controlled virtually every phase of its social, commercial, and political life. As time passed, however, the

authority of the reigning group came to be challenged by a
steadily growing number of newcomers—farmers and small-
scale stock raisers, who had been taking up public lands in
some of the most fertile areas, fencing them, and putting
them under cultivation.

To combat this encroachment on the ranges where they
ran their cattle, the oldtime Wyoming stockmen presently
organized themselves into a group called the Stock Grow-
ers' Association, its announced purpose to protect their
herds against rustlers, whose raids had become progressively more bold and frequent. On the pretext that the
territory's duly constituted authorities had proved themselves unable—or unwilling—to maintain order and punish
the offenders, the Association members took matters into
their own hands. Their method of dispensing "justice" was
that of the frontier; that is, suspected rustlers were rounded
up, brought before impromptu courts, brief hearings held,
and punishment—ranging upward to, and including, the
death sentence—carried out.

Vigilante tactics of that sort were resented alike by Wyoming's judicial and law-enforcement agencies and by the
territory's growing number of small landowners. Another
source of bad blood between the cattle barons and the
newcomers was a belief of the former that the small opera-
tors were systematically raiding their cattle and making off
with such young animals as strayed from the herds to which
they belonged. Commenting on that aspect of the long-
drawn-out—and frequently violent—feud, A. S. Mercer wrote
in his controversial history of the movement, *The Banditti of
the Plains,* published in 1894:

Very soon it seemed to be understood that the owners of
large herds looked upon all the settlers and homeseekers as
rustlers among the herds of mavericks (unbranded animals),

and the name "Rustler" was used as synonymous with settler . . .

Keeping in mind the fact . . . that the settler was an eyesore to the ranchmen, by reason of his fencing up the best lands, it may be seen that the latter was an interested spectator, if not an active promoter, of attaching the disreputable title of "rustler" to all country homeseekers. In fact, public opinion had settled down to the belief that the corporation managers conceived the "Rustler" howl for the purpose of securing public sympathy for their future plan to "run the settler out" by murder, assassination and incendiarism.

> Mercer's indictment of the "Cattle Kings" goes on to cite a long series of crimes against the settlers—crimes, purportedly committed by members of the Association, that included lynchings, shootings from ambush, and the burning of the newcomers' homes. The controversy engendered much hard feeling on both sides and for several years the region was in intermittent turmoil. It was, indeed, not until the mid-1890's that peace was finally achieved.

X
The Southwest

i

One name that looms large in the annals of the Southwest is that of James Ohio Pattie, son and grandson of frontiersmen, who, as a youth, pushed ever farther westward and in the mid-1820's found himself in the Mexican pueblo of Santa Fe. There, while he and his fellow fur hunters were awaiting permission from the governor to set their traps in the streams of the province, he became involved in a highly dramatic adventure. For years the Mexican ranchers who had settled in the upper Rio Grande River valley had been exposed to attack by bands of Apache, Navajo, and Comanche Indians, who slew the men, burned their houses, and made off not only with their livestock but frequently with their womenfolk as well.

During Pattie's stay at Santa Fe one such raid, this one of particular violence, took place. This time the savages—a numerous band of Comanches—killed a number of the ranchers, drove off several hundred sheep, and made captive five young women. When word of this reached the pueblo, an expedition, made up chiefly of members of Pattie's group, was organized and hastened off in pursuit. After traveling

four days, the marauders were sighted and the whites concealed themselves in a narrow mountain canyon through
which the others would have to pass.

Here is Pattie's account of what followed:

My post [he wrote] was in the center of the line. We waited
an hour and a half behind our screens of rocks and trees, before our enemies made their appearance. The first object that
came in sight, were women without any clothing, driving a
large drove of sheep and horses. These were immediately
followed by Indians. When the latter were within thirty or
forty yards of us, the order to fire was given. The women
ran towards us the moment they heard the reports of our
guns. In doing this they encountered the Indians behind
them, and three fell pierced by the spears of these savages.
The cry among us now was, "save the women!" Another
young man and myself sprang forward to rescue the remaining two. My companion fell in the attempt. An Indian
had raised his spear, to inflict death upon another of these
unfortunate captives, when he received a shot from one of
our men, that rendered him incapable of another act of
cruelty. The captives, one of whom was a beautiful young
lady, the daughter of the governor . . . , both reached me.
The gratitude of such captives, so delivered, may be imagined. Fears, thanks, and exclamations in Spanish were the
natural expression of feeling in such a position. My companions aided me in wrapping blankets around them, for it
was quite cold; and making the best arrangements in our
power for their comfort and safety . . .

The aftermath of that rescue was thoroughly in key with the
exploit itself, for one of the women fell in love with a young
trapper who was a member of the party that had saved her.
Whether or not that romance ended in marriage does not
appear; however, the gratitude of the governor was such

that not only was the party's fur-trapping license promptly granted them but on Pattie's subsequent visits to the pueblo he received a hero's welcome.

ii

Of the small group who, in the first half of the nineteenth century, wrote from personal knowledge of life in the Far West, none produced a livelier or more readable account of his adventures than did Lewis H. Garrard. Born in Cincinnati in 1829, Garrard was but seventeen when, having had his interest in the area that lay between the Mississippi and the Pacific stirred by a reading of John C. Frémont's report of his 1842-43 expedition, he made his way to St. Louis, intent on joining one of the trading parties that outfitted there before setting forth on the long ordeal of the Santa Fe trail.

In this the youth was successful, for on arriving in the river town he registered at the Planters' House, there made himself known to a fellow guest, Céran St. Vrain (partner in the flourishing Santa Fe trading firm of Bent & St. Vrain), and, in the words of a later commentator, "almost before he knew it," found himself attached to a train of heavily loaded wagons headed west.

During the year that followed, Garrard, a scholarly youth, made notes of what he saw and heard in the strange new environment in which he found himself, and these formed the basis for his book of frontier reminiscences, *Wah-to-Yah and the Taos Trail*, published six years later. That he observed well and reflected on what he saw is amply evident to readers of that volume, which has been several times reprinted. Here is his tribute to the manner of life to be lived on the plains of the Southwest:

This section of the country I have often heard spoken of as uninteresting [he commented]; but to me there were many attractions. Here, with mule and gun, and a few faithful friends, one experiences such a grand sensation of liberty and a total absence of fear; nobody to say what one shall do; costumed as fancy or comfort dictates; one's blanket one's house; the prairie one's home—money he needs not, except to buy coffee, ammunition, and "Touse" [i.e., the Taos brandy]. No conventional rules of society restrict him to any particular form of dress, manner, or speech—he can swear a blue streak, or pray; it is his own affair entirely. Here, too, one soon learns to say nothing, and do less, but for himself, and the greenhorn is often reminded, amid showers of male-dictions, to confine his philanthropic deeds and conversa-tions to his own dear self. I was quite amused by the kindly intentioned remarks of an old mountaineer to me, shortly after my appearance in the country: "If you see a man's mule running off, don't stop it—let it go; it isn't yourn. If his possible sack [bag containing his personal possessions] falls off, don't tell him of it; he'll find it out. At camp, help cook—get wood and water—make yourself active—get your pipe and smoke it—don't ask too many questions, and you'll pass!"

Obviously young Garrard followed that advice, for it is evident that before he had been many weeks on the trail his traveling companions had come to accept him as a true frontiersman. His narrative makes it clear, too, that the old-timers were ever ready to help him learn the ways of the wilderness. Thus, in his account of his first buffalo hunt, he wrote:

The prairie was black with the herds; and a good chance presenting itself I struck spurs to Paint [his brown-and-white pony], directing him toward fourteen or fifteen of the near-est, distant eight or nine hundred yards. We (Paint and I) soon neared them, giving me a flying view of their unwieldy proportions, and when within fifteen feet of the nearest I raised my rifle half way to the face and fired. Reloading, still in hot pursuit (tough work to load on a full run), I followed, though without catching up. One feels a delightfully wild sensation when in pursuit of a band of buffalo, on a fleet horse, with a good rifle and without a hat, the winds playing around the flushed brow, when with hair streaming the rider nears the frightened herd and with a shout of exultation discharges his rifle. I returned to the party highly gratified with my first, though unsuccessful, chase; but Mr. St. Vrain put a slight damper to my ardor by simply remarking——

"The next time you 'run meat' don't let the horse go in a trot and yourself in a gallop" (I had in my eagerness leaned forward in the saddle, and a stumble of the horse would have pitched me over his head); by which well-timed and laconic advice I afterwards profited.

Toward the end of September the travel-worn party reached their first objective, Bent's Fort, and there, in Garrard's words, "We sat down to a table for the first time in fifty days, and ate with knives, forks, and plates."

The Fort [he wrote] is a quadrangular structure of *adobes*, or sun-dried brick. It is thirty feet in height and one hundred feet square; at the north-east corner and its corresponding diagonal are bastions of a hexagonal form in which are a few cannon. The fort walls serve as the back walls to the rooms, which front inward on a courtyard . . . The roofs of the houses are made of poles, and a layer of mud a foot or more thick, with a slight inclination to run off the water. There was a billiard table in a small house on top of the fort where the *bourgeois* and visitors amused themselves; and in the clerk's office, contiguous, a first-rate spy-glass with which

I viewed the *caballada,* coming from the grazing ground
seven miles up the river.

> After many weeks on the road, the party arrived at Taos,
> and there young Garrard became a guest in the house of his
> employer, Céran St. Vrain.

I was ushered into an oblong, handsomely furnished room
[he wrote] with a fireplace in one corner, and the walls
hung with portraits of holy characters, crosses, etc., showing
the prevailing religion; and to furnish additional evidence, a
padre was taking his *congé* as we opened the door. An introduction to Señora St. Vrain—a dark-eyed, languidly handsome woman—followed my appearance. The Mexican mode
of salutation is to meet, and one arm of the gentleman or
lady is thrown around the other's shoulder; then stepping
back one pace, they shake hands, accompanied with the
usual *comme la va.* But I did not understand this most cor-
dial mode of greeting, and when the Señora sidled alongside
in the expectation of the usual embrace, I thought how
strangely she acted, and only extended my hand, saying in
American, "How do you do?" Most assuredly such a fashion
with our ladies would meet with enthusiastic followers.

At supper I sat at table and ate potatoes for the first time
in several months. A fandango was to be held that night, but
declining an invitation to attend, a mattress was unrolled
from the wall, where in daytime it served as a seat, and I
turned in between sheets. Yes! Sheets! For months I had
enveloped myself with blankets, in the open air, pulling off
no clothing but the blue blanket topcoat which with my saddle served as pillow—but now a change came over the spirit
of my dream. A house, table, vegetables, and sheets—to say
nothing of the charming smiles of women and the Taos
aguardiente.

Shortly after lying down, the room filled with gay ladies,

revelling in the excess of paint and flaunting dress, and partaking of the favorite aguardiente by way of support against
the fatigues of the fandango. I looked at them through my
partially closed eyes to notice more closely, without an im-
putation of rudely staring. The musical tone of their voices
uttering their sweet language fell gently on my ear, and as
perception gradually failed, amid a delicious reverie I sank
to sleep.

iii

Throughout Garrard's stay in the Southwest the youth, who,
in the words of a later writer, "had an uncanny trick of being
on hand whenever anything interesting was going on," saw
—and recorded—numerous incidents that took place during
the eventful year 1846. Thus he reached Taos shortly after a
revolt against the American rule of that newly conquered
town had been forcibly put down; not, however, before a
number of officials, including Governor Bent, had been
killed. At the time of Garrard's arrival, the jail was crowded
with prisoners and he was an interested spectator at their
trials.

The courtroom [he wrote] was a small, oblong apartment
dimly lighted by two narrow windows; a thin railing kept the
bystanders from contact with the functionaries. The prisoners faced the judges, and the three witnesses (Señoras
Bent, Boggs, and Carson) were close to them on a bench by
the wall. When Mrs. Bent gave in her testimony, the eyes of
the culprits were fixed sternly upon her; on pointing out the
Indian who killed the Governor, not a muscle of the chief's
face twitched or betrayed agitation, though he was aware
her evidence unmistakably sealed his death warrant—he sat

with lips gently closed, eyes earnestly centered on her, without a show of malice or hatred—an almost sublime spectacle
of Indian fortitude and of the severe mastery to which the
emotions can be subjected. Truly, it was a noble example
of Indian stoicism.

> Six of the prisoners were sentenced to death by hanging; a
> gallows was erected at the edge of the town and a throng
> of residents, among them Garrard, gathered to witness the
> executions.

The word was passed at last that the criminals were coming
[stated he]. Eighteen soldiers received them at the gate with
their muskets at port arms—the six abreast, with the sheriff on
the right—nine soldiers on each side . . . The poor pelados
marched slowly with downcast eyes, arms tied behind, and
bare heads, with the exception of white cotton caps stuck on
the back part, to be pulled over the face as the last ceremony . . .

When within fifteen paces of the gallows the sideguard,
filing off to the right and left, formed at regular distances
from each other three sides of the hollow square; the mountaineers and myself composed the fourth and front side in
full view of the trembling prisoners, who marched up to the
tree under which was a government wagon with two mules
attached. The driver and sheriff assisted them in, ranging
them on a board placed across the hinder end . . . The
gallows was so narrow they touched. The ropes by reason
of size and stiffness, despite the soaping given them, were
adjusted with difficulty; but through the indefatigable efforts
of the sheriff and the lieutenant all preliminaries were arranged . . .

Bidding each other "adois" with a hope of meeting in
heaven, at a word from the sheriff the mules were started
and the wagon drawn from under the tree. No fall was given,

and their feet remained on the board till the ropes drew
taut . . . After forty minutes of suspension, Col. Willock
ordered his command to quarters . . .

> Throughout his entire stay in the West, Garrard had an
> abiding interest in the Indians of the plains and mountains,
> and missed few opportunities to gain at first hand a knowl-
> edge of their beliefs, customs, and way of life. Thus soon
> after his arrival at Bent's Fort, he made the acquaintance
> of John S. Smith, who had married a woman of the Chey-
> enne tribe, and accompanied Smith on a trading visit to a
> Cheyenne village. Starting on the evening of November 8,
> and riding most of the following day, they at length ap-
> proached their destination.

Toward evening [wrote he] Smith pointed out some objects,
inquiring of me what they were, but I could not guess aright.
"That's the village," said he. Mountain men can distinguish
objects which to a novice . . . have no tangible form or
size. By sundown we were at the lodges, whose conical shape
and dusky yellow hue looked oddly but welcome to our tired
eyes and limbs.

It is Indian rule that the first lodge that a stranger enters
on visiting a village is his home during his stay—whether invited or not it is all the same—and as we wished to be at the
"Lean Chief's," we inquired for him. Without saying a word,
or going in the lodge first, we unsaddled in front of it, putting our "possibles" in the back part, the most honored and
pleasant place, for there is no passing by or other annoyance.

The owner occupies the back of the lodge, which is given
up for a guest, and the Lean Chief's squaw and daughters
removed his robes, etc., to one side. The women and children
crowded around us while unsaddling; the strange dress and
appearance of the boys attracted my attention; which latter
from their infancy to the age of six or seven go without a

particle of clothing . . . a string of beads around the neck . . .

The white man is always welcome with the Cheyenne, as he generally has *mok-ta-bo, mah-pe*—coffee. We went in the lodge; the grave-looking head, *Vip-po-na,* or the Lean Chief, and his two solemn coadjutors, shook hands with us with the salutation of, *Hook-ah-hay! num-whit!*—equivalent to *Welcome, how do you do;* and then relapsed into silence. Water was handed us to drink, as they suppose a traveler must be thirsty after riding; then meat was set before us, as they think a tired man needs refreshment. When we had finished, the pipe was passed around, during which soothing pastime the news was asked . . .

We made known our business and immediately a "crier" was sent out. Throwing back the skin door of the lodge, he protruded his head and then his whole body, and uttered in stentorian voice something . . . meaning . . . that "Blackfoot (Smith), had come for mules; and all who wished to come and trade; that we had tobacco, blue blankets, black (deep blue) blankets, white blankets, knives, and beads."

It is contrary to Indian *medicine* or religion to pass between the landlord (owner of the lodge) and the fire, for they say it dissolves friendship, and any infringement of this custom is looked upon with displeasure . . .

iv

Another engaging picture of the domestic arrangements of the Indians of the Southwest is presented by an early traveler named George D. Brewerton, who, in 1848, made a journey eastward from the Pueblo of Los Angeles. Passing over that historic route, his party spent several days at a settlement of the Eutaw Indians, one of the chiefs of which,

Wacarra—or, as Brewerton called him, Walker—showed
many evidences of friendliness and hospitality.

Before leaving this encampment [wrote Brewerton] I was
invited by Walker to visit his lodge, and accompanied him
accordingly. These lodges are made of skins sewed together,
with an opening in the top which serves as a chimney for the
smoke, the fire being built on the ground in the centre of the
lodge. Upon entering the lodge the children crowded round
me, admiring the gaudy scarlet cloth with which my leathern
hunting-short was lined; most of these young people were
armed with small bows and arrows which they amused themselves by aiming at me. Walker's wife, or wives, for I think he
had several, were busied in their domestic avocations about
the lodge, and one of them (a good-looking squaw of some
eighteen or twenty years, who seemed to be the favorite) was
kind enough to spread a deer-skin for my accommodation.
Wishing to repay her courtesy, I called my servant Juan,
and directed him to get a brass breast-plate with the letters
"U.S." conspicuously displayed, which I had among my
traps, polish it up, and bring it to me. This he did, and I shall
never forget the joy of this belle of the wilderness upon
receiving the shining metal. With the aid of a small mirror,
which had probably been obtained from some passing
trader, she arranged the breast-plate (fully two inches
square) upon her raven locks, and then, with the air of a
tragedy queen, marched up and down in front of the lodge,
looking with great contempt upon her envious companions.
It was certainly an amusing scene, and goes to prove that
vanity may exist as strongly in the character of a Eutaw
squaw as in the breast of a city belle; with this difference
perhaps, that it is exhibited with much less taste among
those whose education should have taught them better
things. . . .

His [that is, "Walker's"] encampment consisted of four

lodges, inhabited by his wives, children, and a suite of inferior warriors and chiefs. This party was awaiting the coming of the great Spanish caravan, from whom they intended
taking the yearly tribute which the tribe extracts as the price
of safe-conduct through their country. I found a vast difference in all respects between these Indians and the miserable beings whom we had hitherto seen. The Eutaws are
perhaps the most powerful and warlike tribe now remaining
on this continent. They appear well provided with fire-
arms, which they are said to use with the precision of veteran riflemen. I remember they expressed their surprise
that the white men should use so much powder in firing at
a mark, while to them every load brought a piece of game or
the scalp of an enemy. Walker . . . received our party very
graciously; in fact their attentions, so far at least as my humble self was concerned, became rather overpowering . . .

That in their dealings with their white guests the Eutaw
braves were uncommonly shrewd bargainers was made
clear to Brewerton by an incident which he related thus:

The reader will probably remember my description of the
horse which I purchased in California . . . I had found him
so worthless upon the road that he had scarcely been ridden;
and now the sharp stones of the desert had injured his hoofs
so seriously that I knew it would be impossible to bring him
over the rugged country which remained to be crossed. Accordingly, I had the miserable beast duly paraded . . . ,
and proceeded, by means of signs and the few words of
Eutaw which I had learned, to open a treaty for his exchange. My Indian friends, after carefully examining the
animal, sent a boy for the horse which they wished to give
for him. Pending the return of their messenger, they employed the time in destroying what little of good character
my steed had ever possessed, shook their heads despond-

ently over his battered hoofs, and grunted in token of their strong disapprobation.

The perfection of horse-flesh (which, alas, was soon to come into my stock), now made his appearance in the shape of a rough-looking Indian pony, which might have been twenty years of age or upward; his Eutaw groom led him by a hair rope, which he had twisted round his nose; but upon a signal from the chief the lad scrambled upon the animal's back, and began putting the old veteran through his paces, which seemed limited to a one-sided walk, and a gallop which would have done credit to a wounded buffalo bull. As a last inducement they exhibited his hoofs, which certainly looked *hard* enough, in all conscience. After considerable hesitation I was about making the trade upon equal terms, when to my great disgust the chief informed me that he could not think of parting with so valuable an animal, unless I gave him some present to boot. This new demand I was fain to comply with, and parted not only with my broken down horse, but with one of my two Mexican blankets; and many was the time while chilled by the cold breezes of the Rocky Mountains that I thought, with a shiver, of my horse-trade . . .

v

Brewerton, a lieutenant in the U.S. Navy, had left San Francisco early in 1848 for the pueblo of Los Angeles, at which place he had joined an overland party led by Kit Carson and set off on the long trek over mountains and deserts that constituted the first leg of the journey to the East Coast. Some five years later he wrote a colorful account of that ride and of the party's frontier-wise leader,

the redoubtable Kit. From that narrative the following excerpts are taken:

It was finally determined [recalled he] that we should take
the road upon the 4th of May; and having procured four
stout mules, already experienced in mountain travel, from
the Quartermaster of Los Angeles (two for riding, and the
same number to pack my baggage and provisions), I purchased, after much bargaining . . . two additional mules
and one horse . . . Having thus got together seven animals
I concluded that so far as horse-flesh was concerned I should
do well enough; but where to procure a proper servant, or
arriero as they are called in Mexico, to pack my mules, and
take charge of the cooking, was a problem which seemed
more than difficult to solve; at last, just as I was beginning to
despair, fortune appeared to favor me, and a Mexican presented himself as a candidate for the office of cook, muleteer,
and man of all work . . .

On the second of May we broke up our camp on the Creek
and returned to Los Angeles from which point we purposed
starting on the morning of the fourth. In the interval we
employed ourselves in making final preparations; drawing
rations and ammunitions for our men, and dividing our provisions into bags of equal size and weight for the greater convenience of packing . . .

It was fully ten o'clock before our party finally got off. We
numbered twenty hired men, three citizens, and three Mexican servants, besides Carson and myself, all well mounted
and armed for the most part with "Whitney's rifle," a weapon
which I cannot too strongly recommend for every description of frontier service . . .

The order of our march, unless altered by circumstances,
or some peculiar feature of the ground, was as follows. Kit
and myself, with one or more of our party came first, then followed in the rear the remainder of our men, who urged the

mules forward by loud cries and an occasional blow from the
ends of their lariats. Our saddles were of the true Mexican
pattern, wooden trees covered with leathers, called *macheers*.
This saddle for service I found superior to those of American
make, being both easier and safer, the great depth of the
seat rendering it almost impossible for the animal to dislodge
his rider . . . Our bridles, formed of twisted hide or horse
hair, were ornamented with pieces of copper, and furnished
with strong Spanish bits. As for our spurs, they were sharp
and heavy . . .

To finish the details of our equipments, I will describe my
own costume as a fair sample of the style of dress which we
wore. I was attired in a check or "hickory" short as they are
called, a pair of buck-skin pants, a fringed hunting shirt of
the same material, gayly lined with red flannel and ornamented with brass buttons (which last I afterwards found
useful in trading with the Indians). As for my head gear,
my hat . . . was a broad-brimmed straw of very ordinary
texture. To go to the other extremity, my feet were cased in
a pair of strong cowhide boots, which reached almost to the
knee. Among my list of sundries I must not forget my water
flask . . . a bottle made of porous leather which . . . suffered so much of the liquid to soak through as was requisite
to keep the outside constantly wet, so that whenever I desired cool water I had only to hang up my flask, or expose it
to a free current of air.

During the first part of the journey their route followed the
old Spanish trail linking California and New Mexico over
which, in the days before the American Conquest, groups
bearing blankets and other goods fabricated in Santa Fe
made their way to the settlements along the coast and, on
their return, drove before them herds of horses and mules,
which found a ready market in the New Mexican capital.
One such caravan had left Los Angeles several days in ad-

vance of Brewerton's party. This, stated he, was "a circumstance which did us great injury, as their large *caballada* (containing nearly a thousand head) ate up or destroyed the grass and consumed the water at the few camping grounds upon the route."

We finally overtook and passed this party [he continued] after about eight days' travel in the Desert. Their appearance was grotesque in the extreme. Imagine upward of two hundred Mexicans dressed in every variety of costume, from the embroidered jacket of the wealthy Californian, with its silver bell-shaped buttons, to the scanty habiliments of the skin-clad Indian. Their *caballada* contained not only horses and mules, but here and there a stray *burro* (Mexican jackass) destined to pack wood across the rugged hills of New Mexico. The line of march of this strange cavalcade occupied an extent of more than a mile; and I could not help thinking, while observing their arms and equipments, that a few resolute men might have captured their property, and driven the traders like a flock of sheep. Many of these people had no fire-arms, being only provided with the short bow and arrow usually carried by New Mexican herdsmen . . .

Near this motley crowd we sojourned for one night; and passing through their camp after dark, I was struck by its picturesque appearance. Their pack-saddles and bales had been taken off and carefully piled, so as not only to protect them from the damp, but to form a sort of barricade or fort for their owner. From one side to the other of these little corrals of goods a Mexican blanket was stretched, under which the trader lay smoking his cigarrito, while his Mexican servant or slave—for they are little better—prepared his coffee and "atole." . . .

Our daily routine of life in the desert had a sort of terrible sameness about it; we rode from fifteen to fifty miles a day, according to the distance from water; occasionally after a long drive halting for twenty-four hours, if the scanty grass near the camping grounds would permit it, to rest and recruit our weary cattle; among our men there was little talking and less laughing and joking, even by the camp-fire while traversing these dreary wastes; the gloomy land by which we were surrounded, scanty food, hard travel, and the consciousness of continual peril, all tended to restrain the exhibition of animal spirits.

Carson, while traveling, scarcely spoke; his keen eye was continually examining the country, and his whole manner was that of a man deeply impressed with a sense of responsibility. We ate but twice a day, and then our food was so coarse and scanty that it was not a pleasure but a necessity. At night every care was taken to prevent surprise; the men took turns in guarding the animals, while our own mess formed the camp guard of the party. In an Indian country it is worthy of remembrance that a mule is by far the best sentry; they discover either by their keen sense of smell, or of vision, the vicinity of the lurking savage long before the mountaineer, experienced as he is, can perceive him. If thus alarmed, the mule shows its uneasiness by snorting and extending the head and ears toward the object of distrust.

During this journey I often watched with great curiosity Carson's preparations for the night. A braver man than Kit perhaps never lived, in fact I doubt if he ever knew what fear was, but with all this he exercised great caution. While arranging his bed, his saddle, which he always used as a pillow, was disposed in such manner as to form a barricade for his head; his pistols, half cocked, were laid above it, and his trusty rifle reposed beneath the blanket by his side, where it was not only ready for instant use, but perfectly protected from the damp. Except now and then to light his pipe, you never caught Kit exposing himself to the full glare of the camp fire. He knew too well the treacherous character of the tribes among whom we were traveling; he had seen men killed at night by an unseen foe, who, veiled in darkness, stood in perfect security while he marked and shot down the mountaineer clearly seen by the fire-light. "No, no, boys," Kit would say, "hang around the fire if you will, it may do for you if you like it, but I don't want to have a Digger slip an arrow into me, when I can't see him."

The routine of life on the early Western trails is well depicted in Brewerton's narrative. Here is his description of how the party got under way mornings:

When the hour for our departure from camp had nearly arrived, Kit would rise from his blanket and cry "Catch up"; two words which in mountain parlance mean, Prepare to start; and these words once uttered, the sooner a man got ready the better; in a moment the whole scene would be changed, the men who just before were lounging about the fires . . . were now upon their feet, and actively employed in bringing up refractory mules, who, due to their obstinate nature, . . . declined any forward movement except under compulsion. This generally called forth a volley of oaths . . . until at length the loads were fairly secured, saddles put on, and the pack-mules, having been gathered together, started upon the trail; the old bell-mare leading off with a gravity quite equal to the responsibility of her office. Kit waited for nobody; and woe to the unfortunate tyro in mountain travel who discovered to his sorrow that packs would work loose, bags fall off, and mules show an utter disregard for the preservation of one's personal property. A man thus circumstanced soon learns to pack his mule as it should be done, put on his saddle as it ought to be put on, and keep his arms in serviceable order; or if he doesn't, Heaven help him; the sooner he gets back to the settlements the better.

In that arid Southwest country the perils of the road included not only hostile Indians but frequently a lack of grass
and water to sustain the animals.

In crossing the desert [wrote Brewerton] it was often necessary to march long distances without water; these dry
stretches were called by the Mexicans "jornadas" . . . On
this "jornada" . . . the distance from one water hole to another cannot be less than eighty miles; and on account of the
animals it is highly important that it should be traveled
at once; to accomplish this we started about three o'clock in
the afternoon and reached the other side of the "jornada"
late in the morning of the following day, the greater part of
the distance being gone over by moonlight. I shall never forget the impression which that night's journey left upon my
mind. Sometimes the trail led us over large basins of deep
sand, where the tramping of mules' feet gave forth no sound;
this added to the almost terrible silence, which ever
reigns in the solitude of the desert, rendered our transit more
like the passage of some airy spectacle where the actors
were shadows instead of men. Nor is this comparison a con-
strained one, for our way-worn voyagers with their tangled
locks and unshorn beards (rendered white as snow by
the fine sand), had a weird and ghost-like look, which the
gloomy scene around, with its frowning rocks and moonlit
sands, tended to enhance and heighten.

vii

Not the least of the dangers faced by those who ventured
westward into the unknown during pioneer days was, of
course, that posed by hostile Indians. Moreover, the annals
of the period made it clear that this peril was an ever-

present one, for few of the narratives of the trail-breakers fail to make reference to brushes with the savages. Although in most cases such attacks were beaten off—usually with but minor casualties on the part of the whites—not always were they so fortunate.

One of the most dramatic of such frontier tragedies was that which befell the Oatmans. This family, numbering nine in all, left Independence, Missouri, in the summer of 1850 as members of a group of Mormons who planned to found a colony in the southeast corner of California. During the journey, dissension arose and the party divided, some following the established trail to Santa Fe, and the others taking a somewhat more northerly route. The Oatman family was in the latter group, and presently, growing impatient at their slow progress, Royce Oatman, his wife, and seven children pushed on ahead. Shortly thereafter they were set on by a band of Apaches, and six of their number slain. One, a teen-aged youth, though badly wounded and left for dead, later recovered and made his escape; and two of the younger girls were taken into captivity. The youngest, Mary Ann, who was but eight at the time of her capture, died two years later. The other, however, fourteen-year-old Olive, remained a chattel of the savages until released after five years of bondage.

Olive's account of her experiences, first published in 1857, graphically describes her life as a prisoner, first of the Apaches, then of the Mohaves. The arrival of the girls at a village of their captors is thus depicted:

On the third day, we came suddenly in sight of a cluster of low, thatched huts, each having an opening near the ground leading into it . . . To two young girls, having traveled on foot two hundred miles in three days; with swollen feet and limbs, lame, exhausted, not yet four days removed from the loss of parents, brothers and sisters . . . the sight of the dwelling places of man, however coarse and unseemly, was no very unwelcome scene. With all the dread possibilities, therefore, that might await them at any moment, nevertheless to get even into an Indian camp was home.

We were soon ushered into camp, amidst shouts and song, wild dancing, and crudest music . . . that ever delighted the ear of unrestrained superstition. We soon saw that these bravadoes had made themselves great men at home. They had made themselves a name by the exploits of the past week . . . That night was nearly all consumed in hallooing, singing, and uproarious dancing over the triumph that had been achieved, the spoils taken . . . They stationed their captives upon an elevated position in the center of a circle, and danced around them in the wildest manner . . .

The Apaches were without any settled habits of industry. They tilled not. It was a marvel to see how little was required to keep them alive; yet they were capable of the greatest endurance . . . Their women were the laborers, the principal burden-bearers, and during all our captivity it was our lot to serve under these enslaved women . . . They invented modes and seemed to create necessities of labor that they might gratify themselves by taxing us to the utmost, and even took unwarranted delight in whipping us on beyond our strength . . . and those days of toil were wrung out of us at the insistence of children, younger than ourselves, who were set as our task-masters . . .

For some time after coming among them, Mary Ann was very ill . . . She would often say to me—"Olive, I must starve unless I can get something more to eat"; yet it was only when she was utterly disabled that they would allow her a respite from some daily menial service. We have taken the time often which was given to gather roots for our lazy captives, to gather and eat ourselves; and had it not been for supplies obtained by such means, we must have perished.

But the physical sufferings of this state were light when com-
pared with the fear and anguish of the mind . . .

After we had been among the Apaches several months,
their conduct towards us somewhat changed. They became
more lenient and merciful, especially to my sister. She always met their abuse with a mild, patient spirit and deportment, and with an intrepidity and fortitude beyond what
might have been expected from her age. This spirit, I could
plainly see, was working its effect upon some of them; so that,
especially on the part of those females connected in some
way with the household of the chief, who had principal control of us, we could plainly see more forebearance, kindness
and interest . . . We had learned their language so as to
hold converse with them quite understandingly, after a few
months . . . They would gather about us frequently in
large numbers, and ply their curious questions with eagerness . . . They wanted to know how women were treated,
and if a man was allowed more than one wife . . .

They had great contempt for one who would complain
under torture or suffering, even though of their own tribe,
and said a person who could not uncomplainingly endure
suffering, was not fit to live. They asked us if we wanted to
get away, and tried by every stratagem to extort from us our
feelings as to our captivity; but we were not long in learning
that any expression of discontent was a signal for new toils,
and tasks and grievances. We made the resolution between
us to avoid any expression of discontent, which at times cost
us no small effort to keep.

> After a year as captives of the Apaches, the girls were sold
> to the chief of a group belonging to a neighboring tribe,
> the Mohaves. The price paid, stated Olive, was "two horses,
> a few vegetables, a few pounds of beads, and three blan-
> kets." Her narrative continues thus:

We were informed at the outset that we had three hundred and fifty miles before us, and all to be made on foot. Our route we soon found to be in no way preferable to the one by which the Apache village had been reached . . . We had not proceeded far ere it was painfully impressed upon our feet, if not our aching hearts, that this trail to a second captivity was no improvement on the first, whatever might be the fate awaiting us at its termination . . . Our feet soon became sore and we were unable, on the second day . . . , to keep up with their rapid pace. A small piece of meat was put into our hands on starting, and this, with the roots we were allowed to dig, and these but few, was our sole sustenance for ten days.

After much complaining, and some threatening from our new captors, we were allowed to rest on the second day a short time. After this we were not compelled to go more than thirty-five miles any one day, and pieces of skin were furnished for our feet, but not until they had been needlessly bruised and mangled without them. The nights were cold, and contrary to our expectations, the daughter of the chief showed us kindness throughout the journey by sharing her blankets with us . . .

On the eleventh day, about two hours before sunset, we made a bold, steep descent . . . from which we had an extensive view on either side. Before us, commencing a little from the foot of our declivity, lay a narrow valley covered with a carpet of green, stretching a distance, seemingly, of twenty miles . . . Very soon there came into the field of our view a large number of huts, clothing the valley in every direction. We could plainly see a large cluster of these huts huddled into a nook in the hills on our right and on the bank of a river . . .

We were soon ushered into the "Mohave Valley," . . . and were conducted immediately to the home of the chief . . . The chief's house was on a beautiful . . . elevation crowning the river bank, from which the eye could sweep a large section of the valley, and survey the entire village, a portion of which lined each bank of the stream.

Although the captives found their new surroundings more attractive than the old, this change of masters did not noticeably improve their lot. Olive's narrative continues thus:

In a few days they began to direct us to work in various ways, such as bringing wood and water, and to perform errands . . . We soon learned that our condition was still that of unmitigated slavery, not to the adults merely, but to the children, [who] soon learned to drive us about with all the authority of an eastern lord . . .

We spent most of this summer in hard work. We were for a long time aroused at break of day, baskets were swung upon our shoulders, and we were obliged to go from six to eight miles for the "Musquite," a seed or berry growing upon a bush about the size of our "Manzanita." We spent from twilight to twilight in gathering this. And often we found it impossible, from the scarcity that year, to fill our basket in a day, as we were required; and for failing to do this we seldom escaped a chastisement . . . I could myself endure the daily task assigned me, but to see the demands and exactions made upon little Mary Ann, when her constitution was already broken down, . . . was a more severe trial than all I had to perform of physical labor . . .

After the younger girl's death—mainly, according to her sister, for lack of nourishment during a period of severe food shortages—life went on much the same for Olive. As time passed, the hope of escape or rescue that had long sustained her gradually died away and she came to accept her lot uncomplainingly. Toward the end of her second year of captivity she, as she later wrote . . .

. . . saw but little reason to expect anything else than the spending of all my years among them . . . I saw around me none but savages, and (dreadful as was the thought) among whom I must spend my days. There were some with whom I had become intimately acquainted, and from whom I had received humane and friendly treatment, exhibiting real kindness. I thought it best now to conciliate the best wishes of all, and by every possible means to avoid all occasions for awakening their displeasure . . . I thought it best to receive my daily allotment with submission, and not darken it with a borrowed trouble . . . [Thereafter] time seemed to take a more rapid flight; I hardly could wake up to the reality of so long a captivity among savages, and really imagined myself happy for short periods.

> The first intimation that her deliverance, after more than five years of bondage, might be near, came to her toward the middle of February, 1856:

One day as I was grinding musquite near the door of our dwelling [she recalled], a lad came running up to me in haste and said that Francisco, a Yuma crier, was on his way to the Mohaves, and that he was coming to try to get me away to the whites. The report caused a momentary, strange sensation, but I thought it probably was a rumor gotten up by these idlers (as they were wont to do) merely to deceive and excite me to their own gratification. In a few moments, however, . . . one of the sub-chiefs came in and said that a Yuma Indian, named Francisco, was on his way with positive orders for my immediate release and safe return . . .

> The messenger duly arrived, bringing with him a letter, signed by Lieutenant Colonel Martin Burke, in command of the army post at Fort Yuma, far to the south. The letter read thus:

Francisco, Yuma Indian, bearer of this, goes to the Mohave
Nation to obtain a white woman there, named Olivia. It is
desirable that she should come to this post, or send her rea-
sons why she does not wish to come.

Upon the arrival of Francisco, the braves of the tribe were
called into counsel, whereupon there followed hours of debate as to whether or not their captive should be released.
Olive was presently summoned to the meeting and thus
described the scene:

I found that they had been representing to Francisco that I
did not wish to go to the whites. As soon as they thought they
had the contents of the letter, there was a breaking out of
scores of voices at once, and our chief found it a troublesome
meeting to preside over. Some advised that I should be
killed, and that Francisco should report that I was dead.
Others that they at once refuse to let me go, and that the
whites could not hurt them. Others were in favor of letting
me go at once. It was not until day-light that one could judge
which counsel would prevail.

In the end the decision was to release her, and Francisco
triumphantly conveyed her to Fort Yuma. There she was
presently joined by her surviving brother Loranzo—who had
long busied himself trying to learn what fate had befallen
his sister. The reunited pair settled at first in Oregon, then
in San Francisco. Olive lived some twenty years after her
deliverance, dying in the mid-1870's.

vii

When, late in 1863, J. Ross Browne, veteran journalist and
globe-trotter, found himself in San Francisco, circumstances

arose that made it possible for him to join a congenial companion on a tour of the Southwest, a visit that resulted in one of the most readable of his books, *Adventures in the Apache Country,* published some years later. Browne's decision to make this journey was, as he himself stated, arrived at on the spur of the moment. "Although it was my intention to visit Arizona some time or other," he wrote, ". . . I had no more idea on Saturday morning, December 5, 1863, of starting on such an important expedition at 4 P.M. of the same day, than I had of going on a prospecting tour through the Mountains of the Moon."

The circumstance that brought about his abrupt change of plans was the meeting on a San Francisco street of an old friend, Charles D. Poston, recently appointed Superintendent of Indian Affairs in Arizona Territory, who was sailing that afternoon to take up his duties. Browne readily agreed to accompany him.

There was no trouble about getting ready [wrote he]. A knapsack, as usual, was my only baggage. The contents were soon packed; a few coarse shirts, a box of pencils and paints, a meerschaum and a plug of tobacco, these were the indispensable parts of my outfit. At 4 P.M. I stood upon the deck of the good steamer *Senator,* fully equipped and prepared for the important enterprise on hand. Poston was true to time. We were favored with the company of Mr. Ammi White, an Indian agent and trader, on his return to the Pimo villages, and two of his wards, Antonio Azul, chief of the Pimos, and Francisco, the interpreter.

The party disembarked at San Pablo, proceeded inland to Los Angeles, where several days were consumed laying in supplies, including firearms, ammunition, clothing, tobacco, cigars, pipes, penknives, pencils, medicines, plus "an abundant supply of coffee, sugar, flour, and beans . . ."

In due time [Browne continued] the outfit was completed. We had everything above specified, and a great many things more, including a guard of five soldiers and a sergeant to fight for us, if necessary, on the way over to Fort Yuma. Our baggage-wagon was filled to the utmost limit of its capacity, and even then our little ambulance and four mules groaned under their precious loads.

Much of the country traversed on the long trek to Fort Yuma was semi-desert. Browne described it thus:

Barren hills of gravel and sand-stone, flung up at random out of the earth, strange jagged mountain-peaks in the distance; yellow banks serrated by floods; sea-shells glittering in the wavy sand-fields that lie between; these overhung by a rich, glowing atmosphere, with glimpses of Indian smokes far off in the horizon, inspired us with a vague feeling of the wonders and characteristic features of the region . . . I could not but think of the brave old Spaniards and their heroic explorations across the Colorado. Here was a glowing and mystic land of sunshine and burning sands, where human enterprise had in centuries past battled with hunger and thirst and savage races; where the silence of utter desolation now reigned supreme. There was a peculiar charm to me in the rich atmospheric tints that hung over this strange land, and the boundless wastes that lay outstretched before us, and I drank in with an almost childish delight the delicate and exquisite odors that filled the air, and thought of my early wanderings, long years past, amid the deserts and palms of Araby the Blest . . .

The face of the country, for the most part, is well covered with mesquite trees, sage bushes, grease-wood, weeds, and cactus. Mountains are in sight all the way across, and the old stage-houses of the Overland Mail Company still stand by the watering-places. Many indications of the dreadful sufferings of emigrant parties and drovers still mark the road; the wrecks of wagons half covered in the drifting sands, skeletons of horses and mules, and the skulls and bones of many a herd of cattle that perished by thirst on the way, or fell victims to the terrible sand-storms that sweep the desert . . .

> Twelve days of dawn-to-dusk travel brought the party to the banks of the Colorado and their first stopping place, Fort Yuma. Browne's account continues:

As soon as we had refreshed ourselves with the customary appliances of civilization at frontier posts—lemonade, if you please—we sallied forth to enjoy a view of the fort and the surrounding country from the opposite side of the river . . .

The fort stands on an elevated bluff, commanding the adjacent country for many miles around, and presents an exceedingly picturesque view with its neat quarters, storehouses, and winding roads. It was with emotions of national pride that we gazed upon the glorious flag of our Union as it swelled out to the evening breeze from the flag-staff that towered above the bluff; and we felt that, so long as that emblem of our liberty floated, there was hope for the future of Colorado and Arizona . . .

Christmas Day came, and with it some natural longings for home and the familiar faces of the family circle. Yet we were not so badly off as one might suppose in this region of drought and desert. Colonel Bennet and his amiable wife got up an excellent dinner at the fort; and in the evening we had a *báile*, or Spanish dance, at which there were several very dusky belles of the Sonoranian race. Unfortunately two Jesuit Padres, attached to the Arizona command, had previously secured the attention of the principal Senoritas in the neighborhood; and what with baptizing and marrying and confessing, it was difficult to get up a quorum at the dance. However, there were plenty of officers, and what the ladies lacked in number they made up in spirit. The fiddlers scraped with an inspiring vim; whisky flowed, and egg-shells, containing dust and gilt-paper, were broken in the true Spanish style upon the heads of the handsome gallants.

Most feared of the Indian tribes of the region, and indeed among the most warlike in the entire nation, were the Apaches, of whose treacherous attacks both on the whites and on their fellow redskins Browne had heard much before setting off. Nor, as he speedily discovered, were the tales of their ferocity exaggerated, for everywhere he saw evidences of the destruction wrought by their raids. Here is his description of one such spot, that of the Santa Cruz Valley, which he termed "one of the richest and most beautiful grazing and agricultural regions I have ever seen."

Three years ago [he wrote] this beautiful valley was well settled by an enterprising set of frontiersmen as far up as the Calabasas ranch, fifteen miles beyond Tubac . . . When the Overland Stage Line was withdrawn . . . the Apaches, supposing they had created a panic among the whites, became more bold and vigorous in their forays than ever. Ranch after ranch was desolated by fire, robbery and murder. No white man's life was secure beyond Tucson; and even there the few inhabitants lived in a state of terror.

I saw on the road between San Xavier and Tubac, a distance of forty miles, almost as many graves of the white men murdered by the Apaches within the past few years. Literally the road-side was marked with the burial-places of these unfortunate settlers. There is not now a single living soul to enliven the solitude. All is silent and death-like; yet strangely calm and beautiful in its desolation. Here were fields with torn-down fences; houses burned or racked to pieces by violence, the walls cast about in heaps over the once-pleasant homes; everywhere ruin, grim and ghastly with associations of sudden death. I have rarely travelled through a country more richly favored, yet more depressing in its associations with the past. Day and night the common subject of conversation was murder; and wherever our attention was attracted by the beauty of the scenery or the richness of the soil a stone-covered grave marked the foreground.

> Browne found Arizona a land of contradictions. At the end of his weeks-long visit he summed up his impressions thus:

No country that I have yet visited presented so many striking anomalies . . . With millions of acres of the finest arable lands, there was not at the time of our visit a single farm under cultivation in the Territory; with the richest gold and silver mines, paper-money is the common currency; with forts innumerable, there is scarcely any protection to life and property; with extensive pastures, there is little or no stock; with the finest natural roads, travelling is beset with difficulties; with rivers through every valley, a stranger may die of thirst. Hay is cut with a hoe, and wood with a spade or mattock. In January one enjoys the luxury of a bath as under a tropical sun, and sleeps under double blankets at night. There are towns without inhabitants, and deserts extensively populated; vegetation where there is no soil, and soil where there is no vegetation. Snow is seen where it is never seen to fall, and ice forms where it never snows. There are Indians the most docile in North America, yet travellers are murdered daily by Indians the most barbarous on earth. The Mexicans have driven the Papagos from their southern homes, and now seek protection from the Apaches in the Papago villages. Fifteen hundred Apache warriors, the most cowardly of the Indian tribes in Arizona, beaten in every fight by the Pimos, Maricopas, and Papagos, keep these and all other Indians closed up in a corral; and the same Apaches have desolated a country inhabited by 120,000 Mexicans.

Mines without miners and forts without soldiers are common.
Politicians without policy, traders without trade, store-
keepers without stores, teamsters without teams, and all without means, form the mass of the white population . . .

Thus Arizona in transition, as it appeared to an experienced
observer during the winter of 1863-64.

viii

It was, of course, the lure of precious metals that drew tens
of thousands westward during the early days and brought
about the settlement of many parts of the country far earlier
than would otherwise have been the case. The most notable
instance of this was the California gold rush of 1849 and the
early 1850's. That, however, was by no means the only such
movement. Indeed, throughout the next half century there
was a series of rushes—to such widely separated places as
New Mexico, Colorado, Idaho, and numerous points in between. One of the most spectacular of these followed the
finding of large quantities of silver on the slopes of Sun
Mountain in western Nevada. This was the famed Comstock
Lode, generally credited with having been the nation's
richest mining strike.

The story of the discovery of the lode is full of ironies. As
early as 1849 emigrant parties bound for California found
traces of gold in the streams flowing into the Carson River,
but the yield was small and all but a few pressed on to the
diggings in the Sierra foothills. Throughout the next decade
Gold Canyon and Six Mile Creek—spots that were soon to
astonish the world by their richness—were known as "poor
men's diggings," the working of which, in the words of
one writer, "gave up a meagre living to a succession of

prospectors too unenterprising to move on to more lucrative
diggings."

All these were gold miners, and in their quest for that
metal they were handicapped by an abundance of a heavy,
bluish sand that clogged their rockers and which they im-
patiently shoveled aside. Not until the summer of 1859 were
samples of this troublesome "blue stuff" sent across the
mountains for analysis. It proved to be an exceedingly rich
silver sulphide, mixed with gold; the specimen examined
assayed close to four thousand dollars a ton!

The lode was named for H. T. P. Comstock, a picturesque
character who was one of the first group to stake out a claim
in the vicinity. None of this group shared in the great fortunes that were presently made there. Years later "Old
Pancake"—as Comstock was known during the early days—
wrote a letter to a St. Louis newspaper relating what purported to be "the true story" of the bonanza's beginnings.
While its writer was not in all respects a reliable historian,
the tale he told was an interesting one, as the following
excerpts will show.

The first discovery of the Comstock Lode was made in this
way [he wrote]: In the middle of January, 1859, I saw some
queer-looking stuff in a gopher hole; I ran my hand in and
took out a handful of dirt and saw silver and gold in it.
At that time John Bishop and Old Virginia [the name by
which another old-timer, James Finney, was known] were
with me; they were sitting upon the side of a hill, Gold
Hill, a couple of hundred yards from me . . . We started
rocking with my water; had only a small quantity to rock
with. We made from five to ten and twelve pounds a day,
and the dust was from $9 to $12 an ounce—sent that at
Brewster's Bank, Placerville, California, where I did my
business.

The most important of the settlements that sprang up on the Lode was Virginia City; here is "Old Pancake's" version of how it acquired its name:

Virginia City was first called Silver City. I named it at the time I gave the Ophir claim its name. Old Virginia and the other boys got on a drunk one night there, and Old Virginia fell down and broke his bottle, and when he got up he said he baptised that ground Virginia—hence Virginia City—and that is the way it got its name. At that time there were a few tents, a few little huts, and a grog-shop; that was all there was. I was camped under a cedar-tree at that time—I and my party.

During the two decades that followed its discovery in 1859, the lode yielded up treasure in such quantities as to focus on it the rapt attention of the rest of the world. Writing in the mid-1870's—when production was at its height—William Wright, editor of the area's leading newspaper, the *Territorial Enterprise*, thus described the yield of a single mine, the famous "Con. Virginia":

The Consolidated Virginia Company extracts five hundred tons of ore per day. This is the average daily yield from all parts of the mine—from the 1500-foot level, and from the levels above. Although much of the ore from the upper levels is of low grade, yet the whole averages $100 per ton in the mills. The yield of the mine has regularly been $50,000 per day, or from $1,500,000 to $1,600,000 per month ever since the work of extracting ore from the bonanza began. Much of the ore on the 1500-foot level is too rich to be economically worked alone by pan process, therefore it is mixed with poorer ore from certain parts of the upper levels. Much more than 500 tons of ore per day might be extracted were it necessary, but that is all that is required to keep the mills of the company in operation.

Opened as it now is, there can easily be extracted from the [adjoining] California Mine as many tons per day as are being taken out of the Consolidated Virginia, and ore that will average even higher, as the upper levels of the California are all intact. There is not the slightest doubt that when the California mill shall be started up, these two mines will produce $3,000,000 per month, or $36,000,000 per year, and not for one or two, but for many years . . . A single foot of ground taken out across the whole widst of the bonanza in its widest part would contain a fortune for any man of moderate desires. Should we go into the centre of the Consolidated Virginia ground and take a slice from the bonanza 250 feet in widst and extending one level below and two levels above the 1500-foot level we should then have a section of ore 300 feet long, 250 feet in widst, and one foot thick. This would contain 75,000 cubic feet, and containing thirteen cubic feet to the ton would weigh a trifle over 5,769 tons, which at $100 per ton would amount to $576,900 for a single slice of the bonanza one foot in widst. By continuing to cut off such slices until we reached the California line—say 230 feet—we should have in all $132,687,000.

Elsewhere in his book *The Big Bonanza,* Wright gave this picture of the underground workings of the Con. Virginia as seen from the 1500-foot level:

Cross-cuts pass through the ore, east and west, and cross-drifts from north to south, cutting it into blocks from fifty to one hundred feet square, as the streets run through and divide a town into blocks. It is indeed a sort of subterranean town, and is more populous than many towns on the surface, as it numbers from 800 to 1,000 souls . . .

We may take our stand here, where the miners are digging

out the ore, and for a distance of seventy-five feet on each side of us all is ore, while we may gaze upward to nearly that height to where the twinkling light of candles shows us miners delving up into the same great mass of wealth. On all sides of the pyramidal scaffold of timbers to its very apex, where the candles twinkle like stars in the heavens, we see the miners cutting their way into the precious ore—battering it with sledge-hammers and cutting it to pieces with their picks as though it were but common sandstone . . . Throughout the mass of ore in many places, the walls of the silver-caverns glitter as though studded with diamonds. But it is not silver that glitters. It is the iron and copper pyrites that are everywhere mingled with the ore, and which, in many places, are found in the form of regular and beautiful crystals that send out from their facets flashes of light that almost rival the fire and splendor of precious stones.

No less picturesque, but in a quite different way, were the sights to be seen above ground, on the streets of Virginia City, Gold Hill, and other towns that sprang up along the length of the lode. In the mid-1860's young Sam Clemens —who had not yet adopted his nom de plume of Mark Twain—joined the staff of Virginia City's *Territorial Enterprise*, and in *Roughing It*, published some years later, he thus pictured the bustling metropolis:

Six months after my entry into journalism [wrote he] the grand "flush times" of Silverland began, and they continued with unabated splendor for three years. All difficulty about filling up the "local department" ceased, and the only trouble now was how to make the lengthened columns hold the world of incidents and happenings that came to our literary net every day. Virginia had grown to be the "livest" town, for its age and population, that America had ever produced. The sidewalks swarmed with people—to such an extent, indeed, that it was generally no easy matter to stem the human tide. The streets themselves were just as crowded with quartz wagons, freight teams and other vehicles. The procession was endless. So great was the pack, that buggies frequently had to wait half an hour to cross the principal street. Joy sat on every countenance, and there was a glad, almost fierce, intensity in every eye, that told of the money-getting schemes that were seething in every brain and the high hope that held sway in every heart.

Money was as plenty as dust; every individual considered himself wealthy, and a melancholy countenance was nowhere to be seen. There were military companies, fire companies, brass bands, banks, hotels, theatres, "hurdy-gurdy houses," wide-open gambling palaces, political pow-wows, civic processions, street fights, murders, inquests, riots, a whiskey mill every fifteen steps, a Board of Aldermen, a Mayor, a City Surveyor, a City Engineer, a Chief of the Fire Department, the First, Second and Third Assistants, a Chief of Police, City Marshal and a large police force, two Boards of Mining Brokers, a dozen breweries and half a dozen jails and station-houses in full operation, and some talk of building a church. The "flush times" were in magnificent flower! Large fire-proof brick buildings were going up in the principal streets, and the wooden suburbs were spreading out in all directions. Town lots soared up to prices that were amazing.

Such was Virginia City at its zenith.

ix

Spurred by the sensational discoveries at Virginia City and elsewhere on the slopes of Nevada's Mount Davidson, parties of prospectors were presently scouring the canyons and creek beds of that area in the hope of making new strikes. For some time they met with but indifferent success; at length, however, having pushed on into the sandy, semi-arid plains of what is now west-central Nevada, their luck changed, rich deposits of gold and silver being uncovered at a number of spots from the vicinity of Lake Tahoe southward for a hundred miles or more.

One of the most productive—and rowdy—of the camps that sprang up in that area was Aurora, where rich ores were discovered in the early 1860's, and the mines of which during the next decade produced some $30,000,000 in bullion.

This town [recalled a pioneer resident, R. K. Colcord, who later became a governor of Nevada] enjoyed its greatest boom in the early spring and summer of 1863. Men swarmed there from all quarters by stage, fast freight, horseback and on foot. My first night's slumber was in a corral, and the next few nights I hit the straw in a quartz mill. It was a wide open town and everybody was happy with the possible exception of those who were sticklers for a generous supply of law and order. One of the two newspapers published there claimed a population of ten thousand, but about half that number would, in my judgment, be nearer the mark . . .

The town that year became notorious as a refuge for the rough element. Two crowds of toughs located there, one from San Francisco and the other from Sacramento, and they did not mix with anything approaching friendship. The good people of the town paid little or no attention to their killing and maiming among themselves, but when they committed a foul murder upon the person of a good citizen, W. R. Johnson, a Vigilance Committee was immediately organized with Captain Palmer as its chief . . . and under his leadership they worked so quickly and quietly that the entire gang found themselves locked up together before they knew what had happened. The place was surrounded by a guard of a hundred armed and determined men and there was no chance for escape.

The primary cause of the necessity for lynching these men was the killing of one of their gang by a young fellow named Johnny Rogers . . . Rogers was in the employ of Johnson, who owned a ranch at Smith's Valley, when three hobos on their way to Aurora, while passing through Wellington Station, took a saddle horse belonging to Johnson. As soon as the discovery was made Johnson told Rogers to saddle the best horse, take a Colt's Navy and capture the stolen horse if he had to kill all of the three men. Rogers struck out at a pony rider's gait and soon came up to them . . . He ordered them to halt, and they replied with bullets. Brave little Rogers limbered up his battery without delay and the two who were riding immediately dismounted. One of them, Jimmy Sayres, is there yet. The others broke for the willows, and Johnny returned with the stolen horse without a scratch. Sayres was an active member of the San Francisco gunmen and was greatly missed, and though they appeared to hold no grudge against Rogers, they notified Johnson that it would not be healthy for him to show up in Aurora. Johnson did not heed their warning and made several trips to town selling produce. He, however, went once too often, and late that fall his body was found one morning lying in the street.

For the murder of Johnson the Vigilance Committee arrested about a dozen of the worst characters, gave all a fair trial, which resulted in the conviction and hanging of Daly, Buckley, Masterson, McDonald and one other whose name I have forgotten. Irish Tom Carberry escaped the hemp by one vote. He was reported killed a few years later in a gun fight at Austin . . .

It has been the custom for all the old timers at Aurora to claim acquaintance with Mark Twain [who, as readers of

Roughing It will recall, spent several months there in the early 1860's]. Unfortunately for me, I did not know him at all except to nod in passing. Many claim to have been partners with him in mining claims, others that they had loaned him money, etc. I was loaded with wild cat stocks and much more likely to want to borrow than to lend, and when he lived at Aurora he did not look like a promising subject to tackle for a loan . . . therefore I missed coming in contact with him . . .

> Colcord's stay at Aurora was brief; however, years later, when he was running for governor, he renewed acquaintance with one of the town's most picturesque citizens.

In 1890 [he recalled] while campaigning throughout the State, it was my privilege to renew my acquaintance with Captain J. A. Palmer, mentioned above as chief of a Vigilance Committee, who presided at our meeting held at Carlin, Elko County. His introductory remarks in presenting me to the audience were quite characteristic of the man, through rather shy on polish. Here is his speech:

"Friends and neighbors: Something like thirty-five years ago, I met a green, hayseed of a boy over in Tuolumne County who had just landed on the coast. He looked as though he wanted to go home. Now after all these years he shows up here, six feet high, with broad shoulders and a big head. It is up to you to judge if there's anything in it. Ladies and gentlemen, I take pleasure in introducing your candidate, Mr. R. K. Colcord of Esmeralda County."

> During the early days—and, indeed, down to comparatively recent times—Nevada's history was one series of mining excitements, with throngs hastening first to the scene of one strike, then to another. Thus the state has seen the rise of scores of bonanza towns—Virginia City, Gold Hill, Aurora,

Austin, Goldfield, Tonapah and many others—most of which prospered for a few months or years. Then, their residents having been drawn elsewhere by rumors of still richer finds, the deserted towns slowly sank back into the sage-covered hills from which they had sprung.

X I

Side-Wheeler, Stagecoach, and Iron Horse

i

Until the completion of the first transcontinental railroad in 1869—and indeed for some time thereafter—a goodly number of those passing from coast to coast went, as we have seen, by water. Those who made the sea voyage in the first years traveled on sailing ships, some breaking their journeys by crossings at Panama or elsewhere, while others endured the months-long cruises round the Horn. As time went on, however, a steadily growing number of steamers were put on the run and, although several decades passed before these entirely supplanted the windjammers, by the early 1850's they were carrying a major share of the passenger traffic.

Many accounts of the voyage from New York to San Francisco aboard these early-day steamers have come down to us. Here are excerpts from that of the West Coast historian Hubert H. Bancroft, who made the passage in 1852. Having proceeded from New York to Aspinwall aboard a steamer of the United States Mail Company, crossed the Isthmus, and boarded the Pacific Mail's *Panama*, which he found much superior to the vessels on the Atlantic side, Bancroft wrote:

Lounging inert and listless under the awning on the upper
deck, with the bay spread out before you in all its glorious
beauties . . . , listening to the friendly waters which lap the
smooth sides of our monster vessel, there comes stealing in
upon the senses a delicious repose . . .

   Late in the afternoon of the 12th of March, the chain
from the buoy was dropped, and clearing the islands, in an
hour we came abreast of Taboga—to Panama what Capri is
to Naples, but more beautiful . . . Steaming lazily along
through the quiet waters, like the chariot of Poseidon, at-
tracting around us myriads of the monsters of the deep sport-
ing and gamboling on every side, with the load of cares behind unburdened, and the load before us not yet put on, time
and observation seemed to expand with the expanding sea.
Gossips took heart; matrons smiled serenely; pater familias
grew jocund; attention turned toward comfort, reading,
and amusements. Gallants mixed huge pitchers of iced punch
and therewith regaled the ladies. Gambling, which in the
earlier voyages monopolized the saloon, had very rightly
been prohibited on board the company's vessels; yet there
was plenty of card-playing in the state-rooms, where the oc-
cupants could gamble to their hearts' content, and lesser
games obtained on capstan, bench, and skylight . . .

   The first stop en route was at the town of Acapulco.

This port [wrote Bancroft] is the best on the western coast
of Mexico, and the half-way station between Panama and San
Francisco, can safely harbor five hundred ships . . . Its
shores are so steep that vessels can lie almost under the
chaparal that overhangs its banks. Surrounded by mountains
rising on every side from six hundred to three thousand feet
. . . the town has the name of being the hottest place on the
route. For weeks the thermometer stands at 120 degrees in
the shade at mid-day . . .

Scarcely does the steamer come to anchor before it is surrounded by canoes laden with fruit, which come swarming
from various parts of the shore, and naked swimmers ready to
begin their aquatic gymnastics . . . While the steamer is
taking on coals, cattle, fowls, fruit, and water, which occupies
several hours, you may if you like go ashore in a boat and visit
the town, less than a mile distant, in a recess of the bay. Near
the landing, and on the shady side of the plaza, you will find
spread out on tables and on the ground fruit and fancy shell-
work which you are solicited to purchase . . . As you walk
along, a charming pensive-eyed senorita throws over your
head a necklace, at the same time saying it is a present, but
should you let it remain you will not have gone far before the
coffee-colored beauty turns up and desires a present in return . . . At night, in the absence of the moon, the town is
lighted by lanterns hung out at the doors. Contentment and
happiness reign; the women, some of them quite beautiful,
gather fruit, and make and sell shell-work; the men lounge in
shady nooks, smoke, and sip aguardiente, and naked children
suck oranges, munch bananas, and roll in the dirt.

> After a second brief stop, this time at San Diego, the
> *Panama* continued north, and on this final leg of the cruise
> a severe storm was met with.

Rearing and plunging like a prairie bison [recalled Ban-
croft], the ship's bow pointed now upward toward the sky,
now downward into the depths . . . Fearing to be driven to
destruction before the wind, the steamer's bow was pointed
athwart the waves, and there in the teeth of the storm the
utmost efforts were made to prevent her being caught and
overturned in the trough of the sea.

Returning to my berth, and bracing myself and holding on,
I lay listening to the creaking timbers and straining joints,
to the thud and rattle of the waters against the ship's planks,

to the crashing of glass and crockery, and the clatter and
bang of loose furniture and baggage . . .

Dawn brought only increased fury to the storm. No tables
could be set that day; indeed, there was little thought of eating, for long before the tempest had spent itself the ship was
despaired of, and such passengers as were out of bed were
beaten about like footballs. All loose canvas was torn to
shreds, and boats were splintered and sent flying from their
fastenings . . .

Next morning our Pacific was all over her passion, though
her bosom yet heaved somewhat, and the sun came out and
smiled upon the sea and changed the black hills off our
larboard bow into hazy purple . . .

> Three days later the storm-tossed *Panama* slipped through
> the Golden Gate and dropped anchor off the San Francisco
> bayfront while her passengers gratefully made their way
> ashore.

ii

During the early years those who broke new trails across the
plains of the trans-Mississippi West and on to the mountains, deserts, and valleys that lay beyond, were under the
necessity of providing their own transportation. Throughout that period a variety of methods were used. Some
traveled afoot; others were mounted on horses or mules.

However, as the tide of emigrants continued to grow
from year to year, and the former trails became reasonably
well-defined roadways, the vehicle that came to be regarded
as a symbol of the winning of the West—namely, the covered
wagon—made its appearance. The annexation of California

in 1846 and Jim Marshall's discovery in the Coloma mill-race, of course, enormously stimulated the westward move-ment—and brought with it a demand for some speedier and less arduous means of travel between the two coasts.

This was answered in part by the organization of pioneer steamship lines, the vessels of which plied both oceans, with crossings at Panama or Nicaragua. The first steamer to fly the flag of the western line, the little *California*, reached San Francisco early in 1849. While this service was far faster than those previously available, cutting weeks from the journey via the overland routes or in the round-the-Horn sailing ships, it was of use primarily to those who lived near the shores of the Pacific. Residents of the region that lay between the Sierra and the Rocky Mountains still had no means of communication with the outer world save the slow-moving vehicles that followed the overland trails.

Throughout the early and middle 1850's agitation for the establishment of a line of stages to carry passengers and mail between the West Coast and the Mississippi River had been continuous. It was not until near the close of that dec-ade, however, that these hopes were realized. On March 3, 1857, Congress passed a law granting a subsidy of $600,-000 per year for a stage company to carry the mail on a twice-weekly basis "from such point on the Mississippi River as the contractors may select, to San Francisco, in the state of California."

The successful bidders were a group headed by John Butterfield. On September 16 of that year the group was awarded the contract, with service to begin a year from that date. "A year of feverish activity followed," wrote a later commentator. "Men were hired; horses, mules, 'mud wagons' and stages were acquired; stations were built along the line, and supplies of hay and grain and food were trekked over the deserts and mountains." On the appointed date, that is,

September 16, 1858, the long-awaited service got under way, with coaches leaving simultaneously from the eastern and western termini.

One passenger over this historic route, who made the trip during the first year of the company's operation, was a young Englishman named William Tallack. On his way home after a visit to Australia, Tallack reached San Francisco early in 1860 and—as he himself later stated—"after considerable hesitation" booked passage on the stages of the Butterfield Overland Mail Company from that city to St. Louis. Later he wrote an account of his journey, which he described as "the longest stage ride in the world" that was published in an English magazine called *The Leisure Hour*. From his narrative the following excerpts have been taken.

Owing to the very limited space for passengers [he wrote at the offset], and the increasing demand for spaces, the writer had to wait ten days before an opportunity for starting presented itself.

Meanwhile, he often felt doubtful as to how far he might be able to endure a continuous ride of five hundred and forty hours, with no other intermission than a stoppage of about forty minutes twice a day, and a walk, from time to time, over the more difficult ground, or up and down stiff hills and mountain passes, and with only such repose at night as could be obtained whilst in sitting posture and closely wedged in by fellow-travellers and tightly-filled mail-bags.

Some other thoughts of not impossible contingencies were also excited by hearing that, although the Indians had never as yet ventured to attack the overland mail, there was no absolute security against such an attempt, whilst murders and robberies were known to be a constant occurrence along the line of route in the cases of solitary or incautious travellers crossing on mules or with only a waggon and team.

A third ground for apprehensive anticipation was the ex-

treme liability of vehicles to overset during a journey
through regions possessing no macadamized roads, and often
by a route the most rugged and steep. In case, too, of any accident or illness occurring, there was the certainty of being
placed in a very unpleasant position by the absence of the
ordinary appliances of civilization . . .

Happily the result was free from any of these contingencies; for, as to sleep, the writer never enjoyed such profound
and delicious repose as often followed days of tremendous
mountain jolting, and no horizontal position in the softest
bed could have given him sounder sleep than when sitting
upright after these jolting days through the clear mountain
and wilderness air . . .

The "stations" of the Overland Company average about
eighteen miles apart; but some are distant only twelve, and
others more than thirty miles. They are mostly log-houses
or adobes, and each tenanted by several men well armed,
whose duty is to look after the mules and their provender, and
have the relays punctually ready on the arrival of the stages.

A conductor and driver accompany each stage, the former
changing every five hundred miles, and the latter at shorter
intervals. Passengers and luggage are shifted into a fresh
waggon about every three hundred miles. The average rate
of travel is one hundred and twenty miles in every twenty-
four hours; but of course the actual speed varies greatly . . .
Over smooth and level prairie lands we sometimes dashed
on at twelve miles an hour, whilst, on rugged or sandy
ground, our advance was only two or three miles in the same
time, and that often on foot . . .

Meals (at extra charge) were provided for the passengers
twice a day. The fare, though rough, is better than could be
expected so far from civilized districts, and consists of bread,
tea, and fried steaks of bacon, venison, antelope, or mule
flesh—the latter tough enough. Milk, butter, and vegetables
can only be met with towards the two ends of the route—that

is, in California and at the "stations" in the settled parts of
the western Mississippi Valley.

Only forty pounds weight of luggage is allowed to each
passenger; but one can easily manage to cross America with
this amount stowed in a handy portmanteau . . . Having
thus made all arrangements . . . the writer started from
San Francisco on the appointed day, with three other through
passengers on board.

As we had to pass through several hundred miles of comparatively settled districts before reaching the wilder parts of
the route, our first stage vehicle was a large one, to accommodate the numerous demands for way-passengers to the towns
and villages of Southern California. So, at starting, our con-
veyance was not a mere waggon, as afterwards, but a regular
coach, holding nine inside (three behind, three in front, and
three in a movable seat, with a swinging leather strap for a
back), by dint of close sitting and tightly dovetailed knees.
Outside was the driver, and an indefinite number of passengers, as, by popular permission, an American vehicle is
never "full," there being always room for "one more." With
these, their luggage, and a heavy mail in strong sacks, stowed
away under and between our feet, or overhead and elsewhere, we started from the Plaza or Grand Square of San
Francisco . . .

> The first four days of travel took Tallack and his fellows
> through the Santa Clara and San Joaquin valleys, thence
> over passes in the Coast Range Mountains to the "sunny
> plains and vineyards of the Ciudad de Los Angeles." The
> fifth and sixth days were occupied in crossing the arid
> country that lay between Los Angeles and the Colorado
> River.

At nightfall [wrote he] we entered the narrow gorge of San
Felipe, just at the entrance of which a large Indian campfire

lighted up the sides of the defile, and beyond which the passage narrowed in, so as just to allow one vehicle to pass between the perpendicular walls rising on either hand. And
now commenced a shaking descent down the long narrow
entrance to the Colorado Desert, over a path uneven in the
extreme, and strewed with loose rocks and stones. Here we
had six horses; and a wild spasmotic pull it was. In the midst
of it, however, some of us managed, as usual, to fall sound
asleep . . . After driving for hours through a wind hot as
from a furnace, we reached a station in the mid-desert—a
miserable adobe, with walls black inside with clustering flies,
but where we were refreshed with coffee. Again starting, we
soon entered the Mexican frontier, as indicated by a line of
iron slabs at wide intervals. The only water at the stations
hereabouts was alkaline and dirty; but, such as it was, we
were glad to fill our canteens with it, both now and further
eastward, when traversing the "journados" of Arizona,
where, for sixty miles at a time, we had no water at all but
that which we carried with us . . . Hour after hour we were
enveloped in clouds of fine clayey dust, as so many times
previously and subsequently, when journeying over low-ly-
ing plains. What with the hot wind, the dust, and the perspiration, our faces and hands became covered with a thin mud,
only removed to be speedily renewed as we proceeded . . .

> A week of continuous travel brought the passengers to the
> banks of the Colorado. After a half-hour stop at Fort Yuma,
> they pushed on across southwestern Arizona, following the
> course of the Gila River. That the Indians of the region con-
> stituted something of a threat to the wayfarers is indicated
> by this passage from Tallack's narrative.

In the afternoon [of the eighth day], whilst passing through
a thicket of mesquite, we met, at intervals, with eight Indians on horseback armed with bows and arrows. The pas-

sengers and conductor got their rifles and revolvers in readiness, should anything unpleasant be threatened, but the Indians soon turned aside amongst the trees, and we saw no more of them. This was just as we were entering a narrow gorge, the Pimo Pass . . . On entering it the conductor pointed out a rock from behind which the Indians had only a fortnight previously killed one of the officials of the Overland Mail Company. We felt easier when we were clear of the pass, and re-emerged on a wide expanse, "the forty mile desert." Hereabouts we passed many skeletons of oxen.

At nightfall we reached the Pimo villages, a settlement of comparatively civilized Indians, very different from their barbarous neighbours, the Apaches . . . Whilst our supper was preparing we washed in an Indian bowl formed of reeds, but quite watertight. Saucepans also of reeds are here made use of. They are filled with water, which is then boiled by dropping hot stones into it . . .

> For another five days and nights the party rolled and bounced eastward across present-day Arizona and New Mexico, with little to relieve the monotony of their journey save brief stops at a succession of widely spaced "overland stations." The thirteenth day found them in Texas.

In leaving the valley of the Rio Grande [wrote Tallack] we proceeded on foot slowly up steep passes to another tableland of yuccas and prairie grass, and were now . . . approaching the eastern spurs of the Rocky Mountains, whose various chains and plateaux we had been successively crossing during the past week.

> That by then their long ordeal had begun to affect the nerves and dispositions of the travelers is indicated by the passage that follows.

Our sameness of posture becoming tedious, we tried various experiments by way of a change, sometimes slinging our feet by loops from the top of the waggon, or letting them hang over the sides between the wheels, and at other times mutually accommodating each other by leaning or lying along the seats, and not seldom all nodding for hours together in attitudes grotesque and diverse.

We had very little interruption to our general harmony. But on one occasion the two front passengers had become wearied with sitting for more than twenty-four hours in an almost horizontal posture, by reason of mail-bags filling up the space between the seats. On our getting out for a meal, one of the two pushed the bags backwards, so as to similarly incommode those sitting in the back of the vehicle, and more particularly "Texas," who stoutly demurred to the change. His neighbour in front persisted in pushing back the bags, and added, with a significant reference to his pistols, that there would be "trouble" unless his arrangement was agreed with. This roused "Texas," who, stopping to grasp his own trusty weapon, remarked, "Well, if you talk about 'trouble,' I can, too; and, as to that matter, I'd as lief have 'trouble' as anything else." This characteristic declaration, with its accompanying gestures, immediately made the first complainant "draw in," and exercise his "prudence as the better part of valour."

Thus the long trek continued. On the nineteenth day the party left Texas and entered Indian Territory, their journey more than two thirds over.

As visitors [commented Tallack] we could not complain of our fare here, as we had sweet green corn and the first potatoes since the commencement of our journey from San Francisco. . . . We found the temperature, though ex-

tremely warm hereabouts (98 degrees in the shade) far
more endurable than that experienced in the Colorado and
Gila deserts.

> The twentieth day—which chanced to be the 4th of July—
> found them in Arkansas, and once more beginning to enjoy
> some of the delicacies of civilization.

After a hot and dusty drag of fifteen miles in six hours [wrote
he], our horses fairly gave in, and we had to walk the last
part of the stage west of Fort Smith. On reaching this town
. . . we found every one holiday-keeping, in honour of "the
Fourth." We were allowed two hours' delay—a very welcome
opportunity for a bath and a leisurely dinner at a regular
hotel. There we emerged on the comforts of ice-water and
ice-cream, both such universal requirements of loyal American citizens in summer . . .

> Two more days of hard driving brought them to the town
> of Syracuse, the western terminus of the Pacific Railroad,
> something more than a hundred miles to the west of St.
> Louis.

A few minutes more [reads Tallack's final entry] and we
had completed our long and uninterrupted ride of twenty
seven hundred miles; and, as we leaped for the last time
from the stage, it was not without feeling some emotion of
thankfulness to that good Providence who had brought us
thus safely to the termination of a journey characterized by
extreme interest and variety, and by more than a little peril
and physical exertion . . .

iii

Another revealing—and frequently amusing—picture of early western travel is given by Mark Twain in *Roughing It*, an account of his stay on the Pacific Coast during the early 1860's. Twain, traveling by stage, was bound for Carson City, Nevada, to join his brother, who had recently been appointed secretary of that territory. En-route stops for meals were made at way-stations set up at irregular points along the line.

The station buildings [wrote he] were long, low huts, made of sun-dried, mud-colored bricks, laid up without mortar (*adobes*, the Spaniards call these bricks, and the Americans shorten it to *'dobies*). The roofs, which had no slant to them worth speaking of, were thatched and then sodded or covered with a thick layer of earth, and from this sprang a pretty rank growth of weeds and grass. It was the first time we had ever seen a man's front yard on top of his house. The buildings consisted of barns, stable-room for twelve or fifteen horses, and a hut for an eating-room for passengers. The latter had bunks in it for the station-keeper and a hostler or two. You could rest your elbow on its eaves, and you had to bend in order to get in the door. . . . There was no stove, but the fire-place served all needful purposes. There were no shelves, no cupboards, no closets. In a corner stood an open sack of flour, and nestling against its base were a couple of black and venerable tin coffee-pots, a tin tea-pot, a little bag of salt, and a side of bacon.

By the door of the station-keeper's den, outside, was a tin wash-basin, on the ground. Near it was a pail of water and a piece of yellow bar soap, and from the eaves hung a hoary blue woolen shirt—but this latter was the station-master's private towel, and only two persons in all the party might

venture to use it—the stage-driver and the conductor . . .
We (and the conductor) used our handkerchiefs, and the
driver his pantaloons and sleeves . . .

The furniture of the hut was neither gorgeous nor much
in the way. The rocking-chairs and sofas were not present,
and never had been, but they were represented by two
three-legged stools, a pine-board bench four feet long, and
two empty candle-boxes. The table was a greasy board on
stilts, and the table-cloth and napkins had not come—and
they were not looking for them, either. A battered tin plat-
ter, a knife and fork, and a tin pint cup, were at each man's
place, and the driver had a queens-ware saucer that had seen
better days. Of course this duke sat at the head of the
table . . .

The station-keeper upended a disk of last week's bread,
of the shape and size of an old-time cheese, and carved some
slabs from it which were as good as Nicholson pavement,
and tenderer. He sliced off a piece of bacon for each man,
but only the experienced old hands made out to eat it, for
it was condemned army bacon which the United States
would not feed to its soldiers in the forts, and the stage company had bought it cheap for the sustenance of their passengers and employees . . .

Then he [the station-keeper] poured us a beverage which
he called *"Slumgullion,"* and it is hard to think that he was
not inspired when he named it. It really pretended to be tea,
but there was too much dish-rag, and sand, and old bacon-
rind in it to deceive the intelligent traveler. He had no sugar
and no milk—not even a spoon to stir the ingredients
with . . .

Our breakfast was before us, but our teeth were idle . . .
We gave up the breakfast, paid our dollar apiece and went
back to our mail-bag bed in the coach, and found comfort
in our pipes . . .

A bit farther on the travelers suffered what Twain termed "the first diminution of our princely state." He described it thus:

We left our six fine horses and took six mules in their place. But they were wild Mexican fellows, and a man had to stand at the head of each of them and hold him fast until the driver gloved and got himself ready. And when at last he grasped the reins and gave the word, the men sprung suddenly away from the mule's heads and the coach shot from the station as if it had issued from a cannon. How the frantic animals did scamper! It was a fierce and furious gallop—and the gait never altered for a moment till we reeled off ten or twelve miles and swept up to the next collection of little station-huts and stables.

The most trying part of the entire journey was a stretch of alkali desert that lay to the west of Salt Lake, close to seventy miles across and with but a single stopping place near its center. Here is Twain's description of the crossing:

The sun beats down with dead, blistering malignity; the perspiration is welling from every pore in man and beast, but scarcely a sign of it finds its way to the surface—it is absorbed before it gets there; there is not the faintest breath of air stirring; there is not a merciful shred of cloud in all the brilliant firmament; there is not a living creature visible in any direction whither one searches the blank level that stretches its monotonous miles on every hand; there is not a sound, not a sigh—not a whisper, not a buzz, or a whir of wings, or distant pipe of bird—not even a sob from the lost souls that doubtless people that dead air . . .

The mules, under violent swearing, coaxing and whip-

cracking, would make at stated intervals a "spurt," and drag
the coach a hundred or may be two hundred yards, stirring
up a billowy cloud of dust that rolled back, enveloping the
vehicle to the wheel-tops or higher, and making it seem to
float in a fog. Then the rest followed, with the usual sneezing
and bit-champing. Then another "spurt" of a hundred yards
and another rest at the end of it. All day long we kept
this up, without water for the mules and without ever changing the team. At least we kept it up ten hours, which, I
take it, is a day, and a pretty honest one, in an alkali desert.
It was from four in the morning till two in the afternoon.
And it was so hot! and so close! and our water canteens
went dry in the middle of the day and we got so thirsty! It
was so stupid and tiresome and dull! and the tedious hours
did lag and drag and limp along with such cruel delibera-
tion! It was so trying to give one's watch a good long undis-
turbed spell and then take it out and find that it had been
fooling away the time and not trying to get ahead any! The
alkali dust cut through our lips, it persecuted our eyes, it ate
through the delicate membranes and made our noses bleed
and *kept* them bleeding—and truly and seriously the romance all faded far away and disappeared, and left the
desert trip nothing but a harsh reality—a thirsty, sweltering,
longing, hateful reality.

Two miles and a quarter an hour for ten hours—that was
what we accomplished. It was hard to bring the comprehen-
sion away down to such a snail-pace as that, when we had
been used to making eight and ten miles an hour. When
we reached the station at the farther verge of the desert, we
were glad, for the first time, that the dictionary was along,
because we never could have found language to tell how glad
we were, in any sort of dictionary but an unabridged one
with pictures in it. But there could not have been found in a
whole library of dictionaries language sufficient to tell how
tired those mules were after their twenty-three mile pull. To

try to give the reader an idea of how *thirsty* they were, would be to "gild refined gold or paint the lily."

While crossing a second stretch of desert farther along—this one in what is now central Nevada—Twain saw many evidences of the California-bound emigrants who had passed that way a few years earlier. Having pronounced it "forty memorable miles of bottomless sand, into which the coach wheels sunk from six inches to a foot," he continued thus:

We worked our passage most of the way across. That is to say, we got out and walked. It was a dreary pull and a long and thirsty one, for we had no water. From one extremity of this desert to the other, the road was white with the bones of oxen and horses. It would hardly be an exaggeration to say that we could have walked the forty miles and set our feet on a bone at every step! The desert was one prodigious graveyard. And the log-chains, wagon tyres, and rotting wrecks of vehicles were almost as thick as the bones. I think we saw log-chains enough rusting there in the desert, to reach across any State in the Union. Do not these relics suggest something of an idea of the fearful suffering and privation the early emigrants to California endured?

Twain reached his destination—Carson City, Nevada—twenty days after setting off from St. Jo., Missouri. Here is his description of the capital of that newly created territory:

It was a "wooden" town; its population two thousand souls. The main street consisted of four or five blocks of little white frame stores which were too high to sit down on, but not too high for various other purposes; in fact, hardly high enough. They were packed close together, side by side, as if room were scarce in that mighty plain. The sidewalk was of boards that were more or less loose and inclined to rattle when walked upon. In the middle of the town, opposite the stores, was the "plaza" which is native to all towns beyond the Rocky Mountains—a large, unfenced, level vacancy, with a liberty pole in it, and very useful as a place for public auctions, horse trades, and mass meetings, and likewise for teamsters to camp in. Two other sides of the plaza were faced by stores, offices and stables. The rest of Carson City was pretty scattering.

iv

Of travel over the Sierra during pioneer times, J. Ross Browne gives this account of a trip made in the early 1860's, from California to the newly opened silver mines of Nevada. Having proceeded from San Francisco to Sacramento by riverboat, and there, "after a hasty breakfast of water bewitched and coffee begrudged," he boarded a train of the state's first railroad, the 22-mile line connecting the state capital with the foothill town of Folsom, and there boarded a transmountain stage for the balance of his journey.

As most passengers desire to get an outside seat, except when it rains [he wrote], it is highly important that you should proceed at once to secure the favorable consideration of the superintendent, who is a gentleman of great suavity and politeness, considering his position. Should you fail in that, I warn you not to climb up on the forewheel with any hope of getting the seat of honor alongside the driver; for whether you be a Minister Plenipotentiary or a member of the Common Council he will exercise the right pertaining to his craft—order you down, and then enjoy your discomfiture for a distance of ten miles . . .

The scene on the arrival of the cars [at Folsom] is quite inspiring. Stages backed up in a long row; prancing horses in front; swearing and sweating porters, baggage-masters, drivers, and passengers all about and behind; John China-men, with long tails rolled up on the backs of their heads, running distractedly through the crowd in search of their lost bundles; anxious ladies, prolific in crinoline and gor-geous in silks and satins (the California traveling costume), fretting and scolding over crushed band-boxes; and stern-looking men of an official cast of countenance shouting fiercely, "This way, gents! 'Ere's the place for your baggage! Bring it along if you want it weighed; if you don't, it won't go—that's all!" And there is the machine that weighs, and there stands the inexorable gentleman that marks off the weights—ten, forty, sixty, ninety pounds per passenger—thirty pounds allowed; all excess baggage twenty-five cents per pound . . . "Quick, if you please, ladies and gents! Stages behind time—won't get to Placerville before dark!" . . . And so on till we are all fairly in and off, looking back, with fervent thanks that we are clear of the smoke and trou-ble and turmoil of the railroad depot at Folsom . . .

It was 5 o'clock P.M., just three hours after the usual time . . . , when we took our places on the stages [at Placer-ville], and girded up our loins for the trip across the moun-tains. I was the lucky recipient of an outside seat. The seat of honor, by the side of that exalted dignitary the driver . . . I was proud and happy to sit by the side of Charlie—es-pecially as the road was supposed to be a little undulating even by its best friends. Possibly I have travelled over worse roads than the first ten miles out of Placerville . . . but there are not many quite so bad on the continent of North America . . . But I had implicit confidence in Old Charlie. The way he handled the reins and peered through the clouds of dust and volumes of darkness and saw trees and stumps and boulders of rock and horses' ears, when I could scarcely see my own hand before me, was a miracle of stage-driving. "Git aeoup!" was the warning cry of this old stager. "Git alang, my beauties!" was the natural outpouring of the poetry that filled his capacious soul.

"Do many people get killed on this route?" said I to Charlie, as we made a sudden lurch in the dark and bowled along the edge of a fearful precipice.

"Nary a kill that I know of. Some of the drivers mashes 'em once in a while, but that's whicky or bad drivin'. Last summer a few stages went over the grade, but nobody was hurt bad—only a few legs'n arms broken. Them was opposition stages. Pioneer stages, as a general thing, travels on the road. Git aeoup!" . . .

And so passed the long hours of the night, Charlie and I gossiping pleasantly about the risks and charms, and mysteries of the stage-driving profession. A hard life is that of the stage-driver; a life of exposure and peril, and wear and tear, such as few other men experience. You, my good friend, who cross the Sierra once or twice in a lifetime, imagine you have done great things—you boast of your qualities as a traveller; you have passed unscathed through the piercing night air; have scarcely shuddered at the narrow bridges, or winced at the fearful precipices . . . But think of Old Charlie! He has crossed the mountains a thousand times; crossed when the roads were at their worst; by night and by day; in storm and gloom and darkness; through snow and sleet and rain, and burning suns and dust . . . his life ballanced on the temper of a horse or the strength of a screw. This is a career worthy of the consideration of the heedless world! Who thinks of Old Charlie? Where is the gazette to herald his achievements? What pen is there to trumpet his praises? . . .

Owing to our late start, we did not reach the summit before two o'clock. The air at this elevation was sharp, though not unpleasantly so. The altitude is estimated at eight thousand feet above the level of the sea . . . The moon, which so kindly befriended us during the greater part of our journey, was still shining brightly, shedding its silver rays over the wilderness of mountains that loomed up around us. . . .

For a distance of five or six miles the road winds around the sides of the mountains, crossing ravines and doubling up occasionally in turns so rapid that the stage seems to run one way and the horses another . . . As we strike the straight road again the driver gives rein to our spirited animals; crack goes the whip, and down we plunge over narrow bridges, along the edges of terrific precipices a thousand feet deep, through dark forests of pine and along frowning banks of granite, hewn from the solid bed of the mountain . . . It is not comfortable to look down when you are flying along at the rate of ten miles per hour and see no bottom short of a thousand or fifteen hundred feet. Yet there is a charm in this dashing, reckless journey by moonlight. The danger is just sufficient to give it a relish. The excitement keeps the blood warm; the fresh mountain air invigorates and inspires every faculty; the spirit rises with the rapidity of motion, and before you get half-way to the valley you find yourself in a condition to sing, shout, or dance . . .

v

Throughout the pioneer era one of the inconveniences that residents of the Far West found hardest to bear was a lack of fast and dependable means of communication with the outer world. Letters to or from the East Coast, whether carried in the lumbering overland stages or on the pioneer steamers that operated via Panama, commonly required three weeks or longer to pass from coast to coast.

The desire for a speedier means of transporting the mails grew more pressing year by year, and as the decade of the 1850's closed resulted in the launching of one of the most interesting—and romantic—ventures in the annals of the early West; that is, the Pony Express. Beginning in the spring of 1860, a corps of young riders, mounted on fleet ponies, began riding on regular schedules between St. Joseph, Missouri, and Sacramento, each youth traveling from fifty to seventy-five miles, changing to fresh mounts at stations set up every ten or fifteen miles, and carrying in their saddle-bags a sheaf of half-ounce letters, for which their senders paid a flat rate of five dollars each.

A spirited picture of that service, and of the men who rode the ponies, was given by young Sam Clemens, who got his first view of the messengers while, as stated earlier, on his way west in the early 1860's, bound for Carson City, Nevada.

The pony rider [wrote he] was usually a little bit of a man, brimful of spirit and endurance. No matter what time of the day or night his watch came on and no matter whether it was winter or summer, raining, snowing, hailing, or sleeting, or whether his beat was a level straight road or a crazy trail over the mountain crags and precipices, or whether it led through peaceful regions or regions that swarmed with hostile Indians, he must always be ready to leap into the saddle and be off like the wind! There was no idling time for a pony rider on duty. He rode fifty miles without stopping, by daylight, moonlight, starlight, or through the blackness of darkness—just as it happened. He rode a splendid horse that was born for a racer and fed and lodged like a gentleman; kept him at his utmost speed for ten miles, and then, as he came crashing up to the station where stood two men holding fast a fresh, impatient steed, the transfer of rider and mail-bag was made in the twinkling of an eye, and away flew the eager pair and were out of sight before the spectator could get hardly the ghost of a look. Both rider and horse went "flying light."

The rider's dress was thin and fitted close; he wore a roundabout and a skullcap and tucked his pantaloons into his boot tops like a race rider. He carried no arms—he carried nothing that was not absolutely necessary, for even the postage on his literary freight was worth *five dollars a letter*. He got but little frivolous correspondence to carry—his bag had business letters in it mostly. His horse was stripped of all unnecessary weight too. He wore light shoes or none at all. The little flat mail pockets strapped under the rider's thighs would each hold about the bulk of a child's primer. They held many and many an important business chapter and newspaper letter, but these were written on paper as airy and thin as gold leaf, nearly, and thus bulk and weight were economized. The stagecoach traveled about a hundred to a hundred and twenty-five miles a day (twenty-four hours), the pony rider about two hundred and fifty. There were about eighty pony riders in the saddle at all times, night and day, stretching in a long, scattering procession from Missouri to California, forty flying eastward and forty toward the west, and among them making four hundred gallant horses earn a stirring livelihood and see a deal of scenery every single day in the year.

We had a consuming desire, from the beginning, to see a pony rider, but somehow or other all that passed us and all that met us managed to streak by in the night, and so we heard only a whiz and a hail, and the swift phantom of the desert was gone before we could get our heads out of the windows. But now we were expecting one every moment and would see him in broad daylight. Presently the driver exclaims:

"*Here he comes!*"

Every neck is stretched farther and every eye strained

wider. Away across the endless level of the prairie a black
speck appears against the sky, and it is plain that it moves.
Well, I should think so! In a second or two it becomes a
horse and rider, rising and falling, rising and falling—sweeping toward us nearer and nearer—growing more and more
distinct, more and more sharply defined—nearer and still
nearer, and the flutter of the hoofs comes faintly to the ear—
another instant a whoop and a hurrah from our upper deck,
a wave of the rider's hand, but no reply, and man and horse
burst past our excited faces and go swinging away like a
belated fragment of a storm!

So sudden is it all and so like a flash of unreal fancy that,
but for the flake of white foam left quivering and perishing
on a mail sack after the vision had passed by and disappeared, we might have doubted whether we had seen any
actual horse and man at all . . .

vi

During that same period other pony express services sprang
up and flourished briefly throughout the West. Typical of
these was that launched by I. Van Dorsey Mossman early
in 1861 to carry letters, papers, and light merchandise between Walla Walla, Washington Territory, and the newly
opened mines of the Oro Fino district in central Idaho.

With only one pony and $5 in money and one pair of blan-
kets [he later recalled] . . . I left Walla Walla about the
fifth of April and started for the diggings. My route was
past Dry Creek to Coppei, Whiskey Creek, and on to the
Pattit and Whetstone Hollow to the Tucannon . . . From
there it was over to Alpowa Creek, and down it to its
mouth. Then I crossed the Snake River at Silcott's Ferry,

near the juncture of the Clearwater and Snake. Thence followed up the Clearwater past the Lapwai Indian Agency of the Nez Perce Indians . . . At the foot of the Bitterroot Mountains, I caught up with a pack-train bound for the mines, and stopped four days to help them shovel the snow so they could proceed . . . We finally worked our way through and found thirty or forty miners at the camp . . . I stayed there two days and received a lot of letters to carry back to Walla Walla, at fifty cents each. This trip proved very hard on me, as there were few houses or stopping places between Walla Walla and the mines.

> After stating that along the entire route at only two or three points could food or shelter for man or beast be had, Mossman continued thus:

Realizing only five dollars out of my first trip, I began to feel blue, but had no intention of giving up. My next trip paid me ten dollars over my expenses, and from that time on business was good. On my third trip down I found a small steamer tied up to the bank of the Clearwater, at the foot of the rapids above the Indian Agency. A man by the name of S. S. Slater was on board with a stock of goods. His first intention was to start a trading post where he had tied up, but changed his mind, dropped back to the junction of the Snake and Clearwater rivers, and unloaded his goods, and opened up the first store where Lewiston now stands . . .

I stayed with my little express . . . and by July [1861] had augmented my train to ten good saddle ponies. They were scattered along the route at convenient distances, so I could change two or three times a day. In the meantime, Tracy & Co., consisting of Ned Tracy, Ned James and Ned Norton, had started an express to Oro Fino, employed some of the best riders to be had . . . and many a hard race I had with him between Oro Fino and Walla Walla. On two

different occasions we raced . . . one hundred and eighty
miles without sleep, and made stops only to change tired
horses for fresh ones. On one of my racing trips my canteen
was broke and a buckskin bag containing eight hundred
dollars in gold dust was lost from it. I was in the lead and
would have won allright, but missing the bag of dust, gave
up the race . . .

> A bit further on in his recollections, Mossman tells how
> Joaquin Miller, the future "Poet of the Sierras," came to be
> associated with him.

I continued in the business . . . [he wrote] until October,
1861, when C. Hiner Miller, now known as Joaquin Miller,
met me at Walla Walla with a letter of introduction to me
from his uncle, Colonel W. W. Chapman. Miller wanted to
join me in the express business. He had one little pony, and
$5 in cash, but he could ride well and was a hustler. I had at
that time eighteen head of good saddle horses, so I gave him
an interest in the business. Soon after that the Salmon River
mines were discovered, and I put Miller on the route from
Lewiston to Florence City . . . while I rode between Walla
Walla, Lewiston and the Oro Fino.

> Continuing, Mossman gave this picture of life in the Idaho
> gold camps during the early 1860's:

The "diggings" at Florence proved to be very rich. There
was a great rush to them, and by December there were many
hundreds of men in there at work, and gold dust was plentiful. About the 10th of December I got Miller to change off
with me one trip, and I went to Florence, while he went to
Walla Walla. I had fifty of the *Sacramento Unions* with me
and expected to get a good price for them. When I arrived
at Slate Creek at the foot of the Salmon River Mountains, I

found quite a camp of miners and packers. The notorious Mat Bledso had just shot and killed a packer named Harmon, better known as Pike. Bledso was taken to Walla Walla, where he had a preliminary examination before a justice and was discharged. He afterwards killed two other men, was in the penitentiary for several years, was pardoned out and was finally killed in Arizona over a game of cards.

Arriving at Florence I sold my newspapers for $2.50 each as fast as I could hand them out. I kept my horse under a shed two nights and a day, and fed him thirty pounds of oats, and when ready to leave, my bill was . . . $30—$1 a pound for oats.

I was away from Walla Walla that trip sixteen days and cleared up $400. Between Lewiston and Walla Walla I met hundreds of men on their way to Florence, a great many of them with land sleds loaded with grub and picks and blankets. Many men were frozen to death that winter. Bewildered by a snow storm, they would lose the trail, and then flounder about in the blinding snow and die.

During the brief time the partnership remained in force the firm was known as Mossman & Miller's Express. In the spring of 1862 the future poet withdrew, Mossman commenting that "I paid him $600 over and above his profits, and presented him with a fine horse, saddled and bridled. He went to Portland and from there to Port Orford, where he was married."

Something more than a year later, in 1863, Mossman sold out to Wells, Fargo & Company and his picturesque early express enterprise passed out of existence.

vii

When on May 10, 1869, the rails of the two halves of the
first transcontinental railroad were joined at Promontory
Point, Utah, one of the speakers at the ceremonies announced that the event marked the close of the pioneer era
in the West and went on to state that, with the nation
bound together by twin bands of steel, the hardships and discomforts of early-day travel between the two coasts were
happily a thing of the past. Be that as it may, the fact remains that during the early years of their operation the
trains that passed over the new-laid tracks were, by present-
day standards, considerably less than luxurious. This was
particularly true of what were called the emigrant cars, in
which those unable—or unwilling—to pay the fares charged
on the regular trains were permitted to travel, at cut rates,
between San Francisco and Council Bluffs, Iowa.

A spirited picture of life aboard these cars has fortunately
been preserved for us, from the pen of no less a literary
craftsman than Robert Louis Stevenson, who, then in his
late twenties, made the trip from east to west in the fall
of 1879.

I suppose [wrote he] the reader has some notion of an American railroad car, that long, narrow wooden box like a flat-
roofed Noah's ark, with a stove and a convenience, one
at either end, a passage down the middle, and transverse
benches upon either hand. Those destined for emigrants on
the Union Pacific are only remarkable for their extreme
plainness, nothing but wood entering in any part of their
constitution, and for the usual inefficacy of the lamps, which
often went out and shed but a dying glimmer even while
they burned. The benches are too short for anything but a
young child. Where there is scarce elbow-room for two to sit,
there will not be space enough for one to lie. Hence the com-

pany, or rather . . . the company's servants, have conceived
a plan for the better accommodation of travelers. They prevail on every two to chum together. To each of the chums
they sell a board and three square cushions stuffed with straw
and covered with thin cotton. The benches can be made to
face each other in pairs, for the backs are reversible. On the
approach of night the boards are laid from bench to bench,
making a couch wide enough for two and long enough for a
man of middle height; and the chums lie down side by side
upon the cushions with the head to the conductor's van and
the feet to the engine. When the train is full, of course this
plan is impossible, for there must not be more than one to
every bench; neither can it be carried out unless the chums
agree. It was to bring about this last condition that our
white-haired official now bestirred himself. He made a most
active master of ceremonies, introducing likely couples and
even guaranteeing the amiability and honesty of each. The
greater the number of happy couples the better for his
pocket, for it was he who sold the raw material of the beds.
His price for one board and three straw cushions began with
two dollars and a half, but before the train left and, I am
sorry to say, long after I had purchased mine, it had fallen
to one dollar and a half.

The day faded; the lamps were lit; a party of wild young
men, who got off next evening at North Platte, stood together on the stern platform, singing "The Sweet By-and-
By" with very tuneful voices; the chums began to put up
their beds; and it seemed as if the business of the day were at
an end. But it was not so, for, the train stopping at some
station, the cars were instantly thronged with the natives,
wives and fathers, young men and maidens, some of them in
a little more than night gear, some with stable lanterns, and
all offering beds for sale. Their charge began with twenty-
five cents a cushion but fell, before the train went on again,
to fifteen, with the bed board gratis, or less than one-fifth of

what I had paid for mine at the transfer. This is my contribution to the economy of future emigrants.

A great personage on an American train is the newsboy. He sells books (such books!), papers, fruit, lollipops, and cigars, and on emigrant journeys soap, towels, tin washing dishes, tin coffee pitchers, coffee, tea, sugar, and tinned eatables, mostly hash or beans and bacon. Early next morning the newsboy went around the cars, and chumming on a more extended principle became the order of the hour. It requires but a copartnery of two to manage beds, but washing and eating can be carried on most economically by a syndicate of three. I myself entered a little after sunrise into articles of agreement and became one of the firm of Pennsylvania, Shakespeare, and Dubuque. Shakespeare was my own nickname on the cars, Pennsylvania that of my bedfellow, and Dubuque . . . that of an amiable young fellow going west to cure an asthma . . . Shakespeare bought a tin washing dish, Dubuque a towel, and Pennsylvania a brick of soap. The partners used these instruments, one after another, according to the order of their first awaking; and when the firm had finished there was no want of borrowers. Each filled the tin dish at the water filter opposite the stove and retired with the whole stock in trade to the platform of the car. There he knelt down, supporting himself by a shoulder against the woodwork or one elbow crooked about the railing, and made shift to wash his face and neck and hands—a cold, and insufficient, and, if the train is moving rapidly, a somewhat dangerous toilet.

On a similar division of expense, the firm of Pennsylvania, Shakespeare, and Dubuque supplied themselves with coffee, sugar, and necessary vessels; and their operations are a type of what went on through all the cars. Before the sun was up the stove would be brightly burning; at the first station the natives would come on board with milk and eggs and coffee cakes; and soon from end to end the car would be filled with little parties breakfasting upon the bed boards . . .

> Despite the informality of life aboard the crowded cars, Stevenson found time to reflect on the significance of this miracle by which it was possible to travel behind the iron horse through thousands of miles of what had recently been an untrodden wilderness.

Mile upon mile, and not a tree, a bird, or a river [he wrote]. Only down the long, sterile canyons the train shot hooting and awoke the resting echo. That train was the one piece of life in all the deadly land; it was the one actor, the one spectacle fit to be observed in this paralysis of man and nature. And when I think how the railroad has been pushed through this unwatered wilderness and haunt of savage tribes and now will bear an emigrant for some twelve pounds from the Atlantic to the Golden Gate; how at each stage of the construction roaring, impromptu cities, full of gold and lust and death, sprang up and then died away again, and now are but wayside stations in the desert; how in these uncouth places pigtailed Chinese pirates worked side by side with border ruffians and broken men from Europe, talking together in a mixed dialect, mostly oaths, gambling, drinking, quarreling, and murdering like wolves; how the plumed hereditary lord of all America heard, in this last fastness, the scream of the "bad medicine wagon" charioting his foes; and then when I go on to remember that all this epical turmoil was conducted by gentlemen in frock coats and with a view to nothing more extraordinary than a fortune and a subsequent visit to Paris, it seems to me, I own, as if this railway were the one typical achievement of the age in which we live, as if it brought together into one plot all the ends of the world and all the degrees of social rank, and offered to some great writer the busiest, the most extended, and the most varied subject for an enduring literary work. If it be romance, if it be contrast, if it be heroism that we require, what was Troy town to this?

Index